INQUESTS

The last year has seen the largest and most compr
since the early nineteenth century. The new Coron
upon every aspect of the Inquest and this compi   out
both the substantive law and new procedure followi   _ation and
authorities.

The whole coronial process is laid out in distinct cha   _.s which consider the
present and developing law.

The book provides practical guidance from the beginning to the end of the
process and includes a special chapter on Military inquests, creating an invaluable
reference for both the practitioner and student of this fast developing area of law.

Volume 9 in the Criminal Law Library series

Criminal Law Library

INQUESTS

JOHN COOPER QC

·HART·
PUBLISHING

OXFORD AND PORTLAND, OREGON
2011

Published in the United Kingdom by Hart Publishing Ltd
16C Worcester Place, Oxford, OX1 2JW
Telephone: +44 (0)1865 517530
Fax: +44 (0)1865 510710
E-mail: mail@hartpub.co.uk
Website: http://www.hartpub.co.uk

Published in North America (US and Canada) by
Hart Publishing
c/o International Specialized Book Services
920 NE 58th Avenue, Suite 300
Portland, OR 97213-3786
USA
Tel: +1 503 287 3093 or toll-free: (1) 800 944 6190
Fax: +1 503 280 8832
E-mail: orders@isbs.com
Website: http://www.isbs.com

British Library Cataloguing in Publication Data
Data Available

ISBN: 978-1-84946-037-8

Typeset by Hope Services, Abingdon
Printed and bound in Great Britain by
TJ International Ltd, Padstow, Cornwall

'Long gone are the days of travel to some dispiriting corner of
St. Pancras or Battersea only to be told peremptorily,
when appearing on behalf of the bereaved "Keep quiet & sit down!"'

Lord Justice Moses in *R (on the Application of Lin & others) v*
The Secretary of State for Transport [2006] EWHC 2575 (Admin)

FOREWORD

by Lord Judge, Lord Chief Justice of England and Wales

The development of the Coroner's responsibilities from inquiring into deaths, imposed in 1276 by De Officio Coronatoris (which office was already ancient) to the consequences of the Human Rights Act 1998 and the incorporation of the European Convention of Human Rights into domestic law in the context of article 2 of the Convention – the right to life – has involved significant changes to the coronial jurisdiction and its processes. Thus, not very many years ago, it would have been utterly astonishing to imagine an open judicial process in this country inquiring into the sad deaths of members of the British armed forces in Iraq (see, for example, R (Gentle) v Prime Minister [2008] 1 AC 1358).

This meant that a legislative overhaul of the entire system was necessary, and the answer was to be found in the Coroners and Justice Act 2009, which received Royal Assent in November 2009. This was a comprehensive attempt at reform of some antiquated arrangements, not sufficiently geared up to the increasing demands placed on the coronial system. This new legislative structure suggested that a careful re-appraisal and analysis of the ramifications and impact of the 2009 Act was required and John Cooper set about the task with characteristic enthusiasm. As he set about his work, he can hardly have anticipated the bombshell that the newly-created office of Chief Coroner might not survive the national financial crisis. He seems to have taken this important change in his stride, but he is unable to try, and perhaps does not wish to deny, his surprise that the office might be, as he puts it, 'one of the shortest lived judicial offices in legal history'.

Notwithstanding the proposed abolition of the office, the 2009 Act continues to represent the latest and most comprehensives changes to the coronial system for very many years. The changes are symbolised in the inquests currently being conducted in the Royal Courts of Justice by Lady Justice Hallett into the ghastly events in London on the 7th July 2005, when so many innocent people were the victims of a terrorist outrage committed in the heart of the London.

This new volume compresses the law relating to Inquests into manageable proportions, and is written in crisp and readily understood language. It will be of great assistance to all those who work in or have an interest in this sensitive area of the legal system.

Igor Judge

PREFACE

The Law is never still.

In the field of Inquests the pace of development has, at times, been frenetic.

A new Act, completely overhauling practice and procedure is enough to keep up with, but add to that a regular diet of new law from narrative verdicts to jurisdictional issues concerning overseas deaths outside of Army bases, then it truly seems that Coronial Law is never at rest.

In attempting to keep as current as possible, through the inexhaustible patience of my publishers, I have been allowed to consider in this book the latest consultation paper on the development of the 2009 Act, seminal cases such as *R(Catherine Smith) v Assistant Deputy Coroner for Oxfordshire,* the invaluable ruling of Lady Justice Hallett in the 7/7 Inquest hearings and the consequent judgment in the High Court just before Christmas 2010 on the extent of Secret Hearings.

All errors and omissions are entirely mine.

I would particularly like to record my deep thanks and appreciation to Shaila Bux, whose enthusiasm and encouragement have meant that this book has been able to cover the range and depth that it does. I owe her a significant debt of gratitude.

It is my hope that this work benefits the growing number of practitioners in this field, as well as those who have the very difficult task of sitting as Coroners and deputies. Additionally, this book aims to assist students of the law who read and hear of the growing number of high-profile inquests and have a curiosity to know exactly what goes on in the Coroner's Court.

I further hope that those who are waiting to be trained in the forthcoming sessions planned to introduce the new Act find the book a helpful aid; it is you who will be responsible for bringing the reforms to life.

John Cooper QC
Visiting Professor of Law at Cardiff University
25 Bedford Row
London
March 2011

SUMMARY CONTENTS

DETAILED CONTENTS

TABLE OF CASES

AUSTRALIA

EUROPEAN UNION

NEW ZEALAND

TABLE OF LEGISLATION

UNITED KINGDOM

Charter

Home Office Circulars

AUSTRALIA

CANADA

UNITED STATES OF AMERICA

INTERNATIONAL

TABLE OF CIVIL PROCEDURE RULES, CORONERS RULES AND CRIMINAL PROCEDURE RULES

Introduction

Those who practise in the Coroner's Court do so at a difficult time in the development of practice and procedure in this most venerable of jurisdictions.

The law, as articulated by the Coroners Act 1988 and Coroners Rules 1984, still governs the court, and new precedents are created at regular intervals which develop and maintain the discipline in the most dynamic of ways.

All this is influenced by the formidable shadow cast by the Coroners and Justice Act 2009, which received Royal Assent in November 2009.

The 2009 Act represented the most fundamental reform of the Coroner's Court for centuries, providing rules and regulations upon many aspects of practice and procedure at inquests.

The Act was intended to address the issues identified by The Shipman Inquiry and the Fundamental Review of Death Certification & Investigation. It had been hoped that it would receive staggered implementation over 2012–13.

During this protracted period the Ministry of Justice stated that it would be developing the new law through consultation, pilot projects and secondary legislation. All this changed abruptly in October 2010. After extensive consultation with those who use the coroner's court, consultees received a letter entitled, 'The Delivery of Coroner Reform' signed by Dr Elizabeth Gibby, the Deputy Director responsible for Coroners, Burials and Legal Services Regulation and Redress at the Ministry of Justice. Although Dr Gibby's title contained a comma between Coroner's and Burials the purport of her communication was in fact to bury the coroner, or at least the Chief Coroner.

The significance of this letter as to the future of the coronial service cannot be underestimated and I make no apology for quoting the full extent of this unexpected communication:

> . . . The Justice Secretary has recently commission an internal review of the scope and timing of the coroner reform plans in the light of the difficult financial situation facing Government as a whole. I am writing to inform you of the decision that has been made.
>
> The Minister is keen to see reform and improvement of the coronial system and to continue the changes that Part One of the Coroner's and Justice Act 2009 sought to address. He recognizes the considerable effort that has been undertaken by all who work within the current system to provide good public service and hopes to continue to work with these people in the future. However, the current financial situation means that these reforms must be brought forward without the national leadership framework and new appeals system, headed by a Chief Coroner (which would have included the Medical Adviser to support the Chief Coroner).

Given the desire to achieve improvement and benefits for the bereaved, some of the functions of the Office of the Chief Coroner need to be transferred to an alternative body. To enable functions to be transferred the Office of the Chief Coroner has to be abolished. The Minister has proposed that the abolition of this role be taken forward alongside the abolition of other Public Bodies in the Public Bodies Bill, announced earlier today by Francis Maude MP.

In making some transfers of functions, great care will be needed to ensure that functions are transferred to appropriate bodies. We have therefore already begun discussions with the senior judiciary about which functions it would, and which it would not, be appropriate to transfer to the judiciary and others with a close interest.

I hope that the Health Secretary's decision to take forward the introduction of medical examiners – to work in parallel with coroners to ensure that poor or criminal certifying practices are detected and addressed – will be a significant improvement and will enhance, as a secondary purpose, the medical knowledge available for coroners to draw on when investigating their own cases . . .[1]

The terms of the letter require close analysis. Contrary to initial reactions, it does not seem that the incoming government are completely reversing the entirety of the 2009 Act in relation to inquests. But the following can be gleaned from Dr Gibby's communication. The Office of Chief Coroner has probably become, with its abolition, one of the shortest lived judicial offices in legal history.[2]

Nevertheless it seems that the government is consulting with the senior judiciary to ascertain whether they can take on any of the roles that had been assigned to the Chief Coroner. We can therefore anticipate that although the title of Chief Coroner has now been consigned, somewhat prematurely, to history, some of his duties may yet be part of the coronial system.

In the light of this, this book contains a consideration of the role and duties that were to be undertaken by the Chief Coroner, in the knowledge that some of these matters will be undertaken by the senior judiciary. Precisely what will and will not be given a second chance of life is at the time of writing unspecified.

It is interesting that Dr Gibby's letter also recognises the inherent dangers of the present system of death certification and seems to be reassured that the 2009 Act introduction of medical examiners, which will be maintained, will in some way address these issues. Time will tell.

What is clear is that the reforms articulated in the 2009 Act may yet, at least in part, come to pass. The question for the next few years, is how many will survive.

Despite this, case-law is taking into account the objectives and rationale of the 2009 Act in deciding whether Coronial law is compliant with the obligations of the United Kingdom under the European Convention on Human Rights, and any future submissions – be they to the Coroner on matters such as disclosure, the calling of witnesses and the structure of narrative verdicts –will be informed by the principles laid down in the 2009 Act.

---

[1] The full statement of the Minister in relation to these matters can be accessed on http://www.justice.gov.uk/consultations/reform-coroner-system.htm.

[2] See *New Law Journal* Vol 160 No 7438 22 October 2010 at page 1437: 'Strangled at Birth' (John Cooper QC).

The attitude of the Coroner's Court to bereaved families is a further example of how the new Act is, even now, impacting upon the inquest process. A key aim of the new legislation is to increase the participation of bereaved families to be properly interested parties. As Bridget Prentice, the then Parliamentary Under Secretary for Justice put it in her Ministerial foreword to the Consultation Paper on *Reform of the Coroner System, Next Stage*,[3] the reforms are designed to provide 'families with the opportunity to participate more extensively in Coroners' investigations', which she describes as 'at the heart of the reform programme'.

The Act, along with the Charter for Bereaved People, already influence the approach of the Coroners Court to those who have lost members of their families and who find themselves thrust into a death investigation at one of the most vulnerable times of their lives.

Time will tell whether the legislation achieves this important objective.

For many who practice in the Coroners Court, although the interests of the bereaved are considered by the court on an individual basis, there has, hitherto, been no structured and principled approach to their treatment.

Yet there remains, within this stated philosophy an hypocrisy within the heart of the Act – the continuing refusal of the legislature to provide properly assessed Public Funding to bereaved families, who face the daunting and complex procedure of the Coronial process as well as the formidable resources of governments, such as the Ministry of Defence or the Prison Service, police or other potential parties, all with legal representation funded at the taxpayers expense.

The reasons given by the Minister[4] are disingenuous. She states that Coronial proceedings 'are generally less formal than a court hearing, and legal representation is considered unnecessary generally'. If this is so, why are government departments represented at great expense to the taxpayer at all major inquests and at some basic cases?

Neither is it expected by government that any significant amount of public funding will be available to bereaved families in the new appeal process, than to the Chief Coroner. They estimate that it will cost the legal aid budget £100,000 a year for exceptional funding,[5] it is clearly anticipated that bereaved families will not be provided with any substantial assistance from the public purse to obtain independent legal representation at any appeal. Given that the Ministry of Justice expects most appeals to be dealt with on paper, even this, the more positive aspect of the 2009 Act, may yet prove to promise more than it delivers.

Generally, between 2007–08 only 12 of 69 applications for legal aid were granted and between 2006–07, 16 of 104 applications, perhaps putting into perspective claims of the bereaved being at the forefront of the system.

Despite these grave misgivings, reform of the Coronial jurisdiction was long overdue following the false dawns of Broderick and Luce, and the stated aim of the

---

[3] Consultation Paper CP06/10. Published on 11 March 2010.
[4] *ibid*, Impact Assessment, paras 5.24–5.26 (p 147).
[5] *ibid*, Impact Assessment, para 5.25 (p 147). Also to include £270,000 for legal help.

legislation to introduce national operational leadership for the first time and to ensure that there is effective local provision is to be welcomed.

There are examples of reforms in the 2009 Act which will, if they survive, without doubt achieve positive change in the way inquests are conducted. Chief amongst these are the new death certification procedures, the relaxation of boundary restrictions, the power to make reports to prevent future deaths and the new powers to secure information, to enter and search premises and to seize material.

This book is intended to provide the first and most comprehensive analysis of law and procedure. In what is without doubt one of the most dynamic periods in the development of the coronial jurisdiction, analysis in the forthcoming chapters will seek to explain the present law and anticipate the future, in a time of great uncertainty. It considers the law as it relates to the Coroners Act 1988 and the 1984 Coroners Rules and applies the growing and up-to-date case law as it affects the whole of the jurisdiction, as an aid to the present and a guide for the future.

1

History

Early History

1.1 It is generally suggested that the coronial process dates back to the reign of Richard 1 when the office of Coroner was created by the Articles of Eyre in 1194. But recent research indicates that the existence of a Coroner could date back to the reign of King Alfred (871–910). At that time the official who was required to maintain order was known as the 'Coronator' or the controller of the 'Corona' or circle of audience.

The role of the Coroner has changed over the centuries. In the mid fourteenth century coroners performed the role of mediators. They provided the safeguard against bias of the medieval sheriffs, particularly concerning empanelling jurors. If the sheriff was considered to be partial, a challenge to the array of the court was sometimes dealt with by the Coroner.

Also around this time, coronial jurisdiction extended into ecclesiastical matters. A particular privilege of the church in the mid-fourteenth century was that of sanctuary. Allowing felons sanctuary upon church property would considerably hamper the administration of criminal justice. The privileges which sanctuary provided were attached by common law to the place and not to the person and were therefore available to any person who was bodily within the boundary of ecclesiastical property. Abjuration was closely associated with sanctuary although it was not an ecclesiastical concept. At the request of the felon, a Coroner would attend upon church property.

With him would be neighbours who he proposed to summon as witnesses. During the process the felon would confess his offence and the confession would be recorded in writing. The Coroner would then take the felon to a port where he would proceed to embarkation and promise never to return to England again, without the King's permission. The felon's possessions were forfeited, except for essential clothing and he was given a wooden cross to serve as a passport.[1]

---

[1] See Sir John Baker, *The Oxford History of the Laws of England* vol IV (1483–1558) (Oxford University Press, 2003).

The reputation of the Coroner was already held in high esteem and protected vociferously, often through the courts of law.[2] Coroners were also responsible for the recording of serious crime throughout the country. It was the community's local duty to identify and produce persons guilty of each crime from within that community. If the community failed in any of its duties to assist the Coroner, then the community as a whole would be punished. Royal justices would visit each county in the Eyres, and the representatives of each hundred and township were called upon to present suspects to them for judgment and their presentations would be checked against the Coroner's rolls. The system became mandatory under the Assizes of Clarendon 1116 and Northampton 1176.[3]

So although the basic functions of the medieval Coroner was concerned with the custody of the King's revenue, particularly that obtained from fines and forfeiture, the Coroner also had a general jurisdiction over the medieval criminal justice system.

The essential duty of a Coroner to enquire into deaths was laid out in the statute De Officio Coronatoris in 1276. It is, perhaps, the first articulation of what is now considered to be the primary function of a Coroner and an inquest:

> A Coroner of Our Lord, the King ought to enquire of these Things: first, when coroners are commended by the Kings Bailiffs or by honest Men of the Country, they shall go to the Places where any be slain, or suddenly dead or wounded, or where Houses are broken, or where Treasure is said to be found, and all forthwith command four of the next Towns, or five or six, to appear before him in such a Place; and when they are come thither, the Coroner upon the Oath of them shall enquire in this matter, that to wit, if it concerns a Man slain, whether they know where the person was slain whether it were in any House, Field, Bed, Tavern or Company, and if any, and who were there . . . and how many soever be found culpable by Inquisition in any of the Manners aforesaid, they should be taken and delivered to the Sheriff . . . and their Names shall be written in the Rolls of the Coroners.

The wide breadth of a Coroner's duty included the requirement that he arrange the funeral of suicides. Those who had taken their own lives were placed in a carriage after the fall of darkness and taken to a crossroads where they were staked through the heart and buried by the official hangman.[4]

The concept of inquests into deaths in custody is similarly not a modern manifestation. In fact it dates back to the late thirteenth century, where it was recorded that 'If any person die in prison, our pleasure is, that the Coroner go and view the body and take a true inquest of his death, in what way it has happened'.[5]

As the role of the coroner developed from this period up until the seminal changes of the nineteenth century, the Coroner continued to find his work varied

---

[2] *Hyggons the botfylde* (1558) CP40/1173, m644, where a Coroner recovered £5 from a 'false perjured knave'.
[3] JH Baker, *An Introduction to English Legal History* (Oxford, Oxford University Press, 1971).
[4] See Sadakat Kadri, *The Trial A History from Socrates to OJ Simpson* (Harper Collins, 2005) 178.
[5] See J le Breton, *Treatise of Common law* (1865).

and diverse. The onerous aspect of his duties was exacerbated by the fact that the Coroner was expected to fund the inquest out of his own pocket. As a result of this, the Coroner developed imaginative ways of raising funds. For instance, a charge would be levied by the coroner on any community, if a murderer from within that society escaped.

The Nineteenth Century

1.2 In the early nineteenth century the Coroners' Courts remained an unstructured and at times ill-disciplined environment. The Coroner, who presided over his individual court, was in essence a law unto himself. Social commentators of the time, including Charles Dickens, observed the idiosyncratic attitudes of different Coroners and the fact that the inquest had become more of a place of gossip and scandal than a forensic and structured inquisitorial process into matters relating to the deaths of individuals.

During this time there were also disputes as to whether the coroner should be legally or medically qualified, indeed the Lancet observed in 1839.[6]

> It will not be expedient for this court to confine the qualifications of the candidates for the Office of Coroner, either to the Legal, Medical, or any particular profession, but that any Gentleman of experience, respectable character, and liberal education, is duly qualified to fill that office.

The inquest developed piecemeal until the Coroners Act of 1887, which attempted to consolidate earlier law.

In 1860 the parliamentary select committee on Coroners[7] recommended that the role of Coroner as the Crown's protector of finances should be abandoned. It was not until the Coroners Act 1887 that this recommendation was acted upon. This important statute attempted to consolidate earlier law and began the process of developing Coronial jurisdiction, as we know it to this day. The Act also took the opportunity of removing from the responsibility of the Coroner some of the more unusual duties. For instance Section 44 of the 1887 Act laid down that,

> A Coroner shall not take pleas of the Crown nor hold inquests of Royal Fish or wreck nor of felonies accept felonies on inquisitions of death; and he shall not enquire of the goods of such as by the inquest are found guilty of murder or manslaughter, nor cause them to be valued and delivered to the Township.

So it was that the Coroner ceased in 1887 to be required to hold an inquest into the death of Royal Fish.

---

[6] See *The Lancet* (1839) 731: reproduced in Freckelton and Ranson, *Death Investigation and the Coroner's Inquest* (Oxford University Press, 2006) 17.
[7] House of Commons Reports 1860, vol 16.

The Local Government Act 1888 abolished the election of Coroners by the freeholders of the county, providing instead that they be appointed by the local authority.

To The Present Day

1.3 One of the most influential statutes of the twentieth century was the Coroners (Amendment) Act 1926.[8] The 1926 Act encompassed the Select Committee's recommendations that the coroner should have the power to order a post-mortem in cases of sudden death, even where there was no suspicion of death being occasioned by violence. Nevertheless the 1926 Act crucially decided that the inquest process should be no longer used as a tool for criminal investigation. The Select Committee had held the contrary point of view that the inquest should play a crucial roll in a criminal investigation and, if appropriate, a pivotal part of any subsequent prosecution. Today the modern inquest strongly adheres to the principles laid down as far back as 1926 and despite all the changes that have occurred in the Coroners and Justice Act 2009, the central ethos of the inquest remains, that is that it does not form any part of a Criminal Investigation.

The connection between the Coronial process and criminal and civil proceedings was further weakened when in 1936 the Report of Home Office Departmental Committee on Coroners[9] recommended that the Coroner's power to commit a matter for trial be abolished. Lord Wright, who chaired this committee, also recommended, that contrary to many views at the time, only Barristers or Solicitors should undertake the role of Coroner, causing a significant amount of controversy within the medical profession.

In 1971 the Broderick Committee[10] laid down central and influential guidance as to the role of the Coroner.[11] Broderick decided that the inquest should seek to achieve five fundamentals:

(i)   to determine the medical cause of death;
(ii) to allay rumours or suspicion;
(iii) to draw attention to the exercise of circumstances which, if unremedied, might lead to further deaths;
(iv) to advance medical knowledge; and
(v)   to preserve the legal interests of the deceased persons family, Heirs or other interested parties.

---

[8] Implementing many of the recommendations of the Select Committee on Coroners (Cd 5004, 1910).
[9] Report of Home Office Departmental Committee on Coroners (Cmd 5070, 1936).
[10] Report of the Committee on Death Certification and Coroners (Cmnd 4810, 1971).
[11] See Freckelton and Ranson, *Death Investigation and the Coroner's Inquest*, 23.

In paragraph 13 of the report[12] the Broderick Committee articulate their vision of the role of the inquest, which chimes with modern times:

> There is still a tendency to regard the Coroners role as being primarily directed to the investigation of suspicious deaths and, in particular, possible homicides. This belief . . . is now completely outmoded . . . we cannot too strongly emphasise our own conclusion that the Coroners primary function, at present, is to help to establish the cause of death in a wide range of situations, few of which have any criminal or even suspicious overtone.

More recently the Luce Report[13] recognised the significant pressures both of time and resources placed upon the modern Coroner and recommended that the Coroner's jurisdiction be divided into about sixty sections and that all Coroners should have medical expertise.

1.4 Modern developments of the Coroner's role and duties have hitherto been case specific. Following the inquests into the deaths surrounding the practice of Dr Harold Shipman, the Coroner, John Pollard, made a reference to the undesirability of single-handed medical practices. The Coroner also made observations about the reporting of deaths to the coronial services, he observed during the course of the Shipman Inquest that

> people do not know the procedure and maybe one of the few benefits of this case will be an education of the general public on what the Coroner does and how he can help resolve problems [and investigate] causes of death.

Following Shipman's conviction, a Commission of Inquiry found that the defendant had killed at least 215 patients.[14]

The Inquiry chaired by Dame Janet Smith enforced the views of the Luce Committee, in criticising the weakness of the death certification and coronial process in relation to the reporting of deaths. Dame Janet Smith was critical of the system which existed at the time, although endorsing, finally, the coronial process.

In general the profession can be relied upon, but not always. The Shipman case revealed that existing procedures failed to protect the public from the risk that, in certifying a death without reporting it to the Coroner, a doctor might successfully conceal homicide, medical error or neglect leading to death. The Shipman Inquiry observed that. It is said by some that Shipman is unique; there will never be another like him, a hope that is so, but other, less prolific killers have been detected in the medical profession and it is not possible to determine how many killings or how many errors by a health professional have gone undetected. Certification of the

---

[12] As helpfully reproduced by Freckelton and Ranson (above n 12) at 23.

[13] *Death Certification and Registration in England, Wales and Northern Ireland: The Report of a Fundamental Review* (Cm 5831, 2003).

[14] *The Shipman Inquiry: Second Report: The Police Investigation of March 1998*, July 2003 (Cm 5853, 2003).

cause of death by a single doctor is no longer acceptable. Cremation certification, as presently practised, was also considered ineffective. The Third Report stated:

> I have concluded that the coronial system should be retained. In that, I am in agreement with the Coroners Review. However, in my view, there must be radical reform and a complete break with the past, as to organisation, philosophy, sense of purpose and mode of operation. The new Coroner Service that I shall recommend will be barely recognisable as the offspring of its parent.[15]

1.5 The essence of the Report in the Shipman Inquiry is reflected in the Coroners and Justice Act 2009. As well as recommending a comprehensive procedure into death certification Janet Smith made recommendations as to the coronial system itself. In doing so she recommended national, regional and district structures and the increased judicial qualifications of Coroners.

Ultimately as a result of the Shipman Inquiry the Home Office felt moved to reflect that funding arrangements applicable to the coronial service were 'Archaic'.[16] They also observed that 'the practices do not allow effective performance management or promote consistently high quality; nor do they deliver a cost effective service across the country'.[17] So it is that from the depths of the reign of Richard the First, into the Victorian age of reform, via medieval England that the wholesale reforms to be implemented by the Coroners and Justice Act 2009 are to be implemented.

1.6 Prior to the 2009 Act, legislation was comprised within the Coroners Act 1988 and the Coroners Rules 1984, many of which will still form the bedrock of practice and procedure within the inquest and remain unaltered. The 2009 Act represents an end to the frustration of many who worked within the Coronial system that much-needed reform had been advised but never implemented. The Luce Report back in 2003 proposed the creation of a Chief Coroner from 'higher levels of the judiciary' and full-time appointments.[18] It argued for change to the existing purposes of death investigation to include ascertaining whether the death had been preventable.[19]

In a letter to the minister at the front of the Home Office review, Luce (and his fellow members of the review committee) observed:

> During the last three-quarters of a century, the Government has twice commissioned reviews of these subjects, in 1936 and 1965. Very little happened in response to their reports. The services are showing the consequences of this neglect. We, and those whom we have consulted, hope that the inaction will not continue.

---

[15] See *The Shipman Inquiry: Third Report* (Cm 5854, 2003) para 19.12.
[16] Home Office, *Reforming the Coroner and Death Certification* (Cm 6159, 2004).
[17] *ibid.*
[18] Luce Report (2003) 73.
[19] *ibid*, 76.

1.7 The 2009 Act seeks to end this neglect and in a very wide-ranging statute – which deals with, amongst other things, anonymity of witnesses, partial defences to murder and the treatment of vulnerable and intimidated witnesses – lays down fundamental changes to the modern-day inquest, which over a period of time and the provision of secondary legislation will overhaul the coronial courts.

2

Coroners' Courts

Appointment of Coroners

2.1 Coroners are appointed and funded by local authorities. The appointment of Senior Coroners, Area Coroners and Assistant Coroners will be governed by the Coroners and Justice Act 2009, section 23 and Schedule 3.

The Lord Chancellor and the Chief Coroner, until he was abolished, were designated by the Act to consent to the appointment of any individual as a Senior Coroner.[1] To be eligible for appointment as a Senior Coroner, Area Coroner, or Assistant Coroner an individual must be under 70 years of age and satisfy the judicial appointment eligibility condition on a five-year basis.[2]

If an individual has been a Councillor for a local authority, or has during the previous six months, held such a position they may not be appointed as a Senior Coroner, or as an Area Coroner or Assistant Coroner for a Coroner Area that is the same as or includes the area of that Local Authority.[3] The Act also lays down[4] that the offices of Senior Coroner, Area Coroner and Assistant Coroner will no longer be regarded as freehold offices.

High Court Judges

2.2 The office of Coroner can also be held by the Lord Chief Justice and/or High Court Judges.[5] This facility has been exercised most recently during the inquest related to the death of Diana, Princess of Wales and Dodi Al-Fayed and the inquest into the deaths as a result of the so-called 7/7 Bombings, where Lady Justice Hallett has undertaken the role of Coroner in that hearing.

---

[1] Coroners and Justice Act 2009 (c 25) Sch 3, para 1(3).
[2] *ibid*, Sch 3, para 3.
[3] *ibid*, Sch 3, para 4(1).
[4] *ibid*, Sch 3, para 9.
[5] Coroners Act 1988 s 33(1).

Vacation of Office

2.3 If implemented, a Senior Coroner, Area Coroner or Assistant Coroner must vacate office on reaching the age of 70 years. This does not apply to persons who are appointed as Coroners under the Coroners Act 1988 who will be treated as appointed as either a Senior Coroner or an Assistant Coroner.

Consideration has been given by the drafters of the 2009 Act as to whether the removal of the status of freehold office could be regarded as a deprivation of property, which may give rise to compensation. It is considered that no material loss will be caused to anyone as a result of the abolition of freehold office status.

Disqualification as a Result of Bias

2.4 As with any person acting in a judicial capacity any bias either perceived or real can result in the disqualification of a Coroner to preside over an inquest.[6] The leading authority on bias remains *Re Medicaments and Related Classes of Goods (No 2)*.[7] The salient principles were made out in paragraph 83 of that report:

(1) If a Judge is shown to have been influenced by actual bias, his decision must be set aside.
(2) Where actual bias has not been established the personal partiality of the judge is to be presumed.
(3) The court then has to decide whether, on an objective appraisal, the material facts give rise to a legitimate fear that the judge might not have been impartial; if they do, the decision of the judge must be set aside.
(4) The material facts are not limited to those which were apparent to the applicant. They are those which are ascertained upon investigation by the Court.
(5) An important consideration in making an objective appraisal of the facts is the desirability that the public should remain confident in the administration of justice.

Whether or not there was a 'legitimate fear that the judge may not have been impartial' will depend on whether a fair minded and informed observer would 'conclude that there was a real possibility, or real danger, the two being the same, that the tribunal was biased'. The Material circumstances will include any explanation given by the Judge under review as to his knowledge or appreciation of those circumstances. Where that

---

[6] This is not a new concept, in medieval times, if some of the Coroners were involved in the litigation or connected with the parties in some way, a situation which was relatively common since Coroners were often lawyers, then the remaining Coroners would be expected to conduct the hearings. See *Vyall v Norris* (1497) KB27/942, m.34 *Abbot of St Augustine's, Canterbury v Goldwyn* (1523) CP40/1038, m.130 (the sheriff and two Coroners were the plaintiff's tenants); *Earl of Northumberland v Wedall* (1523) CP40/1038 m.449; CP40/1039, m.103 (the sheriff was the son-in-law of the plaintiff, and one of the Coroners was his Counsel.) Even now these factual examples may give some guidance as to conflicts which could still occur. See also Sir John Baker, *The Oxford History of the Laws of England* vol VI (1483–1558) (Oxford University Press, 2003) 355.

[7] *Director General of Fair Trading v Proprietary Association of Great Britain and proprietary Articles Trade Association* [2001] 1 WLR 700 (CA).

explanation is accepted by . . . [the parties] it can be treated as accurate. Where it is not accepted, it becomes one further matter to be considered from the viewpoint of the fair-minded observer. The Court does not have to rule whether the explanation should be accepted or rejected. Rather it has to decide whether . . . [a] fair-minded observer would consider that there was a real danger [or real possibility (the two being the same thing)] of bias not withstanding the explanation advanced.[8]

2.5 In *Ex Parte Dallaglio and Lockwood Croft,*[9] a Coroner described one of the relatives of a victim of the Marchioness Pleasure Boat fatality as 'unhinged'. During the course of that inquest the same coroner made a decision not to resume that inquest after it had been adjourned for Criminal Proceedings. The Court of Appeal criticised the word 'unhinged', but also observed that the clinical condition of the relative, that of post-traumatic stress disorder, may have adversely affected the Coroner's judgment process. Lord Justice Simon Brown was also of the view that the Coroner may have thought that the Marchioness Action Group were trouble-makers and so became prejudiced against any application they might make, particularly in the circumstances of their case, as they were applying for the resumption of the inquest.[10]

2.6 In essence an assessment of bias is a matter of fact and degree. In the particular circumstances of an inquest the courts will be particularly vigilant to ensure that the Coroner has not violated the threshold so as to be considered bias. At an inquest a party may still, as a result of the public funding regime, be unrepresented and the Coroner will have a particular duty to ensure that a fair hearing is not only achieved but is perceived to have been achieved. This becomes even more critical when one considers the disclosure obligations of the Coroner. In cases where some parties may argue sensitivity or even national security reasons for documents not be disclosed, the Coroner will consider the materials in the absence of the parties or at least those representing the bereaved. It is therefore particularly incumbent upon any Coroner making a decision as to disclosure without reference to some parties at an inquest to be perceived as exercising his judicial function scrupulously.

It is therefore argued that the strictures as to bias, comprehensively laid down in Criminal Jurisprudence will apply with similar rigour in the Coronial process.

Prohibitions on Hearing a Case

2.7 Coroners are appointed by the County Council and Deputy and Assistant Coroners are appointed at the discretion of the Coroner.[11]

---

[8] For a full explanation of the Criminal Law Principles in relation to bias see *Archibald Criminal Pleading* 2010 para 4-32.

[9] *R v Inner West London Coroner, ex parte Dallaglio and Lockwood Croft* [1994] 4 All ER 139.

[10] *ibid*, 153.

[11] See Home Office Circular HOC 1991–1996.

In many ways the employment conditions of the Coroner are inextricably linked to the local authority. This includes agreement for remuneration.

Despite this even if the Coroner is so linked to the local authority, this does not necessarily debar them from hearing cases which may consider the provision of services of that authority.[12] A common sense approach is taken by Coronial procedure to potential conflicts of interest. For instance the Coroners Act 1988 section 20(3) prohibits medical practitioners from acting as a pathologist where the work of that medical practitioner may be criticised as causing or contributing to the death of the deceased.

Even if the interest of the Coroner is non-financial, proper practice dictates that he should declare it at the start of any proceedings and if there is any substantive argument which may result in him being perceived as inappropriate to adjudicate on the inquest then as a matter of good practice he should stand down.

Local Authorities

2.8 One of the real handicaps of the previous coronial regime was inconsistency both in procedure and decision-making.

Inquests come within the domain of the local authority. When a decision of the Coroner is judicially reviewed, the respondent will be at the local authority.

As a consequence of this there was no lateral infrastructure whereby a consistent approach could be taken as to what happened during an inquest. It is accurate to observe that individual Coroners, within individual boroughs, would conduct their work as it suited them, sometimes with idiosyncratic styles and approaches.

Funding

2.9 Funding remains another consistent problem for the Coroners' Courts and it would be wrong to assume that the Coroners are automatically provided with offices, staff and the ability to perform court functions with expedition.

Indeed, some Coroners continue to complain of chronic under-funding and inadequacy, both of office space and administrative support, and this reality must be borne in mind when dealing with the Coroner and his court, and the maintenance of realistic expectations in terms of expedition or response.

---

[12] See *Carver of South Yorkshire Coroner, ex parte Stringer* (1993) 158 JP 453. The so-called Hillsborough Disaster Inquest at which the local authorities provision of emergency services at a major incident in a football ground was criticised during the hearing.

2.10 The Coroner's relationship with the parties can be equally idiosyncratic and the distinct boundaries drawn between the decision-maker and the parties can be blurred.

In certain sensitive cases, it would not be considered inappropriate for a Coroner to meet a bereaved family, introduce himself and even give them a view and explanation of the courtroom.

The Coroner's 'hands on' approach to the jurisdiction is something of a culture shock to those used to the defined and prescribed procedures of the criminal or civil courts. In such arenas it would be considered inappropriate for a judge to descend from the bench and maintain a direct and personal relationship with the party. The reasons are obvious, the maintenance of impartiality and the perception of even-handedness dictate that there should be distance between the judge and the parties. This is not necessarily so within the inquest. Central to this different approach is the fundamental observation that the Coroner's Court presides over an inquisitorial process and not an adversarial system.

Inquisitorial-Adversarial

2.11 There are, within the legal system of England and Wales, very few courts that hear evidence based on the inquisitorial procedure. The difference between that and the adversarial process is often overstated and there are different approaches even within the numerous interpretations of the inquisitorial system.

Taken at its most basic level, the inquest has nothing to do with the criminal and civil process, it does not deliver a verdict upon criminality and will not hand down a civil judgment. There maybe criminal or civil consequences following inquests, but that is for subsequent and different jurisdictions to decide, it is not for the inquest.

One of the most direct consequences of this is that advocates do not cross-examine and many Coroners will deprecate any reference to such techniques, emphasising the process is not adversarial; it is an inquiry.

But the coronial system in practice can interpret its inquisitorial basis as flexibly as the different continental systems from which it is derived. In 1995, R Scott described the fundamentals of the inquest process:[13]

> In an Inquisitorial Inquiry the questioning of the witnesses by the Inquiry is not an examination-in-chief, nor is it a cross-examination. Hearsay evidence may be sort. Opinions, whether or not expert, may be sought. Questions to which the questioner does not know the answer will frequently be asked – and, indeed, will be asked because the questioner does not know the answer. The techniques of questioning witnesses in adversarial litigation can be set aside. The questioning process is, or should be, a part of a thorough investigation to determine the truth. It is not a process designated either to promote or to demolish a 'case'.

[13] See R Scott, 'Procedures at Enquiries: The Duty to be Fair' (1995) 11 *Law Quarterly Review* 596.

It would be wrong to think in simplistic terms that England and Wales operate an adversarial system and Continental Europe is governed by the inquisitorial approach. The term 'inquisitorial' is defined in a different way, depending upon which country in Europe is approached for a definition.

In some countries an inquisitorial system will be defined as such if the State undertakes the prosecution as opposed to the individual. Under this system the English Criminal jurisdiction could be described as inquisitorial, although this would be misleading.

In some European countries the title 'inquisitorial' is applied to any proceedings that are secret and in writing whereas the 'accusatorial' or adversarial procedure is in public and oral. For some the difference between the adversarial and inquisitorial system is that with the latter the defendant is expected to contribute to the discovery of truth whilst in the adversarial system guilt must be established objectively and by evidence independent of the defendant. This does indeed distinguish the fact-finding process in the criminal courts of England and Wales as opposed to the way criminal courts operate in France, Belgium and Germany. In those Continental European countries at the early stage of proceedings the presiding judge will question a defendant in general terms about the accusation during which the defendant is expected to answer for himself, even if he is represented by a lawyer, the lawyer will not intervene. But the essential difference between the inquisitorial and adversarial approach is in the role played by the court.

In the Inquisitorial tradition the court has a duty actively to seek the truth, whereas in the Accusatorial tradition its role is limited to deciding whether the prosecution has proved the accusation that it made, after hearing the prosecution evidence (and any) called by the defence. To put the matter another way, in an Accusatorial system there is a clear distinction between the functions of investigating and judging, whereas in an Inquisitorial system they are blurred.[14]

It is important that the Inquisitorial system should not be seen as a neutering of powerful argument on either side of a case. There is a tendency in some Coroners' Courts to interpret the Inquisitorial system strictly, with the intent of avoiding partisan approaches to the fact-finding exercise. This not only places a narrow interpretation upon the Inquisitorial approach, it is also unnecessary as such interpretation is not necessarily followed on Continental Europe, and it can unduly restrict the search for truth.

Lord Denning put it succinctly:[15]

> In the system of trial which we have evolved in this country, the judge sits to hear and determine the issues raised by the parties, not to conduct an investigation or examination on behalf of society at large, as happens, we believe, in some foreign countries. Even in England, however, a judge is not a mere umpire to answer the question 'how's that?' his object, is to find out the truth, and to do justice according to law . . . was it not Lord

---

[14] See Mireille Delmas-Marty and JR Spencer (eds), *European Criminal Procedures* (Cambridge University Press, 2008) 25.
[15] See Denning, LJ in *Jones v National Coal Board* [1957] 2 QB 55 (CA).

Eldon LC who said in a notable passage 'truth is best discovered by a powerful statements on both sides of the question'?

But what remain in the present Coronial process are the principal inquisitorial features:

- It is the Coroner who calls witnesses, not the parties, although parties, particularly bereaved or interested parties can make submissions to the Coroner upon appropriate witnesses to be called
- Pure cross-examination is not allowed
- There are no final speeches by advocates to a jury, if a jury has been empanelled.

Court Etiquette

2.12 Another consequence of the inquisitorial approach to Coronial proceedings is that the Coroner will take the lead role in questioning. Having given the parties to the inquest advance notice of the witnesses that the Coroner intends to call, subject only to objection or observation by the parties, these witnesses will take the oath and give their evidence. It is entirely for the Coroner as to how this evidence will be given. Usually statements would have been provided to the parties in advance of the hearing and the Coroner will take the lead in adducing evidence from that statement as he thinks appropriate and relevant. Furthermore the Coroner will decide in leading this evidence, what documentation or exhibits he will refer to or introduce into evidence. It is by no means certain that the Coroner will refer to everything within the statement, and attention will have to paid by the advocate as to what may be left out.

In adducing the evidence the role of the Coroner is to read into the court's proceedings those facts and that evidence which he considers to be relevant. This will have been subjectively decided upon by the Coroner and therefore the role of the advocate in their approach to the questioning of a witness will be vital.

There can at times be tension between the Coroner and the advocate. This tension is again rooted in the inquisitorial basis of the inquest proceedings. All parties are deemed to be endeavouring to obtain the truth within the strict confines of the Coronial objective. When the Coroner has finished asking his questions the advocate should assume that all matters of interest to the Coroner, or known to the Coroner have been covered and therefore a different practical approach is required of the advocate in a conduct of their own questioning. Put succinctly, the advocates' questions in the Coroner's Court are fundamentally designed to bring out new evidence or to clarify any matters that have been dealt with by the Coroner. They are not strictly to be seen as cross-examination or challenges. When an advocate begins questioning in the Coroner's Court (usually seated), his practical approach to questioning should be founded upon the concept that the Coroner will feel that he has asked all the questions that need to be asked, and therefore the advocate must initially couch their approach to the questioning of witnesses to take this into account, to maintain the ear of the court.

The Chief Coroner [Now Abolished]

2.13 The 2009 Act created the new position of Chief Coroner and Deputy Chief Coroner.[16]

In October 2010, the Coalition Government stated that the Chief Coroner would now be abolished, despite the appointment of an individual to that position. Many of the duties of the Chief Coroner and the roles designated to that position are expected to be taken by a Senior judge or a single judge. Both the Chief Coroner and the Deputy Chief Coroner would have been responsible for:

(i)   hearing appeals against decisions of Coroners;
(ii)   establishing and overseeing national performance standards;
(iii) providing leadership to the service in general.

They have also conducted investigations.

This important change was brought about by the 2009 Act introducing, by way of these new appointments, crucial oversight over the Coronial jurisdiction, which was lacking in the previous regime.

Hitherto there would be little continuity between the disparate Coroners' Courts and the old legal adage of equity being judged by the size of the Lord Chancellor's foot, had resonance with the Coroner's Court prior to the 2009 Act.

2.14 The introduction of the Chief Coroner and Deputy Chief Coroner regime was expected to provide leadership and consistency to the Coroner's Court and particularly provide for clear dance and standards, which should be expected of any national court jurisdiction.

The Chief Coroner and the Deputy Chief Coroner were new innovations within the legal system of England and Wales. The effect and influence of these two new positions would have been predicted by looking at other jurisdictions. An analysis in this book is still pertinent given the governments expressed, but unparticularised, statement in their October letter that the judiciary will be expected to carry some, if not all of the burden of the erstwhile Chief Coroner.

2.15 In Australia the Coroners Act 2003 section 71 lays down the State Coroner's functions:

(a) to oversee and coordinate the Coronial system; and
(b) to ensure the Coronial system is administered and operated efficiently; and
(c) to ensure deaths reported to Coroners that are reportable deaths are investigated to an appropriate extent; and

---

[16] Coroners and Justice Act 2009 s 35 and Sch 8.

(d) to ensure an inquest is held if

    (i) the inquest is required to be held under this Act; or
    (ii) it is desirable for the inquest to be held; and

(e) to be responsible, together with the Deputy State Coroner, for all investigations into deaths in custody; and

(f) to issue directions and guidelines about the investigation of deaths under this Act; and

(g) any other function given to the State Coroner or a Coroner under this Act.[17]

In the Australian case of *Von Einem v Ahern*[18] Chief Justice King observed:

> The State Coroner has a further special responsibility by reason of his administrative responsibilities for the Coroner's service throughout the State. It may be that in the discharge of the Coroner's administrative and investigative responsibilities he feels himself required from time to time to be in communication with the press. I would say that as a matter of prudence that it is desirable that he should avoid direct contact with the press so far as it is humanly possible to do so . . . once an inquest is underway I think that the Coroner should observe in relation to the press and others the same constraints so far as possible and applicable to his office which are observed by Judges in relation to cases which come before them. But as I say, by reason of his general administrative responsibilities it may not always be possible for the Coroner to observe those constraints in the same way in which they apply to Judges.

Commentators of comparative jurisdictions have remarked upon the 'unique judicial' status of the State Coroner (Chief Coroner), recognising as they do the 'discreet investigative, administrative, and adjudicative (judicial) responsibilities of Coroners and especially the State Coroner'.[19]

Abolition of Coroner of the Queen's Household

2.16 Section 46 of the 2009 Act abolishes the Office of Coroner of the Queen's Household. Upon implementation, any investigation which would have been carried out by the Coroner of the Queen's Household will be carried out by the Senior Coroner in whose area the deceased is, or by a Coroner directed by a judge exercising the power of the abolished Chief Coroner to carry out the investigation, or by a Corner requested to carry out the investigation as directed under section 2 of the 2009 Act.[20]

---

[17] See also Freckelton and Ranson, *Death Investigation and the Coroner's Inquest* (Oxford University Press, 2006) 99–100.

[18] *Von Einem v Ahern* (1988) 49 SASR 424, 426–7.

[19] See Freckelton and Ranson (n 26 above) 100.

[20] A Senior Coroner was to give to the Chief Coroner notice in writing of any request made by him or her for another Coroner to conduct the investigation, stating whether or not the potential new Coroner agreed to it: s 2(5). This is a general provision where a request is made by one Coroner for another to conduct an investigation.

Senior Coroners, Area Coroners and Assistant Coroners

2.17 Under the Coroners Act 1988 the hierarchy of Coroners (in descending order) consisted of Coroners, Deputy Coroners and Assistant Deputy Coroners. Furthermore, under the previous regime, the relevant local authority appointed Coroners (but not Deputy and Assistant Coroners, who were appointed by the Coroner, with the approval of the Chair of the relevant local authority). It is also the case that the Secretary of State approved certain Coroners' appointments, and where the Coroner's district consisted of two or more such areas, or two or more Welsh principal areas, the relevant local authority consulted the others before making an appointment. Under the 1988 Act, section 6 the Coroner appointed his own Deputy and any Assistant Deputy Coroners.

The 2009 Act seeks to introduce a new regime of Senior Coroners, Area Coroners and Assistant Coroners.

2.18 Under Part 1 of Schedule 3 appointments will be made by the relevant authority for each Coroner area. Additionally, and for the first time the Lord Chancellor must consent to the appointment of all Senior Coroners.

The Lord Chancellor will determine whether the Coroner area requires one or more Area Coroners in addition to the Senior Coroner and how many are required. This process was to be undertaken to determine the minimum number of Assistant Coroners required.[21]

Qualifications of Senior, Area and Assistant Coroners

2.19 As a result of the 2009 Act, all Coroners must be legally qualified. Under the 1988 Act[22] it was also sufficient to be a qualified medical practitioner of five years' standing. This will no longer be appropriate.

Transitional Arrangements

2.20 It is anticipated the transitional arrangements will be made so that the new provisions do not apply in relation to those Coroners who will be treated as appointed under such transitional arrangements. This will probably include Coroners appointed prior to the implementation of the 2009 Act.[23]

---

[21] Coroners and Justice Act 2009, Sch 3, paras 1 and 2(1)–(2).
[22] Coroners Act 1988, s 2(1)(b).
[23] Part 2 of the 2009 Act also disqualifies local councillors from being appointed as a Coroner, if the area in respect for which they were elected falls within the relevant Coronial area.

Vacation and Termination of Office

2.21 The Senior, Area and Assistant Coroner will be directed to retire at the age of 70. Significantly, the Coroner will no longer be regarded as holding a 'freehold office'.

This has been a slow development. The Local Government Act of 1888 abolished the election of Coroners by the freeholders of the county, and substituted appointment by the local authority. Hitherto section 1 of the Coroners Act 1988 provided that the Coroner held a freehold office under the Crown. Under section one, the appointment is made by the 'relevant Council'. Strictly this would mean that the appointment is made by elected councillors and not by paid officers or civil servants. Approval by the Secretary of State was required under section 1(2) of the 1988 Act before the local authority was permitted to appoint its chosen candidate.

2.22 In common with all Coroners, the Lord Chancellor will have the power to remove a Senior Coroner, Area Coroner or Assistant Coroner from office if that Coroner is considered incapable of performing his or her functions or is guilty of misbehaviour. Before the Lord Chancellor can exercise this power he must have the agreement of the Lord Chief Justice.[24]

2.23 Senior Coroners, Area Coroners and Assistant Coroners are subject to the disciplinary provisions of the Constitutional Reform Act 2005, Chapter 3 of Part 4.

This legislation provides the Lord Chancellor with disciplinary powers.[25] The Lord Chief Justice is also given power to exercise disciplinary functions. This includes providing the Coroner with formal advice, or a formal warning or reprimand, for disciplinary purposes.[26] This does not restrict what the Lord Chief Justice may do informally or for other purposes where any advice or warning is not addressed to a particular office-holder.

2.24 Sanctions at the command of the Lord Chief Justice under s 108(4) include suspension from judicial office for any period where any of the following apply:

(a) the Coroner is subject to criminal proceedings;
(b) the Coroner is serving a sentence imposed in criminal proceedings;
(c) the Coroner has been convicted of an offence and is subject to prescribed procedures in relation to the conduct constituting the offence.

The Lord Chief Justice may also suspend a Coroner under s 108(7) for any period during which he

---

[24] Schedule 3, Part 4 Section 13(1)
[25] Constitutional Reform Act 2005 (c 4) s 108 onwards.
[26] *ibid*, s 108(3).

(a) is under investigation for an offence; or

(b) is subjected to prescribed procedures.

Whilst any Coroner is suspended under this section he may not perform any of the functions of his office. Nevertheless his other rights as holder of the office are not affected.

2.25 The Constitutional Reform Act 2005[27] states that a person is subject to criminal proceedings if in any part of the United Kingdom proceedings against him for an offence have been begun and have not come to an end, and the times when proceedings are begun and come to an end for the purpose of that sub-section are such as maybe prescribed.

For the purposes of this legislation 'sentence' includes any sentence other than a fine.[28]

Coroner's Officers

2.26 The role of the Coroner's Officer is both ambiguous and incapable of precise definition.

Despite the significant provisions within the 2009 Act to harmonise Coronial jurisdiction, little or nothing has been done to provide similar consistency and transparency of the role of Coroner's Officer.

This office is both wide-ranging and potentially influential both in the investigation and ultimate administration of the hearing. The Coroner's Officer will work directly with public bodies, government departments, law enforcement agencies, bereaved families and any other interested parties to the proceedings and the perception of even handedness is essential.

The perception is not always easy to maintain. In the Explanatory Notes to the 2009 Act it is recognised that police authorities currently provide 90 per cent of Coroner's Officers to support the work of the Coroner.[29]

Presently where the local police authority is responsible for providing Coroner's Officers, the 2009 legislation expects them to continue to perform those duties. The legislation anticipates that the local authority and local police authority will work together, with the Senior Coroner to secure appropriate staffing levels.[30]

2.27 The Coroner's Officer will usually be the first individual to be seized of a death prior to the inquest beginning. He will be informed of the death and will

---

[27] *ibid*, s 109(2).

[28] *ibid*, s 109(6).

[29] See Explanatory Notes to the Coroners and Justice Act 2005, note 221.

[30] See Explanatory Notes, note 221.

even decide whether the police should be involved in the investigation of the fatality. The practical role of the Coroner's Officer continues with his involvement as to whether the body should be removed from the scene and how and when an undertaker should perform their duties.

It will be the Officer's duty to liaise with the pathologist. He is also most likely to be expected to communicate with the certifying doctor and act as a bridge between these professionals and the bereaved family. If there is to be an inquest into any death then it is for the Coroner's Officer to take or make provision for the taking of witness statements. Sometimes this will necessitate the Coroner's Officer travelling to meet witnesses, taking notes and perfecting the statements.

2.28 Given that the officer will most likely have had police training in the taking of statements, the form and content of the finalised document will be familiar to criminal practitioners.

In criminal law and procedure a police officer is expected to write down the exact words spoken by a person making a statement and they must not edit or paraphrase it.

When a police officer has finished writing the statement the person making it will be expected to read it and make any corrections, alterations or additions required. When this process has been completed the maker of the statement will be asked to write and sign or make their mark upon a declaration that what they have said is true and if they have said anything to the contrary they will be liable to prosecution.

This vigorous procedure required in the criminal courts of any police officer making a statement, should also be required of the Coroner's Officer, particularly given the likelihood that the Coroner's Officer is a former police officer.

2.29 Ultimately it will be the Coroner's Officer's responsibility to inform those witnesses who will be required to attend at the inquest when the inquest is taking place and on what dates and what times those witnesses will be required.

The difficulty with the Coroner's Officer being so closely connected with the police is stark when an inquest does or may involve criticism of the police force. Here again perception comes into play, and despite the best endeavours of Coroner's Officers to portray even-handedness between the parties, the perception, particularly that of the bereaved, can be to the contrary.[31]

---

[31] In the inquest into the death of James Collinson, one of those trainee soldiers who died at Deepcut Barracks, a significant part of the inquest involved criticism of the Surrey Police. As a result of a number of deaths at Deepcut Barracks between 1995 and 2001 the Surrey Police undertook a review of the investigations into the deaths of Private Sean Benton (1995), Private Cheryl James (1995) and Private Geoff Gray (2001). This review revealed that the investigations into these deaths had been unsatisfactory, which in turn led to the recognition that although it was the custom and practice of the day, it was inappropriate to delegate investigations into deaths that appeared to be self-inflicted to the army at an early stage in the process. In response to these findings, the Surrey Police launched an investigation of the first three deaths at Deepcut, which ran concurrently with the investigation into the deaths of a fourth young man, Private James Collinson. The Surrey Police also led the revision of national police policy on the investigation of deaths at military establishments where criminal conduct could not be

There is no standardised training or procedural discipline provided to Coroner's Officers and this inevitably results in an idiosyncratic interpretation of their goal. The advice cannot be avoided, that each practitioner at an inquest must take their Coroner's Officer as they find them.

2.30 In inquests involving documents or sensitivity or national security, again the Coroner's Officer will be given a unique role. Unlike the legal practitioner, the Coroner's Officer is often considered to be a fit and proper individual to see documents of high sensitivity. In this, they share the dispensation with the Coroner, the police, the security services, and her Majesty's Government.

At inquests involving the deaths of military personnel in the theatre of war, often and most usually certain statements are redacted and at times heavily redacted so that legal representatives and bereaved families or interested parties are not aware of what is contained within the statement. In some cases the legal advisor is permitted to view some of the redacted or partially redacted documentation, upon application to the Coroner. As a matter of practice the lawyer will sit in a closed room, with books and writing material, which he is not permitted to remove from that room at any time, and make notes from the redacted material. Invigilating in that room at all times, is the Coroner's Officer, policing the appropriate behaviour of the legal profession.

Accommodation

2.31 The relevant local authority is also obliged to provide, or secure the provision of, necessary accommodation to enable Senior Coroners to carry out their functions. This accommodation must be maintained by the relevant authority, or alternatively the authority must make provision for its maintenance.[32]

The provision contained within section 24 of the 2009 Act recognising that another person may have responsibility for maintaining accommodation, recognises that not all Coroners have a dedicated court to hold inquests and that there will continue to be a need to hire such facilities in the future, including court accommodation where the existing courtroom is insufficient for the purposes of a particular inquest.[33] This situation arises in the case of high-profile or multi-death inquests, where either there is a large amount of public interest and anticipated

---

conclusively ruled out at the outset. Although in the Collinson inquest the Coroner's office was not connected to the police, one can readily see the perceived difficulty that bereaved families might feel should a Coroner's Officer, connected to the police, be taking statement from a police force who may be subject to criticism at the Inquest. Indeed at the Collinson inquest a further conflict presented itself where the criticised Surrey police at the inquest were responsible for providing the Coroner with documents at their discretion and subjective view of relevance.

[32] This provision does not apply if another person has responsibility for maintaining the accommodation. See s 24 of the Coroners and Justice Act 2009.

[33] See Explanatory Notes, note 222.

public attendance in the public court or there are a large number of bereaved families or interested parties who will require accommodation.[34] Under section 31 of the 1988 Act, the relevant council has power to provide accommodation for inquests.

The relevant authorities are required to take into account the views of the Senior Coroner when providing and, where relevant, maintaining accommodation. The 2009 Act allows inquests to be held anywhere in England and Wales, so that there is new flexibility if particular inquests have requirements for the sort of accommodation which is not available within the Coroner's own area. It is nevertheless expected that an inquest will normally be held within the area of the Coroner who is conducting the investigation, as is presently the position.[35] The ability of Coroners in different geographical areas to take the burden of inquests is an important change brought about by the 2009 legislation.

2.32 There were and there continues to be significant delays in the holding of inquests, which at times can take place some years after the death. These delays not only cause considerable distress to bereaved families and interested parties, but it is also arguable that they are in breach of the provisions of the European Convention on Human Rights.[36] Independent Monitoring Boards in relation to deaths in prison have highlighted the damage done by delays to inquest hearings. In their annual report of 2007, the Independent Monitoring Board of HMP Belmarsh observed:

> [T]he delay between deaths in custody and inquests is an absolute disgrace. Belmarsh is still waiting for four inquests relating to deaths over eighteen months ago, including one which took place in January 2005. The effect of waiting for these lengthy periods is devastating for bereaved families and also for the staff who were involved at the time.[37]

The Parliamentary Joint Committee on Human Rights observed in 2004:

> Where the inquest is the means by which the Article 2 duty of investigation is satisfied following a death in custody, then significant delays may breach Article 2, which requires that an investigation into a death be prompt. We are concerned that current delays may in some instances lead to breaches of article 2.[38]

There remains concern that despite the provisions within the 2009 legislation there may not be sufficient resources within the reformed system to enable these powers to make a real difference.[39]

---

[34] In the inquests into the deaths of Diana Princess of Wales and Dodi Al Fayed, the Queen Elizabeth Conference Centre was used. At the inquest into the death of Jean Charles de Menezes a cricket ground was used and at the inquest into the deaths of 10 servicemen personnel, who died as a result of the Hercules aircraft being destroyed by enemy fire, the Trowbridge town hall was seconded for the purposes of the inquest.

[35] See Explanatory Notes to the 2009 Act, note 223.

[36] ECHR Article 2 (Right to Life).

[37] See HMP Belmarsh, *Annual Report of The Independent Monitoring Board (1 July 2007– 30 June 2008)*.

[38] See the Joint Committee on Human Rights, 'Deaths in Custody': Third Report of Session 2004–05 vol I 2004, para 304 (p 87).

[39] Inquest, 'Briefing on Coroners and Justice Bill 2009 – House of Lords Second Reading. 15 May 2009'.

The Courtroom

2.33 The layout of the Inquest will vary depending upon the venue at which the hearing is to be heard. Substantially, advocates will take up their positions in the courtroom as they would in any other tribunal. There is no protocol as to where at the table or bench different parties should sit. Neither is the convention, observed in other courtrooms, that instructing solicitors or clerks should sit behind counsel, adhered to in Coronial proceedings. It is deemed permissible by Coroners for instructing solicitors and those representing the firm to sit next to the advocate and assist them with documentation, instructions or by note taking.

At Military Inquests it is usual for the President of the Board of Inquiry to be seated next to the advocate appearing on behalf of the Ministry of Defence, throughout the hearings.

Representatives of the bereaved family and interested parties will sit directly behind their legal team as will others who may have a direct role to play at the Inquest.

Normally the public and the media are admitted to the Inquest hearing.[40]

2.34 There is no unanimity between Coroners as to court dress.

The majority of Coroners favour formal lounge suit or other such appropriate attire, both for the Coroner and for the advocates.

But this is not universally observed. There are Coroners who direct that advocates should be robed at the Inquest and that the Coroner appears robed as well.[41] It is sensible to contact the particular Coroner's Court in advance of any hearing to ascertain the particular requirements in relation to dress code of the Coroner with conduct of the hearing.

---

[40] See chapter 10 below.
[41] For instance Andrew Walker often insists upon this protocol.

3

The Duties of the Coroner

3.1 The Coroner's duties will only begin when there is a dead body. This might be construed as stating the obvious, but Coroners have been asked to advise whether or not life sustaining machines in hospitals such as ventilators should be turned off. This is not part of the Coroner's role and so long as a body remains alive the Coroner has no role or duties applied to him.

3.2 There is no legal definition of death.

In the majority of cases there is no difficulty in recognising death.

The introduction of organ transplantation, however, and of more effective mechanical means of resuscitation, such as respirators, whereby an individual's heart can be kept beating almost indefinitely, can at times raise difficulties.

To deal with this, the concept of 'Brain Death' has been introduced. In other words, if there is no evidence of brain activity, as shown by the absence of reflexes and the electro-encephalogram, death is assumed to have occurred even though breathing and the beating of the heart can be maintained by artificial methods.[1]

Section 1 of the 2009 Act lays down the duties of the Senior Coroner to investigate certain deaths.[2]

3.3 The 2009 legislation sets out the circumstances when the Senior Coroner must investigate a death. To a certain degree it reflects the requirements of the Coroners Act 1988 Section 8(1), although there is a significant alteration.

Section 8(1)(c) provided that an inquest be held where the deceased 'has died in prison or in such a place or in such circumstances as to require an inquest under any other Act.' This has been amended by section 1 of the 2009 legislation to read

---

[1] See William AR Thomson (ed), *Black's Medical Dictionary*, 33rd edn (Adam & Charles Black, 1981) 243.

[2] It is interesting to compare this with the recommendations of the Parliamentary Select Committee on the Office of Coroner in 1860, which was chaired by Robert Lowe. That Committee recommended 'an inquest ought to be held in every case of violent or unnatural death, and in cases of sudden death where the cause of death is unknown, and also where, though the death is apparently natural, reasonable suspicion of criminality exists'. The Coroners Act 1988 s 8(1) dealt with this issue and laid down that: 'where a coroner is informed that the body of a person . . . is lying within his district and there is reasonable cause to suspect that the deceased (a) has died a violent or an unnatural death; (b) has died a sudden death of which the cause is unknown; or (c) has died in prison or in such a place or in such circumstances as to require an inquest under any other Act, then whether the cause of death arose within his district or not, the coroner shall as soon as practicable hold an inquest into the death of the deceased either with . . . [or] without a jury'.

so that it applies to deaths where the deceased 'died a violent or unnatural death', or 'the cause of death is unknown', 'or died while in custody or otherwise in state detention.'

The effect of section 1 is that the Coroner must investigate fatalities that he suspects were violent or unnatural, where for example, the deceased may have been murdered or taken his own life, or if the cause of death was unknown. Furthermore the Coroner must also investigate a death, whatever the apparent cause, if it occurred in lawful detention, such as whilst the deceased was detained in prison or in police custody.

In short, the circumstances in which a Coroner must investigate a death are similar to those in section 8(1) of the 1988 Act with the exception of the 'state detention' provision. Furthermore the requirement that a death be 'sudden', as well as of a 'cause unknown', has been removed.[3]

Consultation concerning section 1 and the provision that there be an investigation into a death which resulted while the deceased was 'in custody or otherwise in state detention', revealed some important distinctions.

The pressure group Inquest, a charitable trust concerned with the provision of Coronial justice, argued that although the 2009 Act on this point was broader than the current provision in section 8(1)(b) of the 1988 Act, in that the prior requirement that the death be 'sudden' as well as of a 'cause unknown' was removed as was the simple reference to a death 'in prison', from the 1988 Act, concern was nevertheless expressed that those detained in mental health institutions, secure training centres or immigration detention centres as well as those detained within the criminal justice system might not be encompassed by the proposed legislation. It was argued that this may be in violation of European jurisprudence.[4] Inquest argued that the words 'in custody' be removed from section 1(2)(c) of the 2009 Act and that the following sub-section should be inserted: 'this sub-section applies if the coroner has reasonable cause to suspect that the deceased died while in prison or otherwise lawfully detained'.

The legislature opted for the expression 'state detention'.

The Location of the Deceased

3.4 Under the 2009 legislation a Senior Coroner will be allocated to a geographical area.[5]

---

[3] Compare the Coroners Act 1988 s 8(1)(b), which reads: 'has died a sudden death of which the cause is unknown'.

[4] See *Menson v UK* (Application No 47916/99) ECHR, 6 May 2003, which laid down that Art 2 of the European Convention on Human Rights (right to life) applied where the factual circumstances imposed an obligation on the authorities to protect an individual's life, for example where they have assumed responsibility for welfare, which would apply to those in mental health settings as much as to those detained by the police or prisons.

[5] Although these boundary restrictions can be relaxed.

The location of the body of the deceased will determine which Senior Coroner has a duty to investigate the death. In this respect the law has not changed and is the same as laid out in the 1988 Act section 5(1) and section 8(1). The rationale of the law is to ensure that more than one Coroner does not initiate an investigation into death. Section 48(2) of the 2009 Act lays down that a person is in 'State detention' if he or she is compulsorily detained by a public authority within the meaning of section 6 of the Human Rights Act 1998. The Explanatory Notes accompanying the Act state that whilst the deceased is detained in prison, police custody or an immigration detention centre or held under mental health legislation then the Coroner must investigate a death irrespective of whether the detention was lawful or unlawful.[6]

The Explanatory Notes go on to lay down that the circumstances in which a Coroner must investigate a death are broadly similar to those contained in section 8(1) of the 1988 Act.

Where authorities have a statutory requirement to investigate particular deaths, such as the Health and Safety Executive or the Independent Police Complaints Commission, the Coroner will wait for those authorities to report before deciding upon how to proceed. This does not include the commissioning of post-mortem examinations, where appropriate, or associated duties in relation to the body of the deceased person. The duties of the Coroner in respect to these matters remain unchanged.[7]

Section 5(1) of the 1988 Act provides that an inquest into a death shall be held only by the Coroner within whose district the body lies. Furthermore section 5(2) adds that a Coroner shall hold inquests only within his district.

If parts of the same body are found lying over different Coronial geographical areas, the practical solution would seem to be that the Coroners who might be seised of the case will agree between themselves as to who should hear the inquest.

3.5 There maybe uncertainty as to whether the human remains can constitute a body for the purposes of section 8 and there is little case law on this subject. It is suggested that the test must be whether the quantity of remains found is sufficient to prove death. For example, death may be regarded as apparent if a head is found but the same could not necessarily be said upon finding an arm or a leg. As Christopher Dorries, latterly a full-time Coroner for the Western District of South Yorkshire pointed out in his book, the finding of a leg or arm might for example, 'be an amputated limb lost from normal circumstances. Fragments of human tissue at the site of an air crash may be convincing evidence of death, but would be far from certain proof if discovered by themselves on the ground'.[8]

3.6 If no body can be found, but death is believed to have occurred, the Coroner, by virtue of section 15 of the 1988 Act may report to the Home Secretary that he

[6] See Explanatory Notes to the Coroners and Justice Act 2009, note 61.
[7] *ibid*, note 61.
[8] See Christopher Dorries, *Coroners' Courts: A Guide to Law and Practice* (Wiley and Sons, 1999) 23.

has reason to believe that a death has occurred in or near his geographical area and the circumstances of death are such that he believes that an inquest ought to be held and would be held if there was a body. Section 15(2) gives the Home Secretary the power to direct that the Coroner should hold such an inquest on the basis that it is considered 'desirable to do so'.[9]

The provisions in relation to circumstances where no body has been discovered will include circumstances such as where a body has been lost at, or swept away to, sea, or if someone is suspected to have lost their life in a fire and there are no remains, or if the deceased has already been cremated and information previously unavailable comes to light which the Senior Coroner believes should lead him or her to investigate.[10] If it is decided that action should be taken, the Senior Coroner directed to carry out the investigation does not have to be the same Coroner that reported the death, although in most circumstances it is anticipated that it is likely that it would be.[11] This decision is most likely to be delegated to a judge. An example where it maybe appropriate for a different Coroner to conduct the inquest from the Coroner who reported the death, is where a Judge might consider it more convenient for the bereaved relatives for the investigation to take place in an alternative area. The participation of bereaved relatives and interested parties is crucial to a fair hearing in accordance with European jurisprudence[12] and if a hearing is scheduled to take place in such a location as to make it difficult for such parties to attend, then it is arguable that it will be in breach of the European Convention on Human Rights, Article 2.

3.7 A Senior Coroner may make whatever enquiries seem necessary in order to decide whether there should be an investigation into death whether or not a body remains.[13]

A Senior Coroner's initial decision as to whether to conduct an investigation was to be subject to appeal to the Chief Coroner.[14]

Prior to the 2009 legislation the decisions made by Coroners as to whether or not to investigate lacked consistency. There is little guidance as to how Coroners should exercise their discretion and this resulted in diverging decision making. The provisions contained in the 2009 legislation are intended to harmonise the criteria by which such important decisions are taken. Once more, if it is considered that the decision taken not to initiate an inquest is *Wednesbury* unreasonable, then it is susceptible to judicial review,[15] as is the case under the Coroners Act 1988.

---

[9] Should any party consider that the Home Secretary exercised his discretion unreasonably then the matter may be subject to judicial review: See *R v Home Secretary, ex parte Weatherhead* (1996) 160 JP 627.

[10] See Explanatory Notes to the 2009 Act, note 64.

[11] *ibid*, note 66.

[12] See Art 2 of the European Convention on Human Rights.

[13] Section 1(7) of the 2009 Act.

[14] *ibid*, s 40.

[15] See *R (on the application of Touche) v Inner London Coroner* [2001] 3 WLR 148.

The Transfer of Responsibility

3.8 Section 2 of the 2009 legislation gives the Senior Coroner power to transfer responsibility for the investigation of a death to another Coroner, where that Coroner agrees. Section 2 reflects the provisions contained in the 1988 Act at section 14, here it was provided that any application be made in writing,[16] after which the appointed Coroner will assume all powers and duties in relation to that inquest.

The Foetus or Still-Born Child

3.9 Neither the non-viable foetus or a still-born child is recognised in law as a 'body'.

The Births and Deaths Registration Act 1953 (as amended by the Still-birth Definition Act 1992) defines a still-born child as:

> one which has issued forth from its mother after the 24th week of pregnancy and which did not at any time after being completely expelled from its mother breathe or show any other signs of life.

Logically, as life has not been deemed to exist, as a matter of law, death cannot have occurred and therefore the Coroner has no jurisdiction upon the event.

3.10 There is no statutory obligation upon a Coroner to resume any inquests which have been adjourned pursuant to section 16(1) of the 1988 Act.

Section 16(3) provides:

> (3) after the conclusion of the relevant criminal proceedings . . . the Coroner may, subject to the following provisions of this section, resume the adjourned inquest if it in his opinion there is sufficient cause to do so.

In *R v Inner West London Coroner, ex parte Dallaglio*[17] Simon Brown LJ observed: 'The decision to be made under section 16(3) is of a highly discretionary character and in no way circumscribed by a need to find exceptional circumstances, only "sufficient cause"'.

---

[16] Section 14(5) of the Coroners Act 1988.
[17] *R v Inner West London Coroner, ex parte Dallaglio* [1994] 4 All ER 139, 155 D.

4

Entry, Search and Seizure

4.1 Under the Coroners Act 1988, Coroners do not have any power to enter and search premises or to seize evidence.

Furthermore, the Coroners Rules 1984 make no provision for the Coroner to exercise powers of entry, search and seizure.

4.2 By virtue of Schedule 5 of the Coroners and Justice Act 2009,[1] Coroners were expected to have new statutory powers to enter and search land or property and seize items which are relevant to their investigations. These powers are intended for situations either where the police have immediately eliminated the possibility of the death being suspicious but where the information they have provided to the Coroner leads him or her to request the police to seize specific items if the owner of the material is unable or unwilling to consent to the material being removed; or where a Coroner has already received an investigator's report, and the Coroner decides that further evidence is required in relation to the case.

4.3 The new procedure for search and entry is expected to mirror, where appropriate, the Police and Criminal Evidence Act 1984 sections 15 and 16.

Section 15(2) of the 1984 Act lays down that

(2) Where a Constable applies for any such warrant, it shall be his duty –

(a) to state –

(i) the ground on which he makes the application;

(ii) the enactment under which the warrant would be issued;

(iii) if the application is for a warrant authorising entry and search on more than one occasion, the ground on which he applies for such a warrant, whether he seeks a warrant authorising an unlimited number of entries, or (if not) the maximum number of entries desired . . .

Section 15 of the 1984 Act also requires the Constable to identify so far as practicable the articles or person to be sought.

4.4 The legislature anticipates that the Coroner will have to set out in writing, on a prescribed form to be sent previously to the Chief Coroner, and now possibly to a Judge, an application outlining: the premises to which he or she wishes to gain

---

[1] Coroners and Justice act 2009, Sch 5, para 3(1)–(6).

entry; the identity of the person in occupation, the investigation it relates to; the reason for requiring the power to force entry to premises for the purposes of search and seizure; the identity, so far as possible, of the articles or persons to be sought; and the time-scale within which a response is required.

In non-urgent cases the legislature anticipates that a turnaround time for such requests of between 48 hours and five days will be appropriate. However, it is anticipated that in cases of real urgency (as agreed by Parliament) the Coroner may request permission over the telephone. The outcome of the decision for entry, search and seizure must be set out in writing in prescribed form to be sent to the Coroner who makes the application. It is again anticipated that this procedure will apply even if the Coroner has sought permission over the telephone. A hard-copy record will be made and completed for audit trail purposes.

In normal circumstances – for instance when entry and search are not being conducted at the scene of death at the time the death has occurred or has been discovered – a reasonable period of notice could be given to landowners and occupiers before the Coroner carries out entry and search of premises and seizure of items. The legislature anticipates that this period will be in the region of 48 hours. Nevertheless, in situations where the Chief Coroner has given approval for the power to be exercised without notice due to the very strong risk of concealment, loss, damage, alteration or destruction of evidence,[2] no notice will be required.

4.5 It is not anticipated that Coroners will carry out the actual physical activity of entry, search and seizure personally in the majority of cases. These functions will be delegated under provisions to be made by secondary legislation. It is anticipated that these functions will be delegated to Coroner's Officers or to police officers.

Again, the procedures for carrying out entry, search and seizure will rely heavily upon the precedents created by the Police and Criminal Evidence Act 1984 and in particular sections 15, 16 and 21 of that Act. In effect, this means that the Chief Coroner's permission to conduct an entry and search will only permit a single entry and search and that such entries and searches must be conducted at a reasonable time of the day unless it appears that the purpose of the search would be frustrated by delaying its starting. Furthermore the search may only be conducted to the extent required for the purposes of the Coroner's investigation.

4.6 As a result of the provisions within Schedule 5 of the 2009 Act, the Ministry of Justice has indicated[3] that 'seizure could take place at any time of the day, without notice or consent, and if necessary without the owner being present'. Furthermore, once entry has been effected, no further period of notice should need to be given before seizure can take place, the Coroner would merely have to inform the owner of the goods that they have been seized, and the reason for that seizure. In the case of documents or computer files, however, the owner will be given opportunity to

---

[2] *ibid*, Sch 5, para 3(3).
[3] Consultation Paper CP06/10 (Ministry of Justice, March 2010) chapter 4, para 11 (p 41).

make copies before the items are removed from the premises, this again mirrors the provisions within section 21 of the 1984 Act.

The Coroner will be allowed to take with him onto the premises any individuals who he thinks (or his delegate thinks) are necessary to ensure the goods are seized and removed promptly and effectively. For instance this could include locksmiths and removal people but could also require certain specialists if the items are valuable, fragile or are, for example, computer records that require downloading or documentary records that require photocopying. The Coroner or his delegate will be required to compile an inventory in prescribed form to be signed by the Coroner or his delegate and the owner of the goods seized if they are present. Nevertheless, refusal to sign the document will not be allowed to prevent its removal. If the owner is not present or refuses to sign, the inventory should be left in a prominent position within the property in a sealed envelope.

Once a seized or copied document has been put before the inquest as an exhibit it will become subject to provisions on making documents available to interested persons, and copies, according to procedure, could be provided to such interested persons.

5

The Purpose of the Coroner's Court

5.1 The purpose of an investigation as laid out under section 5 of the 2009 legislation can be broken down into five elements:

(a) who the deceased was;
(b) how the deceased came by his death;
(c) when the deceased came by his death;
(d) where the deceased was when he came by his death;
(e) ascertaining in what circumstances the deceased came by his death.

These new provisions represent what was laid down in the 1988 Act section 8(1), as developed by case law and the demands of the European Convention on Human Rights, and represent the existing approach of Coroners' Courts to their investigations. The ambit of the Coroner's investigation has potentially widened in recent years.

5.2 The principle development has been around the issue of 'how' the deceased came about his death.

Until relatively recently, inquest procedure and investigation took a narrow approach to its jurisdiction. The Coroners Rules 1984, Rule 36, laid down the 'who' 'how' 'when' and 'where' parameters for the inquest investigation. Coroners will strictly interpret the straight-jacket which the Coroners Rules 1984, the Coroners Act 1988 and the 2009 legislation places around them. It is for the Coroner to decide which 'witnesses' it is expedient to examine.[1] And although other parties may make suggestions to the Coroner as to further witnesses they require to be called, the initiative is firmly with the Coroner.

The Coroner will not hesitate to rely upon rule 20(1)(b) of the Coroners Rules 1984 which states in terms:

> The Coroner shall disallow any question which in his opinion is not relevant or is otherwise not a proper question.

The combination of the 1988 Act and the Coroners Rules is thereby used to strictly confine Advocates in the line of questioning that they may seek to take. Although different Coroners take different approaches to the interpretation of these provisions they form the central spine which will limit how far a case may be

---

[1] See Coroners Act 1988 s 11(2).

put, often leading to frustration by bereaved parties or interested parties that a full investigation is not being fulfilled by the Coronial process. It is important that the expectations of bereaved families and other interested parties are carefully managed as to how far an inquest can probe into a death.

5.3 During the course of various parliamentary and public debates calling for public inquiries into high-profile fatalities, either abroad in the theatre of war or domestically, politicians have habitually argued that there is no need for a public inquiry given that the investigation at an inquest adequately fulfils that function. This is somewhat disingenuous on behalf of the politicians and others who argue this point. The ambit of the inquest investigation is significantly narrower than a public inquiry.

Jamieson[2]

5.4 The starting point in a consideration of the ambit of an inquest, is the case of Michael Jamieson.

Mr Jamieson hanged himself whilst he was detained in prison at Full Sutton, near York. It was clear on the facts of the case that the deceased had been showing disturbed behaviour for some time, and the inquest recorded a verdict of suicide. The family of the deceased were unhappy with this verdict and argued that the Coroner should have left the issue of 'lack of care', to the jury, given the warning signs that Mr Jamieson had shown prior to his suicide and the lack of steps taken by the prison service to care for this man. In due course the Court of Appeal heard the case and the judgment of Lord Justice Bingham (as he then was) became seminal in the development of an understanding of the purposes of an inquest investigation.

The judgment of Lord Justice Bingham bears close analysis. In his section headed 'General Conclusions' the learned Judge states:

> An inquest is a fact finding inquiry conducted by a Coroner, with or without a jury, to establish reliable answers to four important but limited factual questions. The first of these relates to the identity of the deceased, the second to the place of his death, the third to the time of death. In most cases these questions are not hard to answer but in a minority of cases the answer maybe problematical. The fourth question, and that to which evidence and inquiry are most often and most closely directed, relates to how the deceased came by his death. Rule 36 requires that the proceedings in evidence shall be directed solely at ascertaining these matters and forbids any expression of opinion on any other matters.

Lord Justice Bingham then made the critical observation in the second of his conclusions:

---

[2] *HM Coroner for North Humberside and Scunthorpe, ex parte Jamieson* [1995] QB 1; [1994] 3 All ER 972 (CA).

'How' is to be understood as meaning 'by what means'. It is noteworthy that the task is not to ascertain how the deceased died, which might raise general and far reaching issues, 'but how the deceased came by his death', a more limited question directed to the means by which the deceased came by his death.

Jamieson was a case on neglect, which established that the expression 'lack of care' should be replaced by the concept that death was 'contributed to by neglect'. The Court of Appeal then went on to lay down 14 principles to define neglect.

Lord Justice Bingham observed: 'Neither neglect nor self neglect should ever form any part of any verdict unless a clear and direct causal connection is established between the conduct so described and the cause of death'. This requirement for a direct test of causation was interpreted so as to narrow the purpose of an inquest's investigation.[3] Mr Justice Tomlinson in *R v Coventry Coroner, ex parte Chief Constable of Staffordshire Police* observed that

> the causal connection which is relevant in the context of consideration by an inquest jury of the addition of a neglect rider is, in my judgment, not the same as the causal connection for which one may look in the context of other, perhaps more familiar inquiries. The touchstone in the present context is, I believe, the opportunity of rendering care, in the narrow sense of that word, which would have prevented the death ... that does not mean that a conscientious person would necessarily have done that which would have successfully prevented death. The question is whether he had the opportunity of doing something effective.[4]

Put succinctly, *Jamieson* directed a prescriptive approach to Coronial procedure. *Jamieson* was not the first case to touch upon this restrictive approach. In *R v Coroner for Western District of East Sussex, ex parte Homberg, Roberts and Manner*[5] Lord Justice Simon Brown considered an inquest into the death of five people who died in a fire at a boarding house. The Court held that the inquest should discover, if possible, how the five individuals died but not how the lack of fire precautions resulted in the tragedy. The judge, in many ways previewing what *Jamieson* was to establish, held that the inquest must focus on matters directly causative of death, but this inquiry excluded evidence into any underlying responsibility for circumstances which contributed to the deaths.

He added: 'the duty to inquire "how" the deceased died does not to my mind properly encompass enquiry also into the underlying responsibility for every circumstance which maybe said to have contributed to the death'.[6]

---

[3] Courts were subsequently at pains to distinguish the causation test at inquests from that in the civil jurisdiction, for instance in *R v Coventry Coroner, ex parte Chief Constable of Staffordshire Police* (2000) 164 JP 665, 675–6, affirmed in *Scott v Inner West London Coroner* [2001] EWHC Admin 105, paras 14–15.

[4] See (2000) 164 JP 665, 675–6.

[5] *R v Coroner for Western District of East Sussex, ex parte Homberg, Roberts and Manner* (1994) 158 JP 357.

[6] *ibid,* 372.

Middleton

5.5 The next development in law came as a result of the case of *R v Coroner for the Western District of Somerset, ex parte Middleton.*[7]

Middleton was a response by the domestic jurisdiction to the European Convention on Human Rights.[8]

An influential tribunal in the House of Lords, which included Lord Bingham of Cornhill, Lord Hope of Craighead and Baroness Hale of Richmond, considered the question as to whether domestic law was compliant with the substantive obligations laid down by European jurisprudence. Central to the consideration of the House of Lords was Article 2 of the European Convention on Human Rights. This imposed upon Member States a substantive obligation not to take life without justification and also to establish a framework of laws, precautions, procedures and means of enforcement which would, to the greatest extent reasonably practicable, protect life.[9]

Significantly in the context of inquests, European law has interpreted Article 2 as imposing upon Member States a procedural obligation to initiate an effective public investigation by an independent official body into any death occurring in circumstances in which it appears that one or other of the other substantive obligations articulated within the European Convention has been, or may have been, violated and it appears that agents of the state are, or maybe, in some way implicated.[10]

The House of Lords considered what would constitute a properly conducted official investigation into a death which involved or possibly involved a violation of Article 2. This would include an inquest.

One of the purposes of an Article 2 investigation has been held to be: '. . . that those who have lost their relative may at least have the satisfaction of knowing that lessons learnt from his death may save the lives of others'.[11]

In *Jordan v UK*[12] the Court described the purpose of an investigation required by Article 2 as follows:

> The obligation to protect the right to life under Article 2 of the Convention, read in conjunction with the State's general duty under Article 1 of the Convention to 'Secure

---

[7] *R v Coroner for the Western District of Somerset, ex parte Middleton* [2004] WLR 800; [2004] UKHL 10 on appeal from [2002] EWCA Civ 390; [2003] QB 581.

[8] See also *R v Coroner for the County of West Yorkshire, ex parte Saker* [2004] UKHL 11, on appeal from [2003] EWCA Civ 217; *In re McKerr* [2004] UKHL 12, on appeal from [2002] NICA 1, subsequent to *McKerr v Armagh Coroner* [1990] 1 WLR 649 and *McKerr v UK* (2002) 34 EHRR 20.

[9] See *Osman v United Kingdom* (1998) 29 EHRR 245; *Keenan v UK* (2001) 33 EHRR 913, paras 88–90: and *Edwards v UK* (2002) 35 EHRR 487, para 54.

[10] See for example *Taylor v UK* (1994) 79-A DR 127, 137; *McCann v UK* (1995) 21 EHRR 97, para 161; *Jordan v UK* (2001) 37 EHRR 52, para 105; and *Oneryildiz v Turkey* (Application No 48939/99) unreported, ECtHR, 18 June 2002.

[11] *R(Amin) v Secretary of State for the Home Department* [2003] UKHL 51, [2003] 3 WLR 1169.

[12] *Jordan v UK* (2001) 37 EHRR 52, para 105.

to everyone within [its] jurisdiction the rights and freedoms defined in [the] Convention' also requires by implication that there should be some form of effective official investigation when individuals have been killed as a result of the use of force. The essential purpose of such investigation is to secure the effective implementation of the domestic laws which protect the right to life and, in those cases involving State agents or bodies, to ensure their accountability for deaths occurring under their responsibility. What form of investigation will achieve those purposes may vary in different circumstances. However, whatever mode is employed, the authorities must act of their own motion, once the matter has come to their attention. They cannot leave it to the initiative of the next of kin either to lodge a formal complaint or to take responsibility for the conduct of any investigative procedures . . .

The House of Lords was ultimately of the view that a strict *Jamieson* approach to proceedings would not meet Convention requirements.

5.6 The House of Lords sought to remedy this problem by broadly interpreting the word 'how' in the Coroners Act 1988, section 11(5)(b)(ii) and Rule 36(1)(b) of the Coroners Rules 1984, so that it meant not simply 'by what means' but 'by what means and in what circumstances'.[13]

5.7 The House of Lords emphasised that nothing in their judgment meant that the inquest should find criminal liability or determine any question in a civil dispute.[14]

The Coroners Rules do treat criminal and civil liability differently. Whereas a verdict must not be framed so as to appear to determine any question of criminal liability on the part of a *named* person, thereby, as was pointed out in *Middleton*, legitimising a verdict of unlawful killing provided no one is named, the prohibition on returning a verdict so as to appear to determine any question of civil liability is unqualified, applying whether anyone is named or not.[15] In case of conflict, the statutory duty to ascertain how the deceased came by his death will prevail over the prohibition in Rule 42.[16] Nevertheless the House of Lords in *Middleton* observed that the conflict would be small. Rule 42 applies, and applies only, to

---

[13] The House of Lords at para 31 of their judgment referred to *Keenan v UK* (2001) 33 EHRR 913 as precisely the sort of case which would be cured by the *Middleton* judgment. In *Keenan* the inquest verdict of death by misadventure and the certificate of asphyxiation by hanging as the cause of death did not express the jury's conclusion of the events leading up to the death. Furthermore in Edwards (see above) the jury's verdict of unlawful killing did not enable them to express any conclusion on what would have been a major issue within that inquest, namely the procedures which led in that case to the deceased and his killer sharing a cell.

[14] See the Coroners Rules 1984, rule 42.

[15] The House of Lords justified this position on the grounds of fairness. The court observed that the law accords a defendant accused of crime or a party alleged to have committed a civil wrong certain safeguards rightly regarded as essential to the fairness of the proceedings, among them a clear statement in writing of the alleged wrong doing, a right to call any relevant and admissible evidence and a right to address factual submissions to the tribunal of fact. These rights, the House of Lords observed, are not granted, and the last is expressly denied by the Coroners Rules, to a party who's conduct maybe impugned by evidence given at an inquest. See the General conclusion, para 4 of the *Middleton* judgment in the House of Lords.

[16] General Conclusions, para 5.

the verdict. The Coroner and/or the jury may explore facts bearing on criminal and civil liability. But any verdict may not appear to determine any question of criminal liability on the part of a named person nor any question of civil liability be it a named or unnamed person.

Any verdict must be factual, expressing no judgement or opinion.[17]

As a result of *Middleton* the Coroner is obliged to take into account Article 2 and in particular the implicit procedural obligation for there to be an effective inquiry into the circumstances of a death, at least when there is an alleged involvement of the state in the events which have happened.

Recent Approaches

5.8 The result of *Middleton* is clear that an inquest is a fact-finding inquiry to ascertain by what means and what circumstances the deceased came by his death.

In any Article 2 hearing the inquest will become the mechanism by which the state will seek to discharge its investigative obligations under the Convention.

In *R(Amin) v Secretary of State for the Home Department*[18] Lord Bingham articulated the relationship between any substantive breach of the Article 2 duty to protect life[19] and the investigative requirements, in the following way:

> 2. The European Court of Human Rights has repeatedly interpreted Article 2 of the European Convention as imposing on Member States substantive obligations not to take life without justification and also to establish a framework of laws, precautions, procedures and means of enforcement which will, to the greatest extent reasonably practicable, protect life . . .

> 3. The European Court has also interpreted Article 2 as imposing on Member States a procedural obligation to initiate an effective public investigation by an independent official body into any death occurring in circumstances in which it appears that one or other of the foregoing substantive obligations have been, or may have been, violated and it appears that agents of the state are, or maybe, in some way implicated.

Lord Bingham went on to define the purposes of an Article 2 inquiry as:

> 31. To ensure so far as possible that the full facts are brought to light; that culpable and discreditable conduct is exposed and brought to public notice; that suspicion of deliberate wrong doing (if justified) is allayed; that dangerous practices and procedures are rectified; and that those who have lost their relative may at least have the satisfaction of knowing that lessons learnt from his death may save the lives of others.

---

[17] And neither should the jury prepare detailed factual statements. See the General conclusions paragraph 6.

[18] *R(Amin) v Secretary of State for the Home Department* [2004] 1 AC 653, paras 2 and 3 of Lord Bingham's judgment.

[19] Not, it is to be noted, to prevent death.

In such circumstances it is argued that the proper test of causation should be whether any failing contributed to the death more than minimally, negligibly or trivially.[20]

In *R v Inner South London Coroner, ex parte Douglas-Williams*,[21] the case went to the European Court of Human Rights.[22] The applicant complained that there had been a breach of the procedural aspect of Article 2, submitting that the inquest proceedings were an inadequate investigative mechanism for examining the surrounding circumstances of the deceased's death.[23]

Ultimately the European Convention argument failed on the basis that the main complaint was that the inquest had failed to reach a proper conclusion, namely in that instance a finding of unlawful death rather than accidental death. The European Court observed that the applicant had taken judicial review proceedings alleging that the Coroner had erred in the way in which he had described the various verdicts open to the jury. The European Court in Douglas-Williams noted that the High Court and the Court of Appeal considered that while the Coroner's direction concerning different types of unlawful death might not have been altogether clear, the jury would, even if properly directed, have reached the same verdict. Reviewing the evidence, they found that there was only borderline evidence to justify leaving the verdict of unlawful death to the jury at all. It is therefore important to distinguish between cases that are properly challengeable by virtue of criticism of how a verdict is obtained and cases in which a challenge is entirely misconceived because it is based purely upon dissatisfaction with the result.

5.9 Prior to *Middleton*, Coroners would consider whether the forthcoming inquest would be a '*Jamieson*' hearing or an Article 2 hearing. Certain practical ramifications would arise from the Coroner designating that the hearing was an Article 2 procedure, not the least of which was that legal aid would be available, which was not available under the *Jamieson* hearing. It was not uncommon for advocates to make applications at preliminary hearings for the inquest to be designated an Article 2 procedure, upon the facts, so as to cause the provision of public funding to bite.

Since *Middleton* the necessity to delineate between a *Jamieson* hearing or an Article 2 hearing has dissipated and substantially the *Middleton* approach will encapsulate any Article 2 matters.

---

[20] Other Coroners have taken a more restricted view, in that an act, omission or circumstance is only relevant if but for this act, omission or circumstance the deceased would not have died.

[21] *R v Inner South London Coroner, ex parte Douglas-Williams* [1998] EWCA Civ 1343; [1999] 1 All ER 344, 350.

[22] *Douglas-Williams v UK* (Application No 56413/00).

[23] It should be remembered that the procedural obligation under Article 2 is one of means, not result. See *Hugh Jordan v UK* (2001) 11 BHRC 1. The fact that a court reaches a verdict with which a party does not agree cannot be regarded as depriving the inquest procedure of its effectiveness per se.

Enhanced Inquests

5.10 Since *Middleton* there have been various attempts to further enhance the ambit of the Coronial inquiry. *Middleton* was, of course, the starting point whereby the inquest would be expected, so as to be Article 2 compliant, to go beyond the immediate circumstances in which the deceased met his death and to look at the wider potential failings of the state.

In *R(JL) v Home Secretary*[24] Langstaff J observed that although holding individuals accountable was part of the purpose of the Article 2 obligations, it was not the sole purpose. The Judge also stated that it was necessary to learn about potential systemic problems.

Systemic failure is an important ingredient which can enhance the investigative role of an inquest. Where the threat to life allegedly comes from a state Agent and the individual concerned was in the care or under direct control of the state, then such investigative duty will arise unless it is clear that in the particular circumstances of the case the state could bear no responsibility for what occurred.

The facts of *Lin* are instructive.

The claimants where parents of Chia Hsin Lin, a 29-year-old journalist who was killed in the Potters Bar rail crash, in 2002.[25] Seven people were killed when a train was derailed and many others were injured. The claimants were challenging the decision of the Secretary of State for Transport declining to hold a public inquiry into the incident. The essential submission of the claimants was that the Secretary of State was required to comply with Article 2 of the European Convention on Human Rights, to hold a public inquiry and that the renewed inquest did not fulfil that obligation.[26]

Examples of systemic failure alleged in *Lin* ranged from wide issues in relation to the system for safety management and culture, the selection and control of contractors and the rail industry's response to the tragedy. Further systemic issues referred to by the Administrative Court included the role of the Health and Safety Executive in its role leading up to the Potters Bar accident.

Any finding of systemic failure at an inquest will be significant in relation to any future civil actions by the parties.

---

[24] *R(JL) v Secretary of State for the Home Department* [2006] EWHC 2558 (Admin).

[25] *R (Lin) v Secretary of State for Transport* [2006] Inquest Law Reports 161. This Inquest finally started on 1 June 2010, when the Coroner expressed grave concern at the length of time it had taken [8 years] for the Inquest to begin.

[26] The response of the Secretary of State was that Article 2 did not oblige him to order a public inquiry and that whatever the content of the obligation under that Article, a combination of past inquiry and the future hearing of the inquest would fulfil the obligations under Article 2 however widely they are drawn. This is the usual retort of government in refusing the public inquiry and placing the burden of investigation upon the inquest, despite the relatively narrow confines of the inquisitorial investigation. To some extent this was alleviated by decisions such as *Lin* and *Middleton* in lifting the straight-jacket of the Coronial investigation. Nevertheless as was pointed out in *Lin* at para 56, a distinction between a public inquiry and an inquest is that at a public inquiry parties are free to make submissions on the facts but at an inquest only submissions of law are appropriate, including any potential recommendations that are urged upon the Coroner in accordance with r 43 of the Coroners Rules 1984.

Lin goes on to establish that it is insufficient merely to refer to the obligation to investigate under Article 2, since that says nothing about the extent of investigation required.[27] Only by identifying with precision the nature of the obligation can the scope of the investigation be discerned. European and domestic jurisprudence illustrates that the most intense investigation and the greatest participation of next of kin are required in cases where Agents of the state bear potential responsibility for loss of life.[28] The provisions of the Coroners Rules 1984 Rule 36 as to how the deceased came by his death will bear different meanings depending upon whether the inquest is:

(a) simply playing a part in the discharge of the State's positive obligation under Article 2 of the Convention to set up an affective judicial system for determining the cause of death; or

(b) required in order to discharge a specific procedural investigative obligation under Article 2, otherwise known as an enhanced inquest.

If the inquest is not an enhanced inquest, then the term 'how' is to be interpreted in the narrow sense of 'by what means the deceased came by his death'.[29] If the inquest is enhanced the term is to be read as 'by what means and in what circumstances the deceased came by his death'.[30]

Often the distinction between the two becomes blurred. The term 'how' the deceased came by his death, whether it carried the *Jamieson* or *Middleton* meaning, simply identifies the issue that is to be enquired into and answered by means of the investigation. The scope of the factual investigations that are necessary and appropriate in order to conduct the inquiry and, if possible, to reach a verdict is a separate matter for the Coroner to determine. In *Dallaglio*[31] Simon Brown LJ observed:

> The enquiry is almost bound to stretch wider then strictly required for the purposes of a verdict. How much wider is pre-eminently a matter for the Coroner who's rulings upon the question will only exceptionally be susceptible to Judicial Review.

Further nuances of enhanced or non-enhanced inquests can include 'extended *Jamieson*' inquests.[32] Such an inquest was argued for which covered alleged failings by the intelligence community and by the emergency responders.

The first question in determining whether there will be a *Jamieson* inquest or a *Middleton* inquest is whether the specific investigative obligation under Article 2 of the Convention is engaged. The existence of the investigative duty was referred to in *McCann v United Kingdom*:[33]

---

[27] See para 22.

[28] See para 22 of *Lin*. See also *Middleton* (above n 7). See also *R(Khan) v Secretary of State for Health* [2004] 1 WLR 971, para 62.

[29] See *Jamieson* (above n 2) [1995] QB 1.

[30] See *Middleton* [2004] AC 182.

[31] *R v Inner West London Coroner, ex parte Dallaglio*, [1994] 4 All ER 139, 155 B.

[32] See the arguments made by Counsel for the families in the preliminary hearings of the 7/7 inquest, as referred to in the ruling of Lady Justice Hallett at para 29.

[33] *McCann v United Kingdom* [1995] 21 EHRR 97, para 161 (ECtHR Strasbourg).

The obligation to protect the right to life under [Article 2(1)], read in conjunction with the States general duty under Article 1 of the Convention 'to secure to everyone within their jurisdiction the rights and freedoms defined in [the] Convention', requires by implication that there should be some form of effective official investigation when individuals have been killed as a result of the use of force by, inter alios, agents of the State.

The specific investigative obligations will be engaged if there is an arguable case that the United Kingdom has breached its substantive obligations under Article 2.

Osman v United Kingdom[34] lays down four separate criteria which need to be satisfied if it is to be held that there is a breach of the substantive Article 2 obligation:

(i) knowledge or deemed knowledge on the part of the State of the existence
(ii) of a real and immediate risk to the life of an identified individual or individuals
(iii) from the criminal acts of a third party, and
(iv) a failure to take reasonable measures within the scope of its powers to avoid that risk.

Real and immediate risk is defined in *Re Officer L*[35] as one which is 'present and continuing'.[36]

Is There Any Difference Between *Jamieson* and *Middleton*?

5.11 In *Lin*[37] Moses LJ stated:

32 . . . Coroners nowadays are more concerned to conduct full inquiries with ample opportunity for participation, even absent the obligation to conduct enhanced inquests. Many, I was told, seek to conduct a full and fair inquiry and do not believe in offering the bereaved what may be perceived as a second-class inquest. Thus, following *Takoushis* there will often be little difference in practice between an enhanced *Middleton* type inquest and other inquests following deaths which give rise to concern both to those immediately involved and to their families.

---

[34] *Osman v United Kingdom* [1998] 29 EHRR 245.
[35] *Re Officer L* [2007] 1 WLR 2135.
[36] See also *R (Humberstone) v Legal Services Commission* [2010] EWHC 760 (Admin), a case dealing with a challenge to a decision refusing legal aid to a member of the bereaved family who required to be represented at an inquest. The case is also an authority for the proposition that (para 51) the state may have a duty to hold an investigation into a death or support a mechanism for investigation into a death even where there is no reason to believe that state Agents have failed to form the primary duty imposed by Article 2. This authority also recognises that the state may have a duty to investigate a death which may have arisen in circumstances in which the deceased was not in the particular care of the state, for instance whenever a death occurs to a patient under medical supervision, whether that be public or private.
[37] *R (Lin) v Secretary of State for Transport* (see above) [2006] Inquest Law Reports 161, para 32.

When will an Article 2 Inquest Arise?

5.12 An Article 2 inquest will arise if:

1. there may have been a violation of the state's substantive obligation not to take life without justification; or
2. there may have been a violation of the state's substantive obligation to establish a framework of laws, precautions, procedures or means of enforcement designed, to the greatest extent practicable, to protect life.

If the answer to either of these questions is yes, and state Agents maybe implicated, then the inquest must satisfy the full requirements of a state-instituted investigation as laid down by Lord Bingham between paragraphs 35 and 38 in *Middleton*.

Broader Issues

5.13 In *R(Gentle) v Prime Minister*[38] the claimants, the bereaved family of Fusilier Gordon Gentle, a soldier who died in his 'snatch' Land Rover when that vehicle drove over an improvised explosive in the road whilst performing operations in Iraq, contended that an inquest could examine broader issues of policy such as governmental decisions on allocation and procurement of resources to the theatre of war.

The family of Gordon Gentle contended that it was necessary to investigate whether the government had taken reasonable steps to be satisfied that the war in Iraq was lawful before committing troops to conflict. They emphasised in argument that they were not challenging, for the purposes of their present application, the legality of the war in Iraq. It was argued that an Article 2 investigation, whether it be at an inquest or a public inquiry (the latter being particularly asserted), was a legal right and that it should consider all the circumstances surrounding the invasion of Iraq by British forces in 2003, including in particular the steps taken by the government to obtain timely legal advice concerning the legality of the invasion.

The claimants in *Gentle* sought to argue for the procedural obligation under Article 2 to initiate an effective public investigation by an independent official body into any death occurring in circumstances in which it appears that one or other of the other substantive obligations contained within Article 2 has been, or may have been, violated and it appears that agents of the state are, or maybe, in some way implicated.[39]

The House of Lords in *Gentle* observed[40] that the procedural obligation under Article 2 is 'parasitic' upon the existence of the substantive obligation, and cannot

---

[38] *R(Gentle) v Prime Minister* [2006] EWCA Civ 1690.
[39] See *Middleton* [2004] AC 182, para 3.
[40] *ibid*, para 6.

exist independently. Therefore to make good any procedural right to an inquiry the claimant must show at least an arguable case that the substantive right arises on the facts of the case. If they cannot do so, the House of Lords observed that their claim will fail.[41] The judgment in *Gentle* upon first reading seems to confine itself to the narrow issue that there is no breach of the substantive duty in Article 2 by sending troops to fight what might be an unlawful war. Therefore, it is reasoned, the Article 2 duty to investigate does not arise. Yet a close analysis of the judgment of Lord Bingham of Cornhill[42] indicates that the House of Lords are underlining that Article 2 does not provide for wide-ranging inquiries.

5.14 The House of Lords observes that there is nothing in European jurisprudence pertaining to Article 2, that appears to contemplate such wide-ranging inquiries upon subjects of public or political importance. They cite a number of authorities to support this proposition.[43] Indeed, Lord Bingham reasserted the observations in *Taylor v UK* where it was held that there was no obligation for an inquiry into a death to extend to wider issues of National Health Service organisation and funding, and confirmed the authority of that case.[44]

Lord Bingham referred with approval to the judgment of Lord Justice Arden in *Scholes v Secretary of State for the Home Department*[45] as to the limits of any Article 2 investigation. Lord Justice Arden observed that in *Taylor*, which involved the killing by the State Enrolled Nurse Beverly Allitt, it was not appropriate at an investigation to examine the responsibility of the authorities in the National Health Service for inadequate systems, staff shortages and weak leadership. Neither did the inquiry address the wider issues relating to the organisation and funding of the National Health Service as a whole or the pressure which might have led to a ward being run subject to the shortcomings apparently witnessed in the Beverly Allitt case. Lord Justice Arden approved the view of the inquiry into Allitt's criminality and observed:[46]

> The wider questions raised by the case are within the public domain and any doubts which may consequently arise as to policies adopted in the field of public health are, in the Commission's opinion, that is, for public and political debate which fall outside the scope of Article 2 and the other provisions of the convention.

---

[41] See *Gentle* [2006] EWCA Civ 1690, para 6.

[42] *ibid*, para 9.

[43] *Jordan v United Kingdom* (2001) 37 EHRR 52, para 128; *Bubbins v United Kingdom* (2005) 41 EHRR 458, para 153; *Taylor v United Kingdom* (1994) 79-A DR 127, 137: *McShane v United Kingdom* (2002) 35 EHRR 593, para 122: *Banks v United Kingdom* (Application No 21387/05) 6 February 2007, unreported, pp 12–13; *McBride v United Kingdom* (2006) 43 EHRR 102, para 1 (pp 109–10).

[44] In reaffirming the status of *Taylor*, Lord Bingham specifically referred to *Scholes v Secretary of State for the Home Department* [2006] EWCA Civ 1343, para 67, wherein Lord Justice Pill seemed to throw doubt on the current applicability ruling in *Taylor*. Lord Bingham observed in para 9 of the House of Lords' report in *Gentle*: 'I do not think the authorities justify his doubt and Lord Justice Arden in paragraphs 82–83, applied what I respectfully think is the correct approach'.

[45] See n 44 above.

[46] *Scholes* (above n 44), para 83.

Lord Justice Arden went on to develop his judgment as to the restrictions of wider investigation into issues of policy. He referred to the case of *Jordan v UK*,[47] a decision of the European Court where the applicant alleged that his son had been unjustifiably shot and killed by a police officer in Northern Ireland. Lord Justice Arden recites a section of the judgment in *Jordan* with approval:[48]

> 128. It is also alleged that the inquest in this case is restricted in the scope of its examination. According to the case-law of the national courts, the procedure is a fact finding exercise and is not a method of apportioning guilt. The Coroner is required to confine his investigation to matters directly causative of the death and not to extend his inquiry into the broader circumstances. This was the standard applicable in the McCann inquest also and did not prevent examination of those aspects of the planning and conduct of the operation relevant to the killings of the three IRA suspects. The Court is not persuaded therefore that the approach taken by the domestic courts necessarily contradicts the requirements of Article 2. The domestic courts accept that an essential purpose of the inquest is to allay rumours and suspicions of how a death came about. The Court agrees that a detailed investigation into policy issues or alleged conspiracies may not be justifiable or necessary. Whether an inquest fails to address necessary factual issues will depend on the particular circumstances of the case. It has not been shown in the present application that the scope of the inquest as conducted so far has prevented any particular matters relevant to the death being examined.[49]

The Limits of a Coroner's Powers as to the Scope of an Inquiry

5.15 In *R (Butler and another) v HM Coroner for the Black Country District*[50] the claimants successfully challenged the Coroner's decision as to the scope of the inquest not because the intended scope was unlawfully wide per se but because of the means by which the Coroner reached his decision as to the scope. In that case Beatson J made comment upon the impact of Rule 43, which is used to justify a broader approach:

> [74] ... I do not consider that rule 43 enables a coroner to admit evidence that he cannot properly admit having regard to the provisions in the rules and his common law duties. But, in assessing all the factors relevant in determining the scope of an inquest, and bearing in mind the statement of Lord Lane CJ in *R v South London Coroner ex p Thompson* (1982) 126 SJ 625 ... and his reference to the public interest, the coroner was entitled to take into account the possibility of the need to refer the matter to the relevant person or authority under rule 43.

---

[47] See *Jordan v United Kingdom* (n 43 above).

[48] *Jordan* (above n 43) para 128.

[49] The policy issue referred to within this citation were whether or not there was a policy within the security forces in Northern Ireland, including the Royal Ulster Constabulary, of 'Shoot to Kill'.

[50] *R (Butler and another) v HM Coroner for the Black Country District* [2010] EWHC 43 (Admin), see also para 65 as to how in particular, this Coroner fell into error.

Therefore the power to produce a report under Rule 43 is not conclusive, but it is relevant to the decision on scope.

Comparative Law

5.16 In the New Zealand authority of *TMW Orchard v Osborne and the Attorney General*[51] Patterson J observed:

> The Coroner does not have a role of apportioning guilt but must obviously be able to go beyond the mere cause of death if he is to serve a useful social function. This is recognised in the Act by requiring him to establish, so far as possible, the circumstances of the death.

Impact of the 2009 Act

5.17 Section 5(2) lays down:

> Where necessary in order to avoid a breach of any Convention rights (within the meaning of the Human Rights Act 1998), the purpose mentioned in sub-section (1)(b) [how, when and where the deceased came by his or her death] is to be read as including the purpose of ascertaining in what circumstances the deceased came by his or her death.

The Explanatory Notes to the Act make it clear that the scope of the investigation is to be widened to include an investigation of the 'broad circumstances' of the death, including events leading up to the death in question, where the wider investigation is necessary to ensure that the domestic courts comply with the jurisprudence of the European Convention on Human Rights, and in particular Article 2.

The Explanatory Notes emphasise that the 2009 Act does not define the precise circumstances where a Coroner should conduct an Article 2 investigation. Those who have drafted the legislation envisage that this will allow for flexibility in the future, should case law determine that Article 2 inquests should extend to cover additional matters.

This approach recognises the developing state of law in relation to Article 2 investigations and the trend to broaden the ambit of any inquiry.

---

[51] *TMW Orchard v Osborne and the Attorney General,* unreported, High Court of New Zealand, 19 July 1996.

The Distinction between the Ordinary Inquest and an Article 2 Inquest

5.18 The essential difference between the two varieties of inquest is that the permissible verdict or verdicts in a traditional inquest are significantly narrower than in an Article 2 inquest. Furthermore, the scope of an investigation is likely to be narrower at a traditional inquest.

Yet, apart from this, jurisprudence does not present a clear analysis of the differences between the two types of inquest.

In *Smith*[52] the Court expressed disappointment that the 2009 Act failed to clarify the distinction between the two varieties of inquest. The Court of Appeal stated:

> We think that this is a great pity and that it would be desirable for the new statute to set out clearly the differences between an Article 2 inquest and any other type of inquest. It is surely desirable that parties and practitioners should simply be able to refer to the statue to appreciate the differences (if they are to persist) without the necessity to delve into the jurisprudence. We do, however, appreciate that that is not a matter for us . . .

The roots of the Article 2 inquest can be found within *Middleton*.[53] Lord Bingham delivered the speech of the House of Lords in *Middleton* and referred to the case in his later judgment in *Gentle*[54] in which he summarised the effect of the European jurisprudence with regards to Article 2. The House of Lords in *Middleton* importantly observed[55] that a verdict of an inquest jury (other than an open verdict) which does not express the jury's conclusion on a major issue canvassed in the evidence at the inquest cannot satisfy or meet the expectations of the deceased's family or next of kin. The House of Lords accepted that these parties, like the deceased, may be victims. They have been held to have legitimate interests in the conduct of the investigation,[56] which is why they must be accorded an appropriate level of participation.[57] An uninformative jury verdict will be unlikely to meet what the House in *Amin*[58] held to be one of the purposes of an Article 2 investigation: 'that those who have lost their relative may at least have the satisfaction of knowing that lessons learnt from his death may save the lives of others'.

5.19 The House of Lords in *Middleton* also ruled that while the use of lethal force by an agent of the state must always be a matter of the greatest seriousness, a systemic failure to protect human life may call for an investigation which may be no less important and perhaps even more complex.[59] It does not promote the objects

---

[52] *R (Smith) v Secretary of State for Defence and Others* [2009] EWCA (Civ) 441, para 65.
[53] *R(Middleton) v West Somerset Coroner* [2004] UKHL 10, [2004] 2 AC 182.
[54] See *R(Gentle) v Prime Minister* [2006] EWCA Civ 1690, paras 2–5.
[55] *Middleton* (above n 53) paras 18–19.
[56] See *Jordan* (above n 43) para 109.
[57] See also *R(Amin) v Secretary of State for the Home Department* (n 17 above).
[58] In particular [2004] 1 AC 653, para 31.
[59] See *Amin* [2004] 1 AC 653, paras 21, 41, 50 and 62.

of the Convention if domestic law were to distinguish between cases where an agent of the state may have used lethal force without justification and cases in which a defective system operated by the state may have failed to afford adequate protection to human life.[60] In the case of *Smith*[61] the Court considered the death of a Private in Iraq caused by a defective system operated by the state to afford adequate protection to human life by ensuring, so far as reasonably practicable, that he was an appropriate person, with proper training and equipment, to expose to the extreme heat of Iraq.[62]

5.20 The differences between the traditional inquest and the Article 2 inquest were not reconciled by the House of Lords when it had the opportunity to do so in *Hurst*.[63]

There is a view, which is maintaining credence at Coroners' Courts, that although the verdicts in the two classes of inquest must be approached differently, the investigation carried out should be the same.[64]

Non-Article 2 Inquests

5.21 Even if it is considered that the inquest does not qualify as an Article 2 inquest, any inquest should not be limited to purely and strictly causative matters. The expression 'clear and direct causal connection' which was used in *Jamieson*, was applied in a strict and very narrow sense in such a way that it might be used in contract or tort cases.[65]

Any inquest, be it Article 2 or not, must investigate systemic problems and issues which may reduce the risk of such instances as are investigated in similar circumstances in the future. Any contrary interpretation would seem to fly in the face of Rule 43 of the Coroner's Rules which permits a Coroner to report in writing to 'the person or authority who may have power' that they take any relevant action, in the event that he 'believes that action should be taken to prevent the reoccurrence of fatalities similar to that in respect of which the inquest is being held'. Strictly in such circumstances, the scope of the inquiry is a matter of the Coroner's discretion, nevertheless to satisfy the implied statutory purpose of identifying

---

[60] See *Middleton* [2004] UKHL 10; [2004] 2 AC 182, para 19.

[61] See *Smith* [2009] EWCA (Civ) 441, affirmed in part on appeal [2010] UKSC 29.

[62] Private Smith died of heat stroke.

[63] *Hurst v London Northern District Coroner* [2007] 2 AC 189. See para 64 of *Smith* above.

[64] See the judgments of Baroness Hale (para 21 of *Hurst*), based upon the statements by Croom-Johnson LJ in *R v Southwark Coroner Ex Parte Hicks* [1987] 1 WLR 1632 and Lord Lane CJ in *R v South London Coroner, ex parte Thompson* (1982) 126 SJ 625 and by the Broderick Committee (Cmnd 1480) at para 16.40.

[65] See Tomlinson J, *R v Coventry Coroner, ex parte Chief Constable of Staffordshire Police* (2000) 164 JP 665, 675–6; *Scott v Inner West London Coroner* [2001] EWHC 105 (Admin), paras 14–15 *Hurst v London Northern District Coroner* [2007] 2 AC 189 (HL) Baroness Hale and Lord Mance; and *R (Takoushis) v Inner North London Coroner* [2006] 1 WLR 461, para 45.

systemic failure with a view to preventing further deaths, the scope of any inquiry maybe required to be broader than is strictly necessary for the production of a verdict or conclusion.

Takoushis concerned a person who died of what was argued was medical negligence in a National Health Service hospital. The issue raised at the inquest was whether the State must have a system that provides for the practical and effective investigation of the facts and for the determination of civil liability. The Court held that a full investigation would involve both what the system at the hospital was and how it operated on the day in question.[66]

In *Takoushis*[67] the Court referred to the case of *R v Inner West London Coroner, ex parte Dallaglio,*[68] in which Lord Justice Simon Brown identified the tension between the apparently narrow definition of 'How' in section 11(5)(b)(ii) and the wider provisions of section 8(3)(d) of the 1988 Act, the latter which looks to the future as does Rule 43 of the 1984 Rules. In clarifying this apparent difference, Lord Justice Simon Brown[69] approved the statement of Mr Justice Morland in *R v HM Coroner for Western District of East Sussex ex parte Homberg*[70] that Rule 36 of the Coroner's Rules 1984 should not be interpreted so as to defeat the purpose of Section 8(3)(d) and that if the 'proceedings and evidence are narrowly confined, the answer to the 'How' question will not serve the purpose of the question, namely the prevention or reduction of the risk of future injuries in similar circumstances. In laying down the above Simon Brown LJ emphasised that the responsibility for setting the bounds of the inquiry was the Coroner's. He stated:[71]

> It is the duty of the Coroner as the public official responsible for the conduct of inquests, whether he is sitting with a jury or without, to ensure that the facts are fully, fairly and fearlessly investigated. He is bound to recognise the acute public concern rightly aroused when death occurs in custody. He must ensure that the relevant facts are exposed to public scrutiny, particularly if there is evidence of foul play, abuse or inhumanity. He fails in his duty if his investigation is superficial, slip shod or perfunctory. But the responsibility is his. He must set the bounds of the inquiry.

The above reference from the judgment of Lord Justice Simon Brown is a direct quotation from *Jamieson*[72] and although he recognised that *Jamieson* involved death in custody, it is clear from the text of Simon Brown LJ's judgment that he regarded the same approach as applicable in the context of a case like *Dallaglio*, where the deaths had occurred as a result of the collision between the Marchioness and the Bowbelle, motor vessels on the Thames. He states, with approval of the Court in *Takoushis*, that it is for the individual Coroner to recognise and resolve

---

[66] The new inquest was ordered to investigate why Takoushis was able to leave the hospital before being seen by a doctor.

[67] *Takoushis* (above n 65), para 45.

[68] *R v Inner West London Coroner, ex parte Dallaglio* [1994] 4 All ER 139.

[69] *Dallaglio* [1994] 4 All ER 139, 154.

[70] *R v HM Coroner for Western District of East Sussex, ex parte Homberg* (1994) 158 JP 357, 381.

[71] *Takoushis* (above n 65) para 46.

[72] See *Jamieson* (above n 2) [1995] QB 1.

the tension between the different provisions of the 1988 Act and the Coroners Rules. It was acknowledged by both courts that an inquiry was bound to stretch more widely than strictly required for the purposes of a verdict. Nevertheless how much more widely was a matter for the Coroner.

5.22 Though the Coroner's Court is considered an inferior court, it does have power to punish for contempt. In *R v West Yorkshire Coroner, ex parte Smith*[73] the applicant in a judicial review accused one witness of having murdered his daughter. The accusation was reported and he was fined £50 for contempt of court. The applicant sought judicial review arguing that a Coroner's Court, not being a court of record, had no power of punishment for contempt. It was held that the Court was an inferior court but did have the power to punish a contempt in the face of the Court. Such a power, the Queen's Bench Division ruled, was necessary to keep order in a court.

---

[73] *R v West Yorkshire Coroner, ex parte Smith* [1985] 1 All ER 100; *The Times*, 3 October 1984.

6

The Jury

6.1 As a general principle an inquest into a death must be held without a jury.

Historically the 'right' to a jury is not a constitutional entitlement.[1] Furthermore there is no provision in the European Convention on Human Rights and in particular Article 6, the right to a fair trial, that the lack of a jury will violate those provisions. Indeed, it has been questioned whether a jury that produces an unreasoned decision violates Article 6 of the Convention.[2]

6.2 The jury is a powerful symbol within the criminal justice system.[3]

Juries have a more specialised and particular role to play in the inquest. Their function dates back to the Grand Jury of the medieval period and is distinct from that of the jury that has developed within the criminal justice system. They are and remain, a specialised entity.

As far back as 1250, Bracton directed that the Coroner call a jury in specific terms:[4]

> It is therefore their office that . . . they ought to visit the slain, or the wounded . . . or those who have died suddenly . . . and this they ought to do forthwith and without any delay. And at their coming to those parts they ought to order four, five or six neighbouring townships that they come immediately before them and by their oath make an inquest concerning the man slain.

To begin with the jury would comprise every male person over the age of 12 from four or more neighbouring townships.

During the medieval period the inquest was held in the presence of the deceased. This approach subsisted for sometime and it was considered that when the jury saw the dead body it brought 'a sense of reality and responsibility'.[5]

---

[1] Unlike in the United States of America, where the sixth amendment to Article III of the US Constitution enshrines the right to juries in Federal and State jurisdictions for all offences not deemed to be 'petty'. ('Petty' is defined as offences carrying more than six months imprisonment. A similar constitutional entitlement to a jury is enshrined under the Canadian Charter of Rights and Freedoms for offences punishable by five years imprisonment or more).

[2] See *Condron v United Kingdom* (2000) 31 EHRR 1, para 95.

[3] In the 18th Century Blackstone described it as 'The Palladium' or the 'Grand Bulwark' of the Englishman's liberties. *Blackstone's Commentaries*, vol IV (1776) p 347, see also 349; see also Stephen, *History of the Criminal Law* vol I, 566. Even more graphically and memorably Sir Patrick Devlin spoke of the jury as a 'little parliament' and 'the lamp that shows that freedom lives': *Trial by Jury*, The Hamlyn Lectures, eighth series (1956) p 164.

[4] See Henry de Bracton, *De Legibus et Consuetudinibus Angliae* (1250).

[5] Chalmers Committee 1910, Report of the Departmental Committee appointed to enquire into the law relating to Coroners and Coroners' inquests and into the practice in Coroners' Courts (Cd 5004, 1910).

It was also noted by the same commentators that the jury 'nearly filed past, often with averted faces'. This procedure was ended by the Coroners (Amendment) Act of 1926.[6]

The Coroners Act 1887 placed a requirement upon the Coroner to summon a jury of between 12 and 23 individuals. 12 of the 23 would be required to deliver a verdict. The Coroners (Amendment) Act 1926 reduced the number of jurors to between seven and 11 and the same Act began inroads into whether a jury would be required to sit at an inquest. Prior to the 1926 Act every inquest would be heard before a jury, but the principles laid down in the 1926 Act would form the law that would later be enshrined in the Coroners Act 1988, section 8.

6.3 Section 8 (3) of the 1988 Act provides:

(3) If it appears to a coroner, either before he proceeds to hold an inquest or in the course of an inquest begun without a jury, that there is reason to suspect –

    (a) the death occured in prison or in such a place or in such circumstances as to require an inquest under any other Act;

    (b) that the death occurred whilst the deceased was in police custody, or resulted from an injury caused by a police officer in the purported execution of his duty;

    (c) that the death was caused by an accident, poisoning or disease notice of which is required to be given under any Act to a government department, to any inspector or other officer of a government department or to an inspector appointed under Section 19 of the Health and Safety at work etc. Act 1974; or

    (d) that the death occurred in circumstances the continuance or a possible recurrence of which is prejudicial to the health or safety of the public or any section of the public,

he shall proceed to summon a jury in the manner required . . .

6.4 The 2009 Act at section 7 sets out the circumstances in which a Senior Coroner is required to hold an inquest into a death, assisted by a jury.

It should be emphasised that the general rule is that an inquest must be held without jury. Section 7(2) and (3) lay down the exceptions to this rule.

In many respects section 7(2) reflects the old law under the 1988 Act. It reads:

(2) An inquest into a death must be held with a jury if the senior coroner has reason to suspect –

    (a) that the deceased died while in custody or otherwise in state detention, and that either –

        (i) the death was a violent or unnatural one, or

        (ii) the cause of death is unknown,

---

[6] Nevertheless the ordeal of facing the deceased remained for Coroners for a further 54 years.

(b) that the death resulted from an act or omission of –

    (i) a police officer, or
    (ii) a member of a service police force,

    in the purported execution of the officer's or member's duty as such, or
(c) that the death was caused by a notifiable accident, poisoning or disease.

6.5 A member of a service police force is defined in section 48 of the 2009 Act as a member of the Royal Navy Police, the Royal Military Police or the Royal Air Force Police.

6.6 State detention is defined within section 48 of the 2009 Act as arising if an individual is

compulsorily detained by a public authority within the meaning of section 6 of the Human Rights Act 1998 . . .[7]

That will be interpreted as including those in mental health detention, secure training centres or immigration detention centres as well as in police or prison custody. It was observed in the Al Fayed/Dodi case[8] by Lady Justice Smith that 'in order that there should be public confidence in the outcome of the inquest, a jury should be summoned in cases where the state, by its agents, may have had some responsibility for the death'.[9]

6.7 An inquest into a death may also be held with a jury if the Senior Coroner thinks that there is 'sufficient reason for doing so'.[10] Time will tell how the courts will interpret this. Although the most recent legislation fails to specifically adopt the terms of section 8(3)(d) of the 1988 Act, that a jury should be empanelled if

the death occurred in circumstances the continuance or possible reoccurrence of which is prejudicial to the health or safety of the public or any section of the public,

it is arguable that these circumstances will be highly persuasive in the mind of a Senior Coroner when considering whether there is 'sufficient reason' for summoning a jury.[11]

In *R v Her Majesty's Coroner at Hammersmith, ex parte Peach*[12] the Court of Appeal considered the position where the Coroner and the jury were investigating the death of a man who was watching a demonstration, who was struck a violent blow on the back of his head from which he died. Lord Justice Bridge considered that section 8(3)(d) applied: 'To circumstances of such a kind that their continuance or reoccurence

---

   [7] Section 48(2).

   [8] *Paul and The Ritz Hotel Ltd v Deputy Coroner of the Queen's Household and Deputy Coroner for Surrey; Mohammed Al Fayed v Same* [2007] EWHC 408 (Admin), [2007] 3 WLR 503, para 42.

   [9] *ibid*, para 46.

  [10] See the 2009 Act s 7(3).

  [11] No positive proof or over formulated evidence will be required – See *R v Inner North London Coroner, ex parte Linnane* [1989] 1 WLR 395.

  [12] *R v HM Coroner at Hammersmith, ex parte Peach* [1980] QB 211 (CA).

may reasonably and ought properly to be avoided by taking of appropriate steps which it is in the power of some responsible body to take'.

Lord Denning MR observed: 'When the circumstances are such that similar fatalities may possibly recur in the future, and it is reasonable to expect that some action should be taken to prevent their recurrence . . .' then section 8(3)(d) could be evoked.

The third judge of an influential Court of Appeal, Sir David Cairns, said:

> The difficulty is to find meaning which does not do violence to the words of the Act and which gives effect to what maybe taken to have been the intention of Parliament. The reference to 'continuance or possible recurrence' indicates to my mind that the provision was intended to apply only to circumstances the continuance or the recurrence which was preventable or to some extent controllable. Moreover, since it is prejudice to the health or safety of the public or a section of the public that is referred to, what is envisaged, must I think be something which might be prevented or safeguarded by a public authority or some other person or body whose activities can be said to affect a substantial section of the public. I cannot find any justification in any further limitation of the meaning of the paragraph in question.

The courts make a distinction between circumstances which amount to an isolated incident and those demonstrating a systemic failure. Put simply, a systemic failure may reoccur in the future but could be prevented or safeguarded against by a public authority or some personal body whose activities can be said to affect a substantial number of the general public.[13]

In *R v HM Attorney General, ex parte Ferrante*[14] the Master of the Rolls, Sir Thomas Bingham, observed that the death of a volunteer soldier who received a head injury whilst he was training was not a case of systemic failure. He added that it was 'Plainly a case which in the Coroner's judgment did not appear to be a case of systemic default, in other words, a case in which the system was so much at fault that, if nothing was done, there would be other deaths'.

Appeals Against the Summoning or Non-summoning of a Jury

6.8 An interested person was briefly given the right to appeal to the Chief Coroner against a decision made by a Senior Coroner as to whether there should be a jury at an inquest.[15] Since the government have indicated that some of the duties and rules assigned to the Chief Coroner may be exercised by the judiciary, it is necessary to consider the appeal criteria which may still be implemented.

---

[13] *R v HM Attorney General ex parte Ferrante* (CA), 8 February 1995, [1995] COD 18; sub nom *R v HM Attorney General ex parte Taylor, The Independent*, 3 April 1995.

[14] *ibid.*

[15] Coroners and Justice Act 2009 s 40(2)(g).

Interested person is defined in section 47 of the 2009 Act and includes family members, personal representatives, medical examiners exercising functions in relation to the death of the deceased, beneficiaries under a policy of insurance issued on the life of the deceased, the insurer of such policy and any persons who may have caused or contributed to the death.

Case law will develop as to the criteria to be established for appeals under this section. Clearly, a number of cases will involve argument and interpretation of systemic failure and the cases on section 8(3)(d) of the 1988 Act will remain relevant.

6.9 But there maybe other reasons why certain parties will argue that they either require or do not require a jury.

In practice courts distinguish between matters of public interest and matters of interest to the public. While the former may fall within the ambit either of a public inquiry under the Inquiries Act 2005 or an inquest under the 2009 legislation, simply because a matter is of interest to the public will not, of itself, mean that a jury will be empanelled.

Nevertheless there have been and will be cases whereby the distinction is far from overwhelming.

A case which involves the faulty equipment or scarcity of equipment provided to members of the armed forces in the theatre of war does not necessarily attract the empanelling of a jury. It can be anticipated that in the future appeals will be taken if a Senior Coroner refuses a jury more readily than might be done at present by judicial review.

There are also cases which come before the Coroner's Court, which, because of sensitivity centering either around the facts of the case or the individuals involved, may require, in the eyes of the bereaved family, a jury to achieve the perception of open justice. Such applications, again, may find themselves on appeal to the Chief Coroner, who will have a wider discretion than the Administrative Court on judicial review. Conversely, certain parties may consider that they have a good reason to argue against the provision of a jury.

Some of these reasons may well have been flagged within the text of Lord Justice Auld's *Review of the Criminal Courts of England and Wales* in September 2001.[16]

Potential objections can, perhaps, be distilled into three fundamental complaints: cost, time and complexity.[17]

When considering the criminal jurisdiction, the Auld report considered what was termed the 'financial and human cost of the criminal justice system'.[18] In

---

[16] The Review was announced by the Lord Chancellor, Lord Irvine of Lairg on 14 December 1999. Sir Robin Auld's terms of reference were: 'A review into the practices and procedures of, and the rules and evidence applied by, criminal courts at every level, with a view to ensuring that they deliver justice fairly, by streamlining all their processes, increasing their efficiency and strengthening the effectiveness of their relationships with others across the criminal justice system, and having regard to the interest of parties including victims and witnesses thereby promoting public confidence in the rule of law'. See www.criminal-courts-review.org.uk/

[17] The issue of inquests or hearings held partly or wholly *in camera* are dealt with later in this work.

[18] See *Review of the Criminal Courts of England and Wales*, Chapter 5 Juries, para 167 (p 197).

accepting the argument that cost was a relevant factor when considering whether a defendant would be tried on indictment and before a jury or summarily and before a bench of magistrates only, Auld LJ observed that there are finite resources and that it was a policy decision, according to the nature and seriousness of the offence, and in the light of the public interest, how different offences should be tried. Lord Justice Auld commented that

> There is still the question of where and how . . . Parliament draws the line. Some cases by their very nature justify the facilities and more searching pre-trial and trial proce-dures then magistrates courts can provide. Others do not.[19]

The Report expressed the view that permitting the law or the courts to decide where defendants would be tried would not, in itself, deprive defendants of a fair trial.[20]

The Auld Report was clearly of the view that policy decisions should be taken as to how valuable time and resources of the courts should be utilised.[21]

It is certainly not fanciful to acknowledge that some parties will argue against the empanelment of a jury on the basis of costs and length of time that a hearing will take, it being accepted that in the majority of cases a jury hearing will take longer than one presided over by a Coroner on his own. Furthermore such objec-tions will not necessarily be taken by state or public bodies, conscious of the public purse. In the hearing dealing with the deaths of 10 servicemen as a result of the Hercules aircraft being brought down by enemy fire over Iraq, one of the ser-vicemen was Australian and the family of the bereaved instructed an Australian lawyer. A representative of the bereaved family and the Australian lawyer instructed on their behalf travelled from that country for the duration of the hearing. Upon application by some families for a jury to hear the inquest, such application was opposed by those representing the Australian member of the armed forces on the grounds that the involvement of a jury would lengthen the time that the inquest would take. No jury was sworn in at the Hercules inquest.

Complexity will also be a potential reason for parties to argue against the empanelment of a jury. In a criminal jurisdiction this is vexed question. There are those who argue that in certain trials of complexity, and in particular serious and complex fraud trials, a jury of the general public is ill equipped to understand the issues in the case and therefore to do justice to them. The counter argument opines that an understanding of complex matters can be achieved through a professional and careful presentation by the advocates, and it is the advocates' responsibility to

---

[19] See *ibid*, para 167.

[20] See Dr Penny Darbyshire, 'The lamp that shows that freedom lives – is it worth the candle?' [1991] Crim LR 740, 741.

[21] The report also accepted that there was and continues to be a perception that Crown Court juries are fairer than magistrates. Lord Justice Auld agreed with Professor Andrew Ashworth who urged that any perceived deficiencies in magisterial justice should be dealt with through magistrates' selection, training and courtroom procedures rather than, as Auld put it 'abandoning them for the Crown Court'. See *The Criminal Process: An Evaluation Study*, 2nd edn (Oxford University Press, 1998) 262.

ensure that right-minded and competent members of the public maintain engagement in the legal process.[22]

The issue on complexity is dealt with by Auld in his paragraph concerning fraud and other complex cases.[23] He particularly observes that judges, with their legal and forensic experience, with or without specialist assessors, would be better equipped to deal justly and more expeditiously with such cases.[24] Ultimately Auld recommends that as an alternative to trial by judge and jury in serious and complex fraud cases, a nominated trial judge should be empowered to direct trial by himself sitting with lay members or, where the defendant has opted for trial by judge alone, by himself alone.

The Auld Report also gives some useful hints as to how the appeal system could work. In his review, he considers an appeal process whereby one or other of the prosecution or defence wish to challenge a court's decision to hear a case.[25] If, in circumstances where there is an issue between the parties as to venue – Magistrates Court or Crown Court – Auld suggests that a District Judge should be entrusted with the decisions (or perhaps lay magistrates). He goes on to recommend that both sides should have a right to appeal from the mode of trial decision to the Crown Court. He states:

> It should be brisk and on paper and dealt with by a small panel of experienced Crown Court judges at each court centre, possibly nominated for the purpose. Though an appeal may add some cost and a day or two's delay, it is valuable in two respects. First, it is a safeguard, particularly in border-line cases. Second, it should improve the quality and consistency of District Judges' decisions.

It is anticipated that this system of appeals, in time, will allow parties to understand how Senior Coroners up and down the country will exercise their discretion, and particularly upon what principles.

---

[22] There are also analogies within the criminal law of the facility for trials to be held without a jury when so-called jury tampering threatens due process of the criminal justice system. Interestingly, in the only case so far to have availed itself of this facility, it was accepted that a potential jury could have been protected from interference but that it would have cost approximately £6 million. The criminal Courts were of the view that this was too much money to expend when a better allocation of resources could achieve a safe jury-less trial. There are echoes here of Auld LJ. Lord Judge CJ observed 'in our judgment these protective measure do not sufficiently address the extent of the risk ... Even if it did deal with the dangers posed to the integrity of trial by jury, it would be unreasonable to impose that package with its drain on financial resources'. See *R v T; R v D; R v C; R v H (R v T)* [2009] EWCA Crim 1035, para 33.

[23] See *Review of the Criminal Courts of England and Wales*, Chapter 5 Juries, para 173 onwards (p 200).

[24] *ibid*, para 181 (p 203).

[25] See *ibid*, para 171 (p 199).

The Summoning of a Jury

6.10 There will be no fewer than seven and no more than 11 people comprising a jury at an inquest.[26] Members of the public will be summoned by the Senior Coroner and be told the time and the place where they are needed.

The Coroner's Officer has the power to withdraw or amend any summons if it appears in his discretion that that potential juror is not required.[27] The qualifications for jury service at a Coroner's inquest are exactly the same as at the Crown Court, the High Court and the County Courts and are governed by the Juries Act 1974 section 1.[28]

Section 8(2) of the 2009 Act enables a Senior Coroner to summon persons whether they be within or outside the coronial area for which that Coroner is appointed.

Once the jury are assembled in court, they will be sworn by or before the Coroner, usually by the Coroner's Officer, to inquire into the death of the deceased and to give a true determination according to the evidence.

By section 8(5) of the 2009 Act the Senior Coroner may put to any individuals summoned to serve on a jury any question that appears necessary to establish whether or not that potential juror is qualified to serve as a juror at an inquest.

The Time to Decide whether a Jury Should be Empanelled

The Coroner must decide as to the scope of the inquest before considering whether a jury should be sworn.

As was stated by Lady Justice Smith in *R (Paul and others) v Deputy Coroner for the Queen's Household and the Deputy Coroner for Surrey* 'As a matter of principle, the right course is to determine the scope of the inquest before considering whether to summon a jury'.

The Views of the Family

The opinions of the family of the deceased are very pertinent to the exercise of the Coroner's discretion.

---

[26] This is the same as the minimum and maximum number of jurors required by the 1988 Act s 8(2)(a).
[27] See Coroners Rules 1984, r 47.
[28] This is a direct reproduction of the requirements in the 1988 Act s 9(1).

In the *R (Paul and others)* case Lady Justice Smith observed:[29]

> It was the strongly expressed view of the family of Dodi Al Fayed that there should be a jury. That, of course, can not be determinative but it is a relevant factor. This was recognised in the *National Union of Miners case* [*R v HM Coroner for the Eastern District of the Metropolitan County of West Yorkshire, Ex Parte National Union of Mineworkers* (1985) 150 JP 58] and, in any event, we believe that it is now regarded as good practice for Coroner's to consult the family of the deceased before making a discretionary decision under Section 8(4) . . . We think the views of the Al Fayed family should have been taken into account.

Indeed the imperative of fully involving bereaved families in the investigative process is a central principle of Article 2 of the Convention.

Jurors must be between 18–65 years of age, registered on the electoral register, resident in the United Kingdom for the past five years since the age of 13 and not in one of the categories of professional people that are excluded under the Juries Act 1974.

Determinations of the Inquest

6.11 Any determination must comply with European jurisprudence. Five general principles can be discerned from the authorities.[30] The investigation must be:

- Effective.

Z v United Kingdom stated:[31]

> The essential purpose of such investigation (into death) is to secure the effective implementation of the domestic laws which protect the right to life and, in those cases involving State agents or bodies, to ensure their accountability for deaths occurring under their responsibility . . . the authorities must act of their own motion, once the matter has come to their attention. They cannot leave it to the initiative of the next of kin either to lodge a formal complaint or to take responsibility for the conduct of any investigative procedures.

The investigation must also be 'capable of leading to a determination of whether the force used was or was not justified.[32] Furthermore the investigation must be plausible. In *Tanli v Turkey*[33] the applicant's son was taken away by Gendarme Commanders following a search in his village. Two days later the applicant was informed at the police station that his son had died of a heart attack whilst in custody. The applicant maintained that his son's death was caused by torture. An investigation which was undertaken by the Public Prosecutor failed to establish

---

[29] [2007] EW8C408 (Admin), reported as *R (Paul) v Deputy Coroner of the Queen's Household and the Deputy Coroner for Surrey* [2007] 3 WLR 503; para 44.

[30] See in particular *Z v United Kingdom* (2002) 34 EHRR 3.

[31] *ibid*, para 105.

[32] *ibid*, para 106.

[33] *Tanli v Turkey* (Application No 26129/95), 10 April 2001.

the cause of death and three defendants were acquitted.

The Court in that case observed that the government had not provided a plausible explanation for the death of the applicant's son in custody after he entered in apparently good health. While the applicant and other witnesses referred to seeing bruising on the body, there was no medical substantiation that this was attributable to traumatic injury rather than post-mortem changes in the body. In the circumstances, the Court found that it had not been established that there had been a violation of Article 3. (Reassuringly, it did find a violation of Article 2 in that the authorities had failed to provide any plausible or satisfactory explanation for the death of the applicant's son and that their responsibility over his death was therefore engaged.)

- Independent

Z v UK goes on to state:[34] 'For an investigation . . . to be effective, it may generally be regarded as necessary of the persons responsible for and carrying out the investigation to be independent from those implicated in the events'.

- Prompt and Expeditious

It was further stated:[35]

> A requirement of promptness and reasonable expedition is explicit in this context . . . A prompt response by the authorities in investigating a use of lethal force may generally be regarded as essential in maintaining public confidence in their adherence to the rule of law and in preventing any appearance of pollution or intolerance of unlawful acts.

- Public

It has been held:[36] 'There must be a sufficient element of public scrutiny of the investigation and its results to secure accountability in practice as well as in theory'.

- Participation of Family

Z v UK is also authority for the proposition that:[37] 'In all cases . . . the next of kin of the victim must be involved in the procedure to the extent necessary to safeguard his or her legitimate interests'.

The Lawrence Enquiry[38] recommendations were also pertinent. They stated that:

> This development must be regarded as a positive contribution to the openness and fairness of the inquest procedures . . . the court considers that the right of the family of the deceased whose death is under investigation to participate in the proceedings requires that the procedures adopted ensure the requisite protection of their interests, which may be in direct conflict with those of the police or security forces.

---

[34] See *Z v United Kingdom* (2002) 34 EHRR 3, para 106.
[35] *ibid*, para 108.
[36] *ibid*, para 109.
[37] *ibid*, para 109.
[38] Otherwise known as the *McPherson Report*.

7

Disclosure

7.1 This chapter deals with general issues in relation to disclosure in the Coroner's Court. Particular issues in relation to military inquests are dealt with elsewhere in this book, at chapter 14.

Although the inquest is an inquisitorial process and not adversarial, a proportion of inquests do deal with controversial deaths and there can be tension between various parties before the Coroner.

In the criminal arena, a distinctly adversarial jurisdiction, the Criminal Justice Act 2003 lays down the test for disclosure as relating to any material 'which might reasonably be considered capable of undermining the case for the prosecution against the accused or assisting the case for the accused'.[1]

Furthermore the Attorney-General's Guidelines enforce the fundamental approach to disclosure in criminal cases:[2]

> Disclosure is one of the most important issues in the criminal justice system and the application of proper and fair disclosure is a vital component of a fair criminal justice system. The 'golden rule' is that fairness requires full disclosure should be made of all material held by the prosecution that weakens its case or strengthens that of the defence.

The *MacPherson Report* recommended that 'there should be advance disclosure of evidence and documents as of right to parties who have leave from a Coroner to appear at an Inquest'.[3]

As a result of this the Home Office produced a circular,[4] which was implemented on 28 April 1999 and was addressed to Chief Constables.

Essentially the circular advised that there should be as a great a degree of openness as possible, and that disclosure of documentary material to interested persons before the inquest hearing should be normal practice.[5]

The intervention of the Home Office was meant to strengthen the right of disclosure, especially as the police have a duty to hand over all of the material that touches upon a death to the coroner.[6]

---

[1] Section 37 of the Criminal Justice Act 2003.

[2] *Attorney-General's Guidelines on Disclosure* (April 2005) Foreword.

[3] Recommendation 42, of *The Stephen Lawrence Inquiry: Report of an Inquiry by Sir William Macpherson of Cluny* (Cm 4262-I, 1999).

[4] Home Office Circular 20/1999, *Deaths in Custody: Guidance to the Police on Pre-Inquest Disclosure*.

[5] *ibid*, para 5.

[6] See *Peach v Metropolitan Police Commissioner* [1986] 2 All ER 129, 138 B–C.

7.2 The 1999 circular has now been superseded by another Home Office circular.[7]

Again, the circular confirmed that inquests were non-adversarial. As such in law there are no parties to the hearing, and no issues to be litigated between them. However, the circular recognises the reality that where a death occurs in controversial circumstances, it can be difficult to avoid an adversarial approach arising, particularly for instance, where the deceased was in legal custody or otherwise confined.[8]

In such circumstances, the circular advises that there be disclosure of information held by the authorities in advance of the hearing. Clearly, this is meant to avoid the wholly unacceptable circumstances where documents are either not provided or provided, late, during proceedings.

As was stated in *R v Criminal Injuries Compensation Board, ex parte Leatherland and Others*,[9]

> [a]ny practice which leads to the withholding of material until the day of any judicial or quasi-judicial hearing is calculated to be to the significant disadvantage of the party from whom they have been withheld . . . the argument that any injustice can be cured by the grant of an adjournment is nothing to the point. An adjournment may, or may not be granted, and even if granted will involve a represented appellant and extra costs and delay before the final resolution of the appeal . . . where the straightforward steps can be taken of making available to a party to the appeal material which, it is conceded he will be entitled to receive in any event, it makes no sense at all to say that he must wait and take his chance without obtaining an adjournment of his appeal from the Panel.[10]

The Home Office Circular of 31/2002 also advises that there should continue to be as great a degree of openness as possible, and that disclosure of documentary material to interested persons before the inquest hearings should be normal practice. It goes on: 'in all cases Chief Officers will want to consider whether there are compelling reasons why certain documents, or parts of documents, may not be disclosed. But there should always be a strong presumption in favour of openness'.[11]

7.3 Pre-inquest disclosure to interested persons will be on a confidential basis, purely for the purpose of enabling interested persons to prepare for the inquest. The Home Office Circular advises that this should be explained to all interested persons where disclosure takes place.[12]

Interested persons other than the police, including the family of the deceased, who have in their possession material about the death not otherwise disclosed to

---

[7] Home Office Circular 31/2002: *Deaths in Custody: Guidance to the Police on Pre-Inquest Disclosure* (5 June 2002).

[8] *ibid*, para 3.

[9] *R v Criminal Injuries Compensation Board, ex parte Leatherland and Others*, unreported, 2 July 2000, (Turner J).

[10] This case dealt with the Criminal Injuries Compensation Board's policy of refusing to disclose to the claimants in advance of any hearing witness statements made by the police and available at the Board.

[11] See para 5 of Home Office Circular 31/2002.

[12] *ibid*, para 13.

the police or the coroner, should at the same time bring it to the attention of the coroner and offer to provide similar pre-inquest disclosure to other interested persons.[13] This will also apply to any witness statements taken by interested parties which they assert should form the subject-matter of evidence at the hearing. Any statements taken should be disclosed to the coroner and other interested parties. Occasionally, interested parties will want to call such evidence, obtained by them and independent of either the law enforcement authorities or the Coroner's Court. Procedurally an application should be made to the coroner, following disclosure of the statements, for such witnesses to be called. An effective use of this procedure is used when practitioners require to call members of bereaved families to speak of the deceased and provide any relevant evidence to the court. Sometimes the Coroner's Officer would have taken the statement of the court's own volition, on other occasions no such statement will be taken, and it is good practice for practitioners to ensure, particularly of bereaved families, that all have had an opportunity of addressing the court, not only on a strict evidential basis but also to assist with the process of grieving.

The Coroner's Power to Order Disclosure

7.4 The coroner has no power to order the pre-inquest disclosure of statements taken by the police and other documentary material produced by the police during an investigation of a death, for instance in police custody. The statements are the property of the Force commissioning the investigation. The Home Office Circular 31/2002 observes that disclosure will therefore be on a voluntary basis.[14] Here there is a conflict with *Peach v Metropolitan Police Commissioner*,[15] in which was held the police do have a duty to hand over all of the material that touches upon a death to the coroner. In so far as there is a conflict between the Circular and *Peach*, case law will prevail.

Basic principles dictate circumstances in which the coroner must disclose material to interested parties. The principles developed by case law are guided by basic approaches to fairness in any tribunal and include: the disclosure of statements where a witness relies on that statement as a memory-refreshing document;[16] the rule relating to parity of disclosure – if a statement is disclosed then all parties should have it;[17] and disclosure of pertinent expert reports.[18]

---

[13] *ibid*, para 14.
[14] See para 8 of Home Office Circular 31/2002.
[15] *Peach v Metropolitan Police Commissioner* [1986] 2 All ER 129.
[16] See *Re McKerr's Application* [1993] NI 249, 255 C–H.
[17] In *Maksimovich v Walsh* (1985) 4 NSWLR 318; where any document or statement may undermine the evidence given by a witness in court, a principle lending itself from the criminal arena: *R v Inner North London Coroner, ex parte Cohen* (1994) 158 JP 644
[18] This is laid out in the Coroners Rules 1984, r 57(1).

7.5 In principle, the disclosure of evidence and in particular the disclosure of witness statements, subject to any matters of sensitivity, will continue to be governed by the principles of fairness. In accordance with this approach, if interested parties in an inquest are of the view that certain statements or documentation may contain evidence that is either prejudicial or may undermine or perhaps strengthen witnesses evidence at a hearing, then in accordance with natural justice, application to the court will be well founded.

7.6 Although the above-stated basic principle will apply, there are some kinds of material which will require particular consideration when pre-inquest disclosure is being considered.[19]

Examples of problematic issues of disclosure, as laid out in the circular, deal with issues of material that might have an impact on possible subsequent proceedings, whether criminal, civil or disciplinary. Where the material might have an impact on subsequent criminal proceedings, the matter should be discussed with the Crown Prosecution Service. But the withholding of documentation or parts of documentation should only occur where there is genuine risk and not simply because of a remote possibility that the disclosure would have a prejudicial effect.

Furthermore there maybe material that contains personal or sensitive information about the deceased, or unsubstantiated allegations about the deceased, or other material which may cause concern or distress to the family of the deceased. Such material should be handled with appropriate care and sensitivity, particularly over the way such material is disclosed to the family of deceased. Home Office guidance on the issue accords with basic commonsense principles that the handling of such material should be discussed with the family or the family's legal representatives.

Disclosure also becomes problematic when there is personal information about third parties which is not material to the inquest, for example the addresses of witnesses. These should be, and are as a matter of practice, deleted from documents where there is or may be a matter of sensitivity.

Disclosure of the investigating police officer's report will not normally be expected to form part of pre-inquest disclosure, according to the Home Office Circular.[20] This should not be taken as meaning that it is impossible for such reports to be made available where, for instance, a Chief Officer considers that it would be right to do so. Even if such a report is disclosed, it maybe redacted.

Timing of Disclosure

7.7 The precise timing of pre-inquest disclosure in any particular case will depend upon the circumstances of that case. Some documentation is habitually disclosed

---

[19] These are dealt with at para 10 of Home Office Circular 31/2002.
[20] *ibid*, para 12.

early on in the pre-inquest phase, for instance custody records in the case of deaths in custody or pathologists' reports.

The Crown Prosecution Service or any prosecution authority should exercise caution when it is considering whether any criminal proceedings are appropriate. In such cases, in order to avoid prejudice to a criminal trial, disclosure should not take place until either the Crown Prosecution Service has advised against a prosecution or any criminal proceedings are finished. Subject to that proviso, the Home Office Circular[21] recommends that arrangements should normally be made for pre-inquest disclosure to take place as soon as the Chief Officer is satisfied that the material maybe disclosed and in any case not less than 28 days before the date of the inquest proceedings. However, the Circular goes on to advise that where possible, pre-inquest disclosure should be made as far in advance as possible. It is not considered good practice to delay disclosure to the 28-day point where there is no good reason to do so.[22]

Costs of Disclosure

7.8 In the High Court, Mr Justice Collins in *Smith*[23] in the context of military inquests was of the view that costs, if a problem, could be dealt with by a requirement that those who seek disclosure must pay all reasonable copying charges and it maybe that all that is needed in some cases is for the parties' representatives to have access to the material and take copies of only that which is regarded as essential. But, he added, in any Article 2 case it will be difficult to justify any refusal to disclose relevant material. Paragraph 16 of the Home Office Circular 31/2002, observes that it is not anticipated that pre-inquest disclosure of documentary material will involve substantial additional costs. Indeed, it goes on, pre-inquest disclosure, through saving unnecessary adjournments and avoiding unnecessary suspicion on behalf of interested parties as a result of perceived lack of disclosure, should actually save time and associated costs in many cases. Contrary to the observations of Mr Justice Collins, the Home Office Circular observes in the same paragraph that the police should normally meet the costs of any reproduction of documents which is necessary for disclosure to interested persons.

Post-inquest Disclosure

7.9 Parties may request additional disclosure after the inquest is over. It will be a matter for the investigating officer to decide whether it is appropriate that such

[21] *ibid*, para 15.
[22] See *ibid*, para 15.
[23] *Smith v Assistant Deputy Coroner for Oxfordshire* [2006] EWHC 694 (Admin), para 37.

disclosure should take place. If the investigating officer deems it appropriate to disclose documentation a record must be kept of all the documents that have been disclosed, to whom and when.[24] Claims to class-based public interest immunity in respect of investigating officers' reports are considered no longer sustainable.[25]

Adjournments During the Inquest for Disclosure

7.10 It is conceivable that during the course of an inquest it becomes apparent that certain disclosure has not been made. The coroner does have a power to adjourn the hearing under his inherent powers of adjournment, to allow the production of certain material and time for parties to consider it. Sometimes these adjournments can last for a period of months.[26]

The Police Reform Act 2002

7.11 The Police Reform Act 2002 placed on a statutory footing the entitlement of complainants against the police to information concerning their complaint, including the investigation of a deceased's death and the disclosure of documents, including the report of the investigation.

The 2002 Act at section 20(4) gives the complainant a statutory entitlement to information as to:

(a) the progress of the investigation;
(b) any provisional findings of the person carrying out the investigation;
(c) whether any report has been submitted [upon the conclusion of the investigation];
(d) the action (if any) that is taken in respect of the matters dealt with in any such report; and
(e) the outcome of any such action.

The information maybe withheld from the complainant

on proportionality grounds if its disclosure would cause, directly or indirectly, an adverse effect which would be disproportionate to the benefits arising from its disclosure.[27]

---

[24] See *Disclosure Guidance for Fatal Incident Investigations* (March 2005).
[25] See *Review of Circumstances Surrounding the Deaths of Four Soldiers at Princess Royal Barracks, Deepcut, Between 1995 and 2002* ('The Blake Review') para 16.3.
[26] Whenever a coroner thinks such a course is proper he may adjourn the inquest. Adjournments maybe granted for the collection of further evidence or obtaining of documentation, see for example *Nicholls v Liverpool Coroner*, unreported, 8 November 2001 (Sullivan J). A relatively lengthy adjournment of months was also obtained in the inquest into the death of SAS soldiers on a Puma Helicopter, from Sept–Dec in 2009 to obtain further detailed reports and analysis relating to the Puma fleet.
[27] See s 20(7) of the Police Reform Act 2002.

Paragraphs 23(12) and 24(10) of Schedule 3 to the Act provide specifically for disclosure of relevant information to the complainant in the form of an investigation report 'notwithstanding any obligation of secrecy imposed by any rule of law or otherwise'.

Regulation 12 of the Police (Complaints and Misconduct) Regulations 2004 provides that:

(1) [Disclosure maybe withheld where] the non-disclosure of information is necessary for the purpose of:

    (a) preventing the premature or inappropriate disclosure of information that is relevant to, or maybe used in, any actual or perspective criminal proceedings:

    (b) preventing the disclosure of information in any circumstances in which its non-disclosure:

        (i)   is in the interests of national security;

        (ii) is for the purposes of the prevention or detection of crime, or the apprehension or prosecution of offenders;

        (iii) is required on proportionality grounds; or

        (iv) is otherwise necessary in the public interest.

(2) [Information may not be withheld from the complainant under paragraph (1)] unless . . .:

    (a) there is a real risk of the disclosure of that information causing an adverse effect; and

    (b) that adverse effect would be significant.

The Independent Police Complaints Committee Statutory Guidance clarifies that the 'harm test' will amount to a judgement as to whether releasing the information may cause more harm than good. In the context of inquests, the IPCC guidance provides that decisions about disclosure in advance of inquests should take into account the views of the coroner, who should be consulted in advance, although the final decision is a matter for the IPCC in managed and independent investigations and for the police in local and supervised investigations. The coroner has no power to prohibit or order disclosure of any particular document.

The IPCC guidance also provides that any decision by the police or the IPCC not to disclose some part or all of an investigation report to a complainant should be properly recorded along with the reasons for the decision, which should be given to the complainant, unless this information in itself may lead to harm. The record should set out a factual basis for the decision rather than merely repeating the provisions of the law.

There are appeal procedures available to challenge decisions against disclosure.

Despite this guidance, law enforcement authorities are encouraged, where appropriate, and if at all possible, to make disclosure and to do so swiftly.

The procedures laid out above, including the Police Reform Act 2002 procedures, expressly envisage disclosure to bereaved families of investigation reports, subject to the above-stated 'harm test'. In practice investigation reports are provided as a matter of routine.[28]

Confidentiality

7.12 In any event the strictures of Article 2 of the Convention will outweigh considerations of confidentiality where there is a tension between the two imperatives. But in any event any decision against disclosure should be open, transparent and amenable to legal challenge.

The requirement of bereaved families to sign a confidentiality clause is no longer applicable. It was required under the Home Office Circular 20/1999 but has not been replicated in the 31/2002 Circular and neither does it feature in IPCC or Prison and Probation Ombudsman proceedings. It was considered that the requirement to sign a confidentiality clause gave rise to difficulties of practical application and was, it seems, considered unnecessary. Contempt of court proceedings deal with the risk of onward disclosure of documents once disclosed.

The Position of those who Make the Statements

7.13 In June 2009, the Association of Chief Police Officers and the Prison and Probation Ombudsman published a 'Memorandum of Understanding' which addresses some of the issues which arise when dealing with witness statements and the individuals who make them.

Although there will be no disclosure of statements or documentation if it has potential to compromise criminal investigations or prosecutions, paragraph 19 of the memorandum lays down that the police will tell witnesses that their statements or documents maybe shared with the Prison and Probation Ombudsman investigation team. It is not essential that such consent is obtained before sharing the information and although the information may have been given to the police in confidence, it can still, in accordance with the 2006 memorandum, be shared with the Ombudsman.

There remain two requirements (under paragraph 19 of the MOU) for the police to consider

whether the public interest to assist the PPO's investigation outweighs the public interest in keeping the information confidential. As the PPO's investigation is considered to

---

[28] The only remaining controversy seems to relate to transitional case reports; that is those reports completed under the Police Act 1996. But in practice even these transitional reports are being disclosed to bereaved families, even though disclosure had sometimes taken threatened judicial review proceedings.

partially satisfy the State's obligation under Article 2 of the European Convention on Human Rights to conduct an independent investigation into a death in custody (the inquest is the other part of meeting this obligation), it will nearly always be in the public interest to assist the PPO's investigation.

whether the statement or document contains information which might cause particular prejudice to the person who made it (for example, serious harm to their business interests). In the rare case that there might such prejudice, the police can still disclose the information, but should give the person prior written notice that this will be done.

The PPO Disclosure guidance contains a clear presumption in favour of disclosure to bereaved families and disclosure will only be withheld on a content specific basis and where it is expressly envisaged that serious harm will result.

Even so where there is a real risk of serious harm to the interests of third party through disclosure, consideration must be given to any means by which such harm maybe minimised or even extinguished and then disclosure achieved.

Disclosure in Custody Death Cases

7.14 The above provisions assist in cases where individuals have died while in state custody. As a matter of practice the views of the bereaved family will be sought at an early stage and their full participation in the investigation must be achieved.

Disclosure of any documentation relevant as to how the deceased lost their life is now habitually disclosed. The investigation plan and all investigative tools, timelines and logistical reconstructions are provided to the families. They are also provided with contemporaneous documents which include for example custody records, occurrence logs, and medical records and documentation.

Following the completion of the investigation, the investigation report will be disclosed to the family together with documents that have been relied upon in the preparation of that report. These documents will include witness statements, interviews of those whose conduct has been called into question and other contemporaneous documents that have been obtained for the purposes of the investigation.

Such norms are required throughout the panoply of inquest cases, including those held as a result of the deaths of military personnel.[29]

---

[29] There has been criticism that there still remains effectively a voluntary code of compliance for disclosure and there remains no disclosure obligation in the 2009 Act. In '*Deaths in Custody: Remedies and Redress*' the pressure group 'Liberty' called for a 'stronger statutory [disclosure] obligation which would standardise practices and create more confidence in the system'. See also Liberty's second reading briefing on the Coroners and Justice Bill in the House of Lords: (May 2009).

8

Witnesses

8.1 The Coroner alone has the power to call witnesses at an inquest.[1] As a matter of practice any witness required by the Coroner will be informed by the Coroner's Officer or where there is provision, for a Coroner's summons or a summons from the High Court or County Court.

Should any summons be disobeyed, it is for the Coroner at the inquest to decide what the appropriate remedy or punishment will be.[2]

In practice the Coroner will provide a list to interested parties at the inquest of the witnesses which he proposes to call. It is open for any interested party to make submissions, usually and initially in writing but later subject to oral argument if appropriate. The Coroner is not bound to accept any suggestion by interested parties as to what witnesses are to be called, and ultimately his decision will be final.

In any event, the Coroner must be cognisant of the provisions of Article 2 of the Convention in requiring a full and effective hearing. This will be particularly relevant to his decision as to what witnesses to call. In *Edwards v United Kingdom*[3] the European Court of Human Rights considered the case of an individual who died in prison after being attacked by a fellow prisoner. In the deceased's case, there was no inquest although there was a non-statutory Inquiry into how it came to pass that the deceased was placed in the cell of a mentally ill prisoner, diagnosed as schizophrenic with a history of violent outbursts and assault. During this inquiry the applicants were not legally represented or able to have witnesses cross-examined. Furthermore, the inquiry had no power to compel witnesses. Indeed, a number of witnesses failed to appear including a crucial witness, a prison officer, who had passed by the cell shortly before the deceased died. The European Court concluded that the inquiry was deprived of potentially significant evidence and was in violation of Article 2 of the Convention.[4]

---

[1] Coroners Act 1988 s 11(2).
[2] Coroners Act 1988 s 10(2), as amended by the Criminal Justice Act 1991 s 17(3) and Sch 4 part 1.
[3] *Edwards v United Kingdom* (2002) 35 EHRR 19.
[4] *ibid*, para 79.

The Production of Documents

8.2 The Civil Procedure Rules 1998, rule 34.4 provides the means whereby the Coroner can obtain documentation for the purposes of an inquest.

The principles in the context of witness summonses relating to civil litigation and the production of documentation are laid down in *South Tyneside Borough Council v Wickes Building Supplies Limited*[5] and can be summarised into four points:

1 The object is to obtain documents, and a summons should not be used to obtain disclosure; nor should it be of a 'fishing' or speculative nature.
2 The production of the documents must be necessary for the fair disposal of the matter or to save costs.
3 The fact that documents are relevant is not to be decisive.
4 The fact that the specified documents may contain confidential information is not an absolute bar to production (although it is plainly a factor which must be taken into account).

Tajik Aluminium Plant v Hydro Aluminium AS[6] laid down that the documents, or class of documents, must be sufficiently identified to leave no real doubt in the mind of the person to whom the summons is directed. Any doubts as to the adequacy of the description must be resolved in that person's favour.

It should be emphasised that the above-cited cases refer to the civil jurisdiction as distinct from the Coroner's inquest. In relation to a witness summons in civil litigation it is possible to define both relevance and necessity by reference to the statements of claim where the issues are identified. There is nothing comparable to this in the Coroner's inquest, which is inquisitorial in nature.

8.3 One of the duties of a Coroner is to allay, or confirm rumour and suspicion.[7] This was particularly relevant for the Coroner in the case of *Inner West London Assistant Deputy Coroner v Channel 4 Television Corporation (Practice Note)*,[8] the inquest into the deaths of Diana, Princess of Wales and Dodi Al Fayed. One of the matters which the Coroner wished to explore as exhaustively as possible, included whether there was any kind of conspiracy to murder or harm the Princess of Wales and/or Mr Al Fayed and also whether security services were involved in any improper or unlawful activity in connection with the deaths. Mr Justice Eady in the High Court[9] observed that any lingering doubts amongst sections of the public about such matters would only be confirmed or allayed following the most rigorous scrutiny.

[5] *South Tyneside Borough Council v Wickes Building Supplies Limited* [2004] New Property Cases 164; [2004] EWHC 2428.
[6] *Tajik Aluminium Plant v Hydro Aluminium AS (Practice Note)* [2006] 1 WLR 767; [2005] EWCA (Civ) 1218, para 29.
[7] See *R v HM Coroner for Western District of East Sussex ex parte Homberg* (1994) 158 JP 357, 380–81.
[8] *Inner West London Assistant Deputy Coroner v Channel 4 Television Corporation (Practice Note)* [2007] EWHC 2513 (QB), [2008] 1 WLR 945.
[9] *ibid*, para 7.

The Court was also considering the need to address means by which lessons may be learned for the greater protection of the public in future. In *R(Paul) v Deputy Coroner of the Queen's Household and Assistant Deputy Coroner for Surrey*[10] the particular matter under consideration was addressed:

> It is likely that there will be a recurrence of the type of event in which the paparazzi on wheels pursued the Princess and Dodi Al Fayed. It is not only members of the Royal family and their friends who receive this unwelcome attention; any celebrity is vulnerable.
>
> Not only is the safety of the person pursued potentially put at risk but there may well be a risk to bystanders. In our view, occurrences such as this are prejudicial to the safety of a section of the public. It is possible that this danger could be prevented by legislation or other means.[11]

In the *Channel 4* case the Coroner sought an order that if witnesses to certain specified events immediately prior to the deaths of the Princess and Mr Al Fayed had seen or recorded any relevant evidence, and in particular Channel 4, they should produce to the Coroner a copy of any documents produced or obtained for any programme in so far as it recorded or contained such evidence.

During the course of the Coroner's negotiations with Channel 4, the request for such material was defined and became more specific, or as specific as it could be, given the Coroner had not seen any of this material. The High Court was sympathetic to the Coroner's position and balanced certain factors as to whether a witness summons with compulsion to produce documentation should be issued.[12]

On one side of the argument was the public interest in the Coroner and the jury being able to carry out their task with the toughness which the circumstances justified. It is necessary to avoid, so far as possible, the opportunity for allegations to be made later that they proceeded on an incomplete or partial account of the evidence, or that they had been the victim of a 'cover up'. On the other side of the argument, Mr Justice Eady took into account 'any chilling effect on our freedom of speech and the obligations of confidentiality undertaken by Channel 4 and the interests towards whom such an obligation is owed'.[13]

The High Court concluded that such a summons should be issued and that it was proportionate to the advantages to be achieved for the transparency of the coronial process.

It is significant that the Court observed that the witness summons was restricted and relatively specific. The effect of the summons which was granted was that the Coroner only, in the first instance, would receive the documentation and then 'filter the material paying proper regard to the repeating considerations which I have had to take into account'.[14]

---

[10] *R (Paul) v Deputy Coroner of the Queen's Household and Assistant Deputy Coroner for Surrey* [2008] QB 172, paras 37–40.

[11] See also *R v Inner West London Coroner, ex parte Dallaglio* [1994] 4 All ER 139, 155 and 164.

[12] See above n 8, para 26.

[13] *ibid*, para 26.

[14] *ibid*, para 27.

Hearsay

8.4 Rule 37 of the Coroners Rules 1984 is the complete code for the admission of all documentary evidence in the Coroner's Court.

In terms, the Coroner may admit documentary evidence at an inquest when it is relevant to the purposes of the inquest, from any living person, and which in the Coroner's opinion is unlikely to be disputed, unless a person who in the opinion of the Coroner is designated within rule 20(2) objects to the documentary evidence being admitted.[15]

Procedurally at the start of the inquest the Coroner must announce that the documentary evidence maybe admitted and give details of it. It will then, at the appropriate time in the hearing be read aloud at the inquest.

Documentary hearsay cannot be put into evidence in the Coroner's Court directed by the Coroner unless he's permitted it by rule 37.

In *R (Paul and others) v Assistant Deputy Coroner for Inner West London*[16] the Court of Appeal considered the decision of the Coroner investigating the death of Henri Paul, a driver employed by the Ritz Hotel who was driving the Princess of Wales and Dodi Al Fayed at the time of the fatal car crash. The Coroner sought to read various documents to the jury in this inquest including statements of witnesses made in proceedings in France, statements of witnesses made to the Metropolitan Police and interviews of witnesses to media organisations. The Coroner also sought to make reference to books written by witnesses.

Significantly the contents of these documents could be proven by the calling of witnesses, not necessarily the maker of the document nor indeed the person who took the statements. This mirrors the approach taken in the criminal courts for the giving of multiple hearsay evidence.

The Court ruled that the words 'unlikely to be disputed' contained in rule 37(1) meant 'uncontroversial' and not 'unlikely to be challenged in oral proceedings by interested persons'. Since rule 37(1) permitted the admission of documentary evidence from a living person only if in the Coroner's opinion it was unlikely to be disputed, and since in the case of Paul, the Coroner was not of that opinion, the Court of Appeal held that the statements did not fall within the provisions of rule 37 and could not be read to the jury by the Coroner.

---

[15] Rule 20(2) deals with categories of individuals who are entitled to examine witnesses at inquests.
[16] *R (Paul and others) v Assistant Deputy Coroner for Inner West London* [2007] EWCA Civ 1259; [2008] 1 WLR 1335.

Witnesses in Court Awaiting Evidence

8.5 There is no rule or practice or procedure in the Coroner's Court whereby witnesses who have not given evidence should remain outside of Court, and the Coroner will in most circumstances allow witnesses to be in Court listening to evidence before they give their own evidence.[17]

This general rule is subject to variation if the Coroner is of the view that a witness's evidence may be undermined or devalued by the fact that they have sat in Court and listened to evidence prior to their own. The Coroner's overriding duty to perform a thorough investigation into death in accordance with principles of Article 2 of the Convention may found an application by an interested party to the hearing that a witness remain outside of Court. But this still remains the exception rather then the rule.

The Rule Against Self-incrimination

8.6 The Coroners Rules 1984, rule 22(1) specifically applies to potential self-incrimination regarding criminal liability. It does not deal with civil liability.

Rule 22 does not compel a witness to answer any questions, although there is no prohibition upon that witness being asked questions.[18]

Indeed if certain evidence has been tendered by the witness as a result of questions by the Coroner, who as a matter of practice will begin the procedure by asking questions first, followed by the questions of interested parties, it will be perfectly permissible for parties to ask questions of a witness which may flow from the Coroner's examination.

---

[17] See *Moore v Lambeth County Court Registrar* [1969] 1 WLR 141, 142 (CA) and *Tomlinson v Tomlinson* [1980] 1 WLR 322.

[18] See *R v Lincolnshire Coroner Ex Parte Hay* (1999) 163 JP 666, 679–82.

9

Interested Parties

9.1 The law in relation to interested parties is substantially contained in the case of *R v Greater London (South District) Coroner, ex parte Driscoll*.[1]

This case concerned the decision of the Coroner that the sisters of the deceased were not properly interested persons in accordance with the Coroners Rules 1984, rule 20. That is the rule which enables a Coroner to decide who is entitled to examine any witness at an inquest. It lays down a series of individuals including a parent, child, spouse and any person representative of the deceased who may be designated as individuals entitled to examine witnesses at the inquest.

There is no definition of a properly interested person to be found in the Coroners Act 1988 or in the 1984 Rules, but a Coroner considering how to exercise his jurisdiction under rule 20 should look at the object of the inquest and then at the categories of persons referred to by the Rules to assist him to decide when he ought to regard the individual applicant as a properly interested person.

In ruling that the sisters were properly interested parties, the Court distinguished *R v Her Majesty's Coroner for Portsmouth ex parte John Keane*[2] In *Keane* there was not a significant history of contact before death between the sisters and the deceased and the High Court in *Driscoll* reminded itself that *Keane* had been confined to the particular circumstances of the case.[3]

The Court in *Driscoll* observed that they doubted whether it was possible to define in general terms what a properly interested person was.[4] The reasons for this were that the circumstances will vary so much and that the expression 'properly interested person' are ordinary English words to which the Coroner must be allowed to give an ordinary meaning.[5] Lord Justice Kennedy (sitting with Mr Justice Pill) in *Driscoll* observed obiter, that it is unhelpful to define 'interest' for the purposes of rule 20(2)(h) by looking at what constitutes locus standi for the purposes of judicial review.

9.2 A properly interested person must establish more than idle curiosity. The mere fact of being a witness will rarely be enough.[6] The Court observed in *Driscoll*

---

[1] *R v Greater London (South District) Coroner ex parte Driscoll* (1993) 159 JP 45 (heard on 22 October 1993).

[2] *R v HM Coroner for Portsmouth ex parte John Keane* (1989) 153 JP 659.

[3] See the judgment of Pill J (as he then was) *ibid*, 661 F.

[4] See the transcript of the *Driscoll* judgment, p 17 F–G.

[5] See also *R v East Sussex Coroner, ex parte Healy* [1989] 1 WLR 1194 (Ct).

[6] See the official Court transcript of *Driscoll*, p 18, para 10.

that what an individual must show is a genuine desire to participate more than the mere giving of relevant evidence in the determination of how, when and where the deceased came by his death. These parameters will be extended to take into account of the broader ambit of an inquest as a result of the *Middleton* judgment and Article 2 jurisprudence.

The Coroner should form an opinion as to who the interested parties are, before the day of the hearing. As the Broderick Report pointed out, if the Coroner forms the opinion that the person seeking to be heard is a properly interested person the discretion of the Coroner is then at an end and the interested person must be afforded all rights set out in rule 20(1) of the Coroners Rules 1984, entitling him to examine any witnesses at an inquest either in person or through an advocate.

It should be emphasised that the expression 'properly interested person' in rule 20(2)(h) of the Coroners Rules should not be given a narrow or technical meaning. It is not confined to a proprietary right or a financial interest in the estate of the deceased. It can cover a variety of concerns about or resulting from the circumstances in which the death occurred. The word 'interested' is not used in the Coroners Rules to describe or identify the persons laid out in the categories in rule 20(2)(a)–(g) but it maybe said that they each have an interest in the sense contemplated.

Such position arises in the case of a parent, child and spouse out of the nature and closeness of the personal relationship to the deceased in each category. The personal representative has a legal duty in relation to the estate of the deceased. Beneficiaries under insurance policies and insurers may have a financial interest in the circumstances of the death. Someone who may have caused or contributed to the death has an obvious concern. Though of differing natures, the concerns of the deceased's trade union, the Chief Officer of Police and the government are readily understood by the courts.

9.3 Of course individuals who come within the above categories may have an interest in the matters laid out within Rule 36 of the Coroners Rules. The categories of persons laid out in rule 20(2)(a)–(g) provide a guide to the types of interest envisaged as relevant for the purposes of paragraph (h).[7]

9.4 The Court in *Driscoll* also considered the significance to be attached to the word 'properly' in paragraph (h). It was held in that case that the context imports not only the notion that the interest must be reasonable and substantial, and not trivial or contrived; it also imports the notion that the Coroner may need to be satisfied that the concern of the person seeking to intervene is one genuinely directed to the scope of an inquest as defined in rule 36.[8]

Driscoll is further authority that rule 20(2)(h), which refers to interested persons being

---

[7] See the transcript of the judgment of Pill J (as he then was) in Driscoll, pp 19(C)–20(D).
[8] *ibid*, p 20(D)–(F).

> any other person who, in the opinion of the coroner, is a properly interested person,

permits and requires the Coroner to form an opinion as to whether a person is properly interested. In the case of close relations the Court in *Driscoll* did not expect a Coroner normally to adopt a restrictive approach, but the Court accepted that there were likely to be circumstances in which a Coroner could properly form an opinion that even a close relative is not properly interested in the proceedings in accordance with the meaning of rule 20(2)(b).

9.5 The position of potentially interested parties was considered by Lady Justice Hallett in preliminary hearings in relation to the deaths of individuals as a result of the so-called 7/7 bombings. A close analysis of the judgment of Lady Justice Hallett[9] is illuminating as to the up-to-date position of Coroners in relation to interested parties.

Lady Justice Hallett accepts in paragraph 2 of her official judgment that asking questions and being part of the investigation into death can be part of a healing process. She highlighted the process of designation of interested parties. Automatic designation is provided by rule 20(2)(a) and comprises individuals who form a category of those associated by blood, marriage, civil partnership, executor status or because the Coroner is satisfied that they lived as a partner of the deceased in an enduring family relationship.

Designation under rule 20(2)(d) deals with

> any person who's act or omission or that of his agent or servant may in the opinion of the coroner have caused, or contributed to, the death of the deceased.

In the 7/7 preliminary inquests there were applications from the East London Bus and Coach Company and another from the driver of the number 20 bus involved in the incident. The application on behalf of the bus company was pursued on the basis that their act of allowing one of the alleged terrorist bombers to board the bus may have 'caused or contributed to the deaths'.

For the applicant – in that case the bus company – to fall within the relevant paragraph, the Coroner must be of the opinion that the applicant holds some 'responsibility' by action or omission that may have been causative of the death. In the particular case of the 7/7 inquest, no parties suggested that they did so. The bus driver's action 'of allowing Hussain (one of the alleged bombers) to board the bus' was, in the opinion of Lady Justice Hallett, too remote in the chain of causation to be properly and purposively construed as an act or omission that 'caused or contributed to the deaths' of the deceased. As such the applications relating to the bus company and bus driver were refused in the 7/7 preliminary hearing.

The Chief Officers of the Metropolitan Police Force, of the City of London Police and of the British Transport Police applied for designation of interested party status under rule 20(2)(g),

---

[9] Transcript of judgment following pre-inquest hearing on 26–30 April 2010.

an inspector appointed by, or a representative of, an enforcing authority, or any person appointed by a government department to attend the inquest.

The Chief Officer of Police is defined by rule 2(1) of the Coroners Rules 1984 as:

the chief officer of police for the area in which the coroner's jurisdiction is comprised.

Lady Justice Hallett designated the Metropolitan Police Force under rule 20(2)(g) and the other two designated forces, indicating that she could have done so under rule 20(2)(g) or using her discretion under rule 20(2)(h). It was observed by the Court in the 7/7 preliminary hearings that those authorities each and independently of each other had a great deal to offer the inquiry in relation to the emergency response and other matters.

The remaining applications for interested party status were made under the discretionary rule 20(2)(h) and broadly fell into four categories. First, relatives of the deceased who do not have an automatic entitlement under rule 20(2)(a) to examine witnesses; secondly, organisations responsible for planning, preparing, rehearsing and implementing the emergency response to a major incident; thirdly, other organisation or government body, and last, the survivors of the 7/7 bombings. Again, Lady Justice Hallett in April 2010 referred to *Driscoll* as the leading authority on rule 20(2)(h).

Assistance was also obtained from *Re Northern Ireland Human Rights Commission*,[10] where the House of Lords considered the test to be applied in determining whether a third party should be allowed to intervene in an inquest in Northern Ireland (to which a different statutory coronial scheme applies). Lord Woolf observed at paragraph 32:

The practice of allowing third persons to intervene in proceedings brought by and against other persons which do not directly involve the person seeking to intervene has become more common in recent years but is still a relatively rare event. The intervention is always subject to the control of the court and whether the third person is allowed by the court to intervene is usually dependent upon the court's judgment as to whether the interests of justice will be promoted by allowing the intervention. Frequently the answer will depend upon whether the intervention will assist the court itself to perform the role upon which it is engaged. The court has always to balance the benefits which are to be derived from the intervention as against the inconvenience, delay and expense which an intervention by a third person can cause to the existing parties.

In the 7/7 preliminary hearings, the Court received a number of applications from the brothers and sisters of the deceased. In some cases, these applications were in addition to other family members who had received automatic entitlement to examine witnesses pursuant to rule 20(2)(a). In other instances, there were no family members with an automatic entitlement and in one case a sister of the deceased applied where there was no one to qualify under rule 20(2)(a) to represent her brother.

---

[10] *Re Northern Ireland Human Rights Commission* [2002] UKHL 25, sub nom *R v Greater Belfast Coroner ex parte Northern Ireland Human Rights Commission*.

Parliament have deliberately excluded siblings from those with an automatic entitlement under rule 20(2)(a). Nevertheless the 7/7 inquest concluded that as a result of 'the closeness of their relationship to the deceased, the promptness of their applications and their expressed concerns for the process', siblings met, in the circumstances of the 7/7 inquest, the criteria for properly interested persons.[11]

Central, it seems, to the judgment of Lady Justice Hallett is that the siblings indicated a genuine desire to participate, and proved that they might be able to assist the process. The Court was mindful that not many of them were involved (under 10) and for the most part submissions on their behalf would be unlikely to differ from those made on behalf of the rest of the families. The Court in the 7/7 preliminary hearings indicated that by designating them then, little, if any, inconvenience or additional cost would be occasioned.

This aspect of the judgment does seem somewhat contradictory, in that it seems that the siblings might duplicate the submissions and approaches made by other designated interested persons, and therefore may be likely to extend the length of the hearing if those questions are repeated (and often they will be if individual representation is provided) and therefore mitigate against the inclusion of siblings in this instance as interested parties.

Indeed, Lady Justice Hallett was aware of the contradiction when she stated:[12] 'I appreciate that some may think I may have been somewhat generous to them in so doing, but they are all very closely related to the deceased into whose deaths I am appointed to inquire'.

The London Ambulance Service, the London Fire and Emergency Planning Authority, Transport for London and Tube Lines Limited were also granted interested party status under the discretion of the Coroner. The Court observed[13] that each of the organisations 'had significant operational roles on the 7th July 2005 as first / emergency responders in the initial aftermath of the explosion'. The Court recognised that each had specialist knowledge and should be in a position to provide considerable help to the inquest. Further perceived benefits were that 'they should know what questions should be asked to assist the process in so far as the planning for and the actual emergency response are concerned'. They could be asked 'to explain alleged systemic failings and/or failings of individuals'.

Conversely, the Coroner was not persuaded that the same argument applied to other organisations or government departments who did not demonstrate a significant role in any operational response. Furthermore certain organisations which were not provided with designation were not anticipated to be the subject of criticism at the forthcoming inquest.

The West Yorkshire Police were granted discretionary designation in the 7/7 inquest on the basis that the alleged bombers all resided within their area. The Coroner noted that the inquest might touch upon their background, and their community. Furthermore the role of the West Yorkshire Police in events prior to

[11] See para 123 of the 7/7 preliminary inquest hearing transcript.
[12] *ibid*, para 124.
[13] *ibid*, para 126.

7 July 2005 and what knowledge or information they had about the alleged bombers would most likely be the subject of scrutiny at the inquest.

Lady Justice Hallett considered the position of the survivors of the bombing and their application for interested party status in some detail.

Submissions on behalf of the survivors involved applications upon the purported engagement of Article 2 of the European Convention and on the breadth of the Coroner's discretion under rule 20(2)(h). It was argued by those representing the interested parties that if they did not receive designation, 'their lawyers will receive no further funding to represent them and will not, therefore, help prepare them for the inquest'.[14]

During the submissions of counsel representing the survivors (who also represented the bereaved families), counsel was unable to identify any additional issues that the survivors would wish to raise or any further lines of enquiry they would wish to pursue over and above those being raised on behalf of the bereaved families. Counsel conceded that their interests coincided. Indeed had they not done so, counsel for the survivors indicated that he and his instructing solicitors felt that they would be unable to represent them all in the previous judicial review proceedings. Quite how the position of the interested parties differs from siblings, when both agreed that there was a duplication of interests, is unclear.

Crucial to the Court's consideration of the submissions was the ruling made by the Coroner that the Article 2 investigative duty did not arise as a consequence of the deaths and therefore cannot be prayed in aid by the survivor applicants.

Article 2 Investigation in 'Near Death' Cases

9.6 Lady Justice Hallett was unconvinced, on the limited argument that she heard in the preliminary hearings in relation to the 7/7 inquest that the survivors in that case could be treated as falling within the category of 'near miss'. She observed[15] that obvious distinctions could reasonably be drawn between those travelling in the carriages or on the bus in which the explosions occurred and those who were not. She also referred to distinctions made by domestic and European law between cases where death has occurred and cases where it has not.

The requirements of an Article 2 investigation in 'near death' cases are less stringent than in cases where death has occurred.[16] In a case where death has occurred the interests of the bereaved family have a 'further dimension of gravity'.

---

[14] *ibid*, para 132.

[15] *ibid*, para 134.

[16] See *R on the application of JL v Secretary of State for Justice* [2008] UKHL 68 (Lord Phillips and Lord Brown).

Concessions to Non-Interested Parties

9.7 In refusing the survivors designated interested parties status, the Coroner in 7/7 attempted to ameliorate that decision by emphasising that she intended to make the survivors 'feel they are a proper part of the process'.[17]

To achieve this lady Justice Hallett authorised the release of the Scene Reports to those survivors who had signed the confidentiality undertaking. She further emphasised that survivors might attend the proceedings whenever they wish and some would be called to give evidence. She encouraged them to use the services of her Specialised Inquest Team, consisting particularly of Counsel and a solicitor and she indicated that the Court would pursue all legitimate lines of inquiry and ask all relevant questions.

The Court also indicated that it would read and hear submissions from survivors if they wished to submit them and the Court would ensure that the process would be as open as possible. To this end, the Court indicated that a transcript of the public proceedings would be published each day on a website, enabling the survivors to follow them in detail, and that the Court would treat all survivors with 'care and sensitivity'.[18]

Significantly, there were a number of bereaved families who opposed the application to designate the 19 survivors as interested parties.

---

[17] At para 135 of the official 7/7 preliminary inquest hearing transcript.
[18] *ibid.*

10

Public Access and Reporting of Proceedings in Coroners' Courts

10.1 'Every inquest shall be held in public', but the coroner 'may direct that the public should be excluded from an inquest or any part of that inquest if the coroner considers that it would be in the interest of national security to do so'.[1]

National Security

10.2 It should be emphasised that the issue of national security cannot simply be raised by those seeking the exclusion of the public and does not necessary arise simply because the deceased is alleged to have worked for the security services.[2] Furthermore, national security should not be confused with issues which may cause embarrassment to the government or any other organisation. In those circumstances there is no good reason to hold the inquest in private.

Strictly, inquests should only be held in private on the basis of national security, where the secret information in issue concerns the defence of the country. In practice, States are given a wide margin of appreciation in matters of national security. In *Grady v United Kingdom*[3] the European Court stated:

> When the core of the national security aim pursued is the operational effectiveness of the armed forces, it is accepted that each State is competent to organise its own system of military discipline and enjoys a certain margin of appreciation in this respect . . .

By contrast, courts in the United Kingdom have recognised the weakness of the doctrine of 'margin of appreciation' in European law, preferring common law principles that require the Human Rights Act 1998 to be interpreted in context as robustly as possible. To this extent, European jurisprudence places particular emphasis upon the need for a full and fearless enquiry.[4] The courts will consider the principle of proportionality, when assessing whether a court hearing should be held in private on the basis of national security. In *Krone Verlag GmbH and Co KG*

---

[1] Coroners Rules 1984 r 17.
[2] *R v McHugh, ex parte Trelford*, unreported, 22 March 1984 (DC).
[3] *Grady v United Kingdom* (1999) 29 EHRR 493, 530, para 89.
[4] *R v Director of Public Prosecutions, ex parte Kebilene* [2000] 2 AC 326, 380–81.

v Austria (No 3)[5] the Court observed that 'the Court's task is therefore confined to ascertaining whether the measures taken at national level are justifiable in principle and proportionate'.

10.3 Article 6 of the Convention which relates to the rights to a fair trial does not directly apply to Coroners' Courts because the inquest hearing does not involve the determination of an individual's civil rights and obligations.

Nevertheless the principles behind Article 6, which, in part, protects citizens from secret hearings and reserves their rights to a public and open hearing, will be of persuasive assistance in coronial proceedings. In *Axen v Germany*[6] the European Court stated:

> The public character of proceedings before the judicial bodies referred to in Article 6(i) protects litigants against the administration of justice in secret and with no public scrutiny. It is also one of the means whereby confidence in the courts, superior and inferior, can be maintained. By rendering the administration of justice visible, publicity contributes to the achievement of the aim of Article 6(i), namely a fair trial, the guarantee of which is one of the fundamental principles of any democratic society, within the meaning of the Convention.[7]

10.4 When an applicant seeks an order that the inquest be held in private or parts of it be held in private it is incumbent upon them to prove that the basic principle of public hearings should be restricted. Normally such applications will be heard *in camera* and will usually be accompanied with advanced written arguments by both sides.

The decision of the court should be given in open hearing.[8]

Any decision by the coroner can be taken to judicial review.

Challenges by the Media to *in Camera* Hearings

10.5 There will be occasions when interested parties to the inquest do not object to proceedings being held *in camera*. This can sometimes arise in the context of military inquests, where bereaved families have been persuaded, at times by representatives of the armed forces, that any publicity could be detrimental to those presently serving in any theatre of conflict.

If this is a realistic fear or risk then all parties should be aware of the care required as to what evidence does reach the public arena.

But sometimes there is a conflict between the rigid but understandable fears of interested parties and the perfectly proper requirement of the media to report to the public at large information that may be in the public interest.

---

[5] *Krone Verlag GmbH & Co KG v Austria (No 3)* (Application no 39069/97) ECHR 2003-XII, para 30.
[6] *Axen v Federal Republic of Germany* Series A No 72 (1983) 6 EHRR 195, para 25.
[7] See also *Pretto v Italy* (1983) 6 EHRR 182.
[8] *R v Ealing Justices ex parte Weafer* (1982) 74 Cr App R 204 (DC); *R v Tower Bridge Justices ex parte Osborne* (1989) 88 Cr App R 28 (DC).

Should this conflict arise then the media, either individually through their outlet or newspaper or collectively by the appointment of a single advocate, have a right to address the coroner as to whether the hearing should be held *in camera*.

The coroner has an inherent right to regulate his own proceedings and it is this starting point by which he may, following argument, decide that proceedings be held completely or partially *in camera* or provide for the prohibition on publication of certain facts or details which may emerge during evidence.

10.6 There is authority for the proposition that a case cannot be said to be held publicly if the media have been excluded. In *Denbigh Justices, ex parte Williams and Evans*[9] it was stated by the Court:

> I find it difficult to imagine a case which can be said to be held publicly if the press have been actively excluded. Today, as everybody knows, the great body of the British public get their news of how justice is administered through the press and other mass media. The presence or absence of the press is a vital factor in deciding whether a particular hearing was or was not in open court.

In a case considering the Contempt of Court Act 1981 section 11, the Court put it explicitly that save in exceptional circumstances, court proceedings should take place in public where the press were free to report. The Court expressed this as a principle of 'fundamental importance'. The commentary to that case observed that any exception 'must be founded on a policy which can assert a greater claim to the court's respect than that of open justice'.[10]

10.7 The principal case upon public hearings remains *Attorney-General v Leveller Magazine Limited*.[11] This case reasserted the principal that as a general rule the English system of administering justice requires that it be done in public. Lord Diplock went on:

> The application of this principal of open justice has two aspects: as respects proceedings in the court itself it requires that they should be held in open court to which press and public are admitted and that in criminal cases at any rate all evidence communicated to the court is communicated publicly. As respects the publication to a wider public of fair and accurate reports of proceedings that have taken place in court the principal requires that nothing should be done to discourage this ... before it departs in anyway from the general rule, the departure is justified to the extent and no more than the extent that the court reasonably believes it to be necessary in order to serve the ends of justice.

10.8 Distilling the above authorities, six basic principles can be extracted:

---

[9] *Denbigh Justices, ex parte Williams and Evans* [1974] QB 759 (DC) 765.

[10] See *R v Dover Justices ex parte Dover District Council and Wells* [1992] Crim LR 371 (DC) 372: See also *Three Rivers District Council and Others v Governor and Company of the Bank of England* [2005] EWCA Civ 993, where the Court observed that the importance of publicity to the judicial process was fundamental.

[11] *Attorney-General v Leveller Magazine Limited* [1979] AC 440 (HL) 449 H–450D; see also *Scott v Scott* [1913] AC 417 (HL).

(a) The normal rule is that hearings should be conducted publicly. There is a fundamental assumption of open hearings.[12]

(b) Nonetheless, courts do have power by virtue of their general right to control their own procedure, to order the public to be excluded which includes the print, digital and broadcast media and the press.

(c) However, the exercise of the power, in common with any other derogation from the principles of open hearings, should be strictly confined to cases where the public's presence would genuinely frustrate the administration of justice, and should not be used merely to save parties, witnesses or others from embarrassment or to conceal facts which might, on more general grounds, be desirable to be kept secret.[13]

(d) Any discretion that the tribunal may have should only be exercised in narrowly circumscribed circumstances and proportionately. The discretion should be exercised consistently with the general spirit of English jurisprudence, which is overwhelmingly in favour of open hearings.

(e) Those applying to depart from the fundamental principal of open hearings must convince the court that without such a restriction it is a reasonable conclusion that justice would not be done.[14]

(f) The embarrassing nature of any evidence is no good reason to exclude or restrict the press.

Any court will be expected to trust the broadcasting authorities and newspaper editors to fulfil their responsibilities accurately to inform the public of court proceedings and to exercise sensible judgement about comment which may interfere with the administration of justice.[15]

Secret Inquests

10.9 By virtue of Schedule 1, paragraphs 3–4 of the 2009 Coroners and Justice Act the Lord Chancellor may request a Senior Coroner to suspend an investigation into a person's death if the Lord Chancellor is of the view that

> the cause of death is likely to be adequately investigated by an inquiry under the Inquiries Act 2005 . . . that is being or is to be held.[16]

This provision appeared in the 2009 legislation as a result of the highly controversial proposals relating to secret inquests.

---

[12] See also *Malik v Central Criminal Court and Crown Prosecution Service* [2006] EWHC 1539 (Admin), para 40.

[13] See *Attorney-General v Leveller Magazine Limited* (n 11 above) 450C–451E.

[14] See *Attorney-General v Leveller Magazine Limited* (above n 11) 471B–E.

[15] See *R v B* [2006] EWCA Crim 2692, [2007] EMLR 145, para 25.

[16] See Coroners and Justice Act 2009 Sch 1, para 3(1)(a).

Originally the previous government had proposed that relatives of the deceased could be excluded from inquest proceedings if that was required in the interest of national security or the general combating of crime. This measure was defeated in the Houses of Lords but the tenor of a ministerial statement made by the then Lord Chancellor and Secretary of State for Justice, Jack Straw, on 15 May 2009 remains in the 2009 Act. The Lord Chancellor said:

> Where it is not possible to proceed with an inquest under the current arrangements, the government will consider establishing an inquiry under the Inquiries Act 2005 to ascertain the circumstances in which the deceased came by his or her death. Each case will be looked at on its own individual merits. As with the provisions in respect of the certification of Coroners' investigations, we would expect to resort to such a procedure only in very exceptional and rare circumstances.

The potential use of this provision was elaborated upon following the Act's Royal Assent on 12 November 2009 when the Ministry of Justice issued a statement which included the following reference:

> There is provision, carefully circumscribed, for the establishment of a Judicial Inquiry under the 2005 Inquiries Act to take the place of an inquest, where there is highly sensitive evidence (typically intercept) and it would not be possible to have an Article 2 compliant inquest. These provisions will be used in rare cases only.

The remaining provision in Schedule 1 relating to the potential use of the Inquiries Act 2005 reflects a determination by the previous government to provide for a form of secret inquest. This can be traced back to the counter-terrorism legislation during which the provision of secret hearings was first mooted. This course was rejected but returned to during the debates over Coroners' reform. Previous clauses in the 2009 Bill[17] which related to secret inquests in circumstance of perceived national security were comprehensively rejected by Parliament but it is clear that the available use of the Inquiries Act 2005 maintains within the 2009 Act the possibility of recourse to inquests without the attendance of bereaved families or juries and in an environment which is not Article 2 compliant.

These provisions also potentially ignore all of the protocols laid down in the Charter for Bereaved People, which sets out guidance for those bereaved, including their rights and roles during the investigations of the Coroner and subsequent inquest. As has been stated, the 2005 Inquiries Act will only be used in exceptional circumstances and only time will tell whether its use will contravene European Convention requirements. Potential violations could be found under Article 2 (right to life), Article 8 (right to respect for private and family life), or Article 10 (freedom of expression).

Article 2 will only be engaged in relation to inquests carried out in order to fulfill obligations under that provision.[18] In their explanatory notes to the 2009 Bill

---

[17] And in particular Clause 11.
[18] In any event, any legislature making rules must do so in a way that respects Convention Rights: see s 6 of the Human Rights Act 1998.

the government considers the potential impact of Article 10.[19] It observes that 'the key is the extent to which Article 10 includes the right to receive information'.

The European Court of Human Rights in *Leander v Sweden*[20] held that Article 10 was understood to include a right to receive information that others wish to impart, but it does not impose an obligation on any authority to provide any particular information. The note in relation to the 2009 Bill considers that there are conflicting authorities but that

> the Government considers that the better view is that Article 10 is not engaged by a decision to hold a statutory inquiry in private, except possibly in the most special and unusual cases (the only example of which has been the Shipman Inquiry).[21]

Furthermore it is the government's view[22] that it is most unlikely that Article 10 would be engaged by this decision to hold an inquest or part of an inquest in private in the interests of national security. They observe that in the event that Article 10 is engaged, this falls squarely within Article 10(2), which ensures that there will be no violation of Convention Rights if the freedoms referred to in the Article are subject to

> such formalities, conditions, restrictions or penalties as are prescribed by law and are necessary in a democratic society, in the interests of national security, territorial integrity or public safety, for the prevention of disorder or crime, for the protection of health or morals, for the protection of the reputation or rights of others, for preventing the disclosure of information received in confidence, or for maintaining the authority and impartiality of the judiciary.[23]

On the 3 November, 2010 Lady Justice Hallett, the Coroner in the 7/7 Inquest ruled that she would not consider closed hearings at the inquest concerning secret intelligence documents which lawyers for the Security Services had argued would damage national security if made public. Lady Justice Hallett observed that the evidence could be edited to remove names of sources and other confidential information.

One of the options available to the Home Secretary would have been to close down the inquest and order instead a Public Inquiry into the events of the 7 July 2005. The legal advantage in doing this would be that there could be greater access to closed hearings to facilitate the alleged concerns of the Security Services. Such a decision, if made, would be controversial because in those circumstances all the evidence would have to be heard again including the traumatic material already heard by the family at the inquest.

---

[19] See Coroners and Justice Bill Explanatory Notes, note 839 onwards.

[20] *Leander v Sweden* [1987] 9 EHRR 433.

[21] Explanatory Notes to the Coroners and Justice Bill, note 839. References made (in fn 8) to *Persey v Secretary of State for Environment, Food and Rural Affairs* [2002] EWHC 371: *R (on the application of Howard) v Secretary of State for Health*; *R (on the application Wright-Hogeland) v Secretary of State for Health* [2002] EWHC 396, distinguishing *R v Secretary of State for Health, ex parte Wagstaff*; *R v Secretary of State for Health, ex parte Associated Newspapers Limited* [2001] 1 WLR 292.

[22] *ibid*, para 840.

[23] European Convention, Art 10(2). Text of Article 10(2) does not appear in the explanatory notes.

In fact, the matter came before the High Court in *R (On the Application of the Secretary of State for the Home Department) v Assistant Deputy Coroner for Inner West London.*[24]

The High Court upheld the decision of Lady Justice Hallett. The crux of their decision involved an interpretation of Rule 17 of the Coroners Rules 1984, which lays down that every inquest should be held in public.

Furthermore, the High Court construed Rule 57, which provides that the coroner, upon application and payment of a fee, supply to any properly interested person a copy of any report or post mortem examination, special examination, any notes of evidence, or any document put in evidence at the inquest.

Finally, the court considered Rule 20(1), which provides that any person who satisfies the coroner that they are properly interested, shall be entitled to examine any witness at an inquest.

Lord Justice Stanley Burnton observed that in this context, absolute rights were given to properly interested parties within the rules expressed in mandatory language – 'shall' – with no exceptions expressed in relation to national security.

The case further established that a 'closed' hearing should be defined as in the absence of properly interested parties and their legal representatives and that if a closed hearing was to occur, it should be attended only by members of the Security Services and their legal representatives, together with counsel to the inquest and those instructing them [per Lord Justice Maurice Kay].

Lord Justice Stanley Burnton defined 'public', in the context of Rule 17, as persons other than properly interested persons [at paragraph 35].

---

[24] [2010] EWHC 3098 (Admin).

11

The Verdict

Determinations of the Inquest

11.1 Any determination must comply with European jurisprudence. Five general principles can be discerned from the authorities.[1] The investigation must be:

- Effective.

Z v United Kingdom stated:[2]

> The essential purpose of such investigation (into death) is to secure the effective implementation of the domestic laws which protect the right to life and, in those cases involving State agents or bodies, to ensure their accountability for deaths occurring under their responsibility . . . the authorities must act of their own motion, once the matter has come to their attention. They cannot leave it to the initiative of the next of kin either to lodge a formal complaint or to take responsibility for the conduct of any investigative procedures.

The investigation must also be 'capable of leading to a determination of whether the force used was or was not justified'.[3]

Furthermore the investigation must be plausible. In *Tanli v Turkey*[4] the applicant's son was taken away by Gendarme Commanders following a search in his village. Two days later the applicant was informed at the police station that his son had died of a heart attack whilst in custody. The applicant maintained that his son's death was caused by torture. An investigation, which was undertaken by the Public Prosecutor, failed to establish the cause of death and three defendants were acquitted.

The Court in that case observed that the government had not provided a plausible explanation for the death of the applicant's son in custody after he entered in apparently good health. While the applicant and other witnesses referred to seeing bruising on the body, there was no medical substantiation that this was attributable to traumatic injury rather than post-mortem changes in the body. In the circumstances, the Court found that it had not been established that there had been a violation of Article 3. (Reassuringly, it did find a violation of Article 2 in that the

---

[1] See in particular *Z v United Kingdom* (2002) 34 EHRR 3.
[2] *ibid*, para 105.
[3] *ibid*, para 106.
[4] *Tanli v Turkey* (Application no 26129/95), 10 April 2001.

authorities had failed to provide any plausible or satisfactory explanation for the death of the applicant's son and that their responsibility over his death was therefore engaged.)

- Independent

Z goes on to state:[5] 'For an investigation . . . to be effective, it may generally be regarded as necessary for the persons responsible for and carrying out the investigation to be independent from those implicated in the events'.

- Prompt and Expeditious

It was further stated:[6]

> A requirement of promptness and reasonable expedition is explicit in this context . . . a prompt response by the authorities in investigating a use of lethal force may generally be regarded as essential in maintaining public confidence in their adherence to the rule of law and in preventing any appearance of pollution or intolerance of unlawful acts.

- Public

It has been held:[7] 'There must be a sufficient element of public scrutiny of the investigation and its results to secure accountability in practice as well as in theory'.

- Participation of Family

Z is also authority for the proposition that:[8] 'In all cases . . . the next of kin of the victim must be involved in the procedure to the extent necessary to safeguard his or her legitimate interests'.

The *Lawrence Enquiry*[9] recommendations were also pertinent. They stated that:

> This development must be regarded as a positive contribution to the openness and fairness of the inquest procedures . . . the court considers that the right of the family of the deceased whose death is under investigation to participate in the proceedings requires that the procedures adopted ensure the requisite protection of their interests, which may be in direct conflict with those of the police or security forces.

The Standard of Proof

11.2 Generally the standard of proof is on the balance of probabilities, the civil standard. Lord Denning defined the standard in *Miller v Minister of Pensions*:[10]

> It must carry a reasonable degree of probability, but not so high as is required in a criminal case. If the evidence is such that the tribunal can say: 'We think it is more

---

[5] See para 106.
[6] See para 108.
[7] See para 109.
[8] See para 109.
[9] Otherwise known as the *McPherson Report*.
[10] *Miller v Minister of Pensions* [1947] 2 All ER 372, 374: Denning J (as he then was).

probable than not', the burden is discharged, but if the probabilities are equal it is not.

It is suggested[11] that the civil standard is flexible in its application. The more serious the allegation, or the more serious the consequences if the allegation is proved, the stronger must be the evidence before a court will find the allegation proved on the balance of probabilities. It seems then, that although there are indications in some of the authorities that the flexibility of the civil standard lies in an adjustment of the degree of probability required for an allegation to be proved,[12] the flexibility lies not in any adjustment, but in the strength or quality of the evidence required for the allegation to be proved on the balance of probabilities.[13]

It was further stated in *Re Dellow's Will Trusts*[14] that '[t]he more serious the allegation the more cogent is the evidence required to overcome the unlikelihood of what is alleged and thus to prove it'.[15]

11.3 There are exceptions to the above general principle that any determination will be found by the civil standard of proof.

Verdicts of unlawful killing or suicide must be reached beyond reasonable doubt, or put another way, so that the tribunal are satisfied so that they are sure. This is the criminal standard of proof.

Where an inquest tribunal does return a verdict of unlawful killing it will be for the Director of Public Prosecutions to decide whether criminal proceedings will be brought. If the DPP does not decide to initiate criminal proceedings he must offer an adequate explanation to the bereaved family as to why this has not been done.[16]

In the criminal courts, judges are discouraged from defining 'beyond reasonable doubt' or 'satisfied so that you are sure' to the jury. The words are to be given their ordinary and natural meanings.[17] Any breach of Article 2 must be proved beyond reasonable doubt.

In *Ireland v United Kingdom*[18] the Court observed that proof can: '[f]ollow from the co-existence of a sufficiently strong, clear and concordant inferences or of similar unrebutted presumptions of fact . . . the conduct of the parties when evidence is being obtained has to be taken into account'.

---

[11] See *Blackstone's Civil Practice* (Oxford University Press, 2009) 643.

[12] See Denning LJ (as he then was) in *Bater v Bater* [1951] P 35 (CA) 37; *Hornall v Neuberger Products Limited* [1957] 1 QB 247 (HL).

[13] See Richards LJ in *R(N) v Mental Health Review Tribunal (Northern Region)* [2005] EWCA Civ 1605, [2006] QB 468.

[14] *Re Dellow's Will Trusts* [1964] 1 WLR 451, Ungoed-Thomas J.

[15] It was also stated by Lord Morris in *Hornall v Neuberger Products Limited* (n 12 above, at 266) – a dictum approved and adopted by the House of Lords in *Khera v Secretary of State for the Home Department* [1984] AC 74, 113–14 – that 'the very elements of gravity become part of the whole range of circumstances which have to be weighed in the scale when deciding as to the balance of probabilities'.

[16] See *R v Director of Public Prosecutions ex parte Manning* [2000] 3 WLR 463.

[17] The courts have been less reluctant to give examples of what does not reach the appropriate threshold for the criminal standard of proof, indicating that: 'Reasonably sure', 'Pretty sure', 'Pretty certain', and 'Sure, which is less than being certain' are disapproved, see *R v Head and Warrener* (1961) 45 Cr App R 225, *R v Woods* [1961] Crim LR 324, *R v Law* [1961] Crim LR 52 and *R v Stephens* (2002) *The Times*, 27 June 2002 respectively.

[18] *Ireland v United Kingdom* (1978) 2 EHRR 25, para 161.

For instance in cases of death in custody, where an applicant is in good health at the time of the fatality and then clearly suffers injuries and death, the State will be expected to provide a plausible explanation for those injuries and any suggestion that they were self-inflicted or in some way legitimately inflicted will have to be overcome by medical evidence to the contrary.[19]

In *Selmouni*[20] the Court recognised several medical certificates which were 'precise and concordant' as to the injuries suffered and the absence of any plausible explanation as to their cause were together considered sufficient for the Court to conclude that the majority of the applicant's allegations were proved to the required standard of proof, beyond reasonable doubt.[21]

In cases where the events in issue lie wholly, or in a large part, within the exclusive knowledge of the State, such as in instances where individuals die in custody, there will be strong presumptions of the fact in respect of the injuries and death occurring in that detention. Furthermore the burden of proof may rest on the authorities to provide a satisfactory and convincing explanation.[22]

The Jury's Power to Deliver a Verdict

11.4 Section 9 of the 2009 Act directs that a jury will be initially directed by the Senior Coroner to reach a unanimous determination or finding. There maybe circumstances in which the Senior Coroner comes to the view that certain specific verdicts are not available, on the evidence, to the jury. If the Senior Coroner concludes that a specific verdict is technically available to the jury that will not reflect the evidence that has been part of the investigation, the Senior Coroner will have a discretion to withdraw the jury's power to come to that verdict.[23]

The Court of Appeal in *Douglas-Williams*[24] considered the case of a man who had died in a police station after he had been arrested for aggravated burglary. The appeal included the point as to whether the coroner was right in refusing to leave a verdict of neglect to the jury. Lord Woolf MR ruled that the coroner was perfectly entitled to take the view that neglect would be an inappropriate verdict.[25] Ultimately it is a matter for the Coroner's discretion.

---

[19] See *Tomasi v France* (1992) 15 EHRR 1 and *Ribisch v Austria* (1999) 21 EHRR 573. See also *Klass v Germany* (1994) 2 EHRR 305, a case where no violation of Article 3 was found on a basis that the medical evidence could not rule out an alternative explanation of ill treatment.

[20] *Selmouni v France* (2000) 29 EHRR 403.

[21] For a full analysis of standards of proof in the European Court see John Cooper, *Cruelty-An Analysis of Article 3* (Sweet & Maxwell, 2003).

[22] See *Salman v Turkey* (2002) 34 EHRR 17, para 100.

[23] See *R v Inner South London Coroner ex parte Douglas-Williams* [1999] 1 All ER 344.

[24] *ibid.*

[25] Lord Woolf also commented that even if that Court had ruled that a verdict of neglect should have been left to the jury, that error could hardly justify a new inquest.

The principles outlined in the well-known criminal case of *R v Galbraith*[26] will guide the approach of a Coroner as to the exercise of his discretion.

The Principles in *Galbraith*[27]

This case, well known within the criminal jurisdiction, directs how a judge in a criminal trial should consider whether or not the prosecution has, at the close of the prosecution's case, presented enough evidence to be left before a criminal tribunal or whether the case should be dismissed without the need for the defence to challenge it.

The proper approach was laid down by Lord Lane CJ.[28] He stated:

(1) If there is no evidence that the crime alleged has been committed by the defendant there is no difficulty – the judge will stop the case.

(2) The difficulty arises where there is some evidence but it is of a tenuous character, for example, because of inherit weakness or vagueness or because it is inconsistent with other evidence.

> (a) Where the judge concludes that the prosecution evidence, taken at its highest, is such that a jury properly directed could not properly convict on it, it is his duty, upon a submission being made, to stop the case.
> (b) Where however the prosecution evidence is such that its strength or weakness depends on the view to be taken on a witnesses reliability, or other matters which are generally speaking within the province of the jury and where on one possible view of the facts there is evidence on which the jury could properly come to the conclusion that the defendant is guilty, then the judge should allow the matter to be tried by the jury.

Lord Lane went on in *Galbraith* to state that borderline cases should be left to the discretion of the judge and fall within the legitimate exercise of his discretion.[29]

In *R v Inner South London Coroner, ex parte Douglas-Williams*[30] the approach was endorsed by Lord Woolf MR, who stated[31] that so far as evidence called before a jury is concerned, a coroner should adopt the *Galbraith* approach in deciding whether to leave a verdict to the jury. He distinguished coronial procedures from that of criminal courts and went on to observe that there is no prosecutor in relation to an inquest and, while an inquest is at court, the Coroner's role is more inquisitorial, even when sitting with a jury, than that of a judge. A prosecutor has a considerable discretion as to what charges he prefers and the trial takes place on

---

[26] *R v Galbraith* [1991] 1 WLR 1039 will apply to the reasoning of the Senior Coroner as much as they would to any judge in the criminal courts, when considering the strength of evidence that has been heard.

[27] *R v Galbraith* (1991) 73 Cr App R 124 (CA).

[28] *ibid*, 127.

[29] See *R v Lesley* [1996] 1 Cr App R 39 (CA).

[30] *R v Inner South London Coroner, ex parte Douglas-Williams* [1999] 1 All ER 344.

[31] *ibid*, 349.

those charges. Conversely, the Court in *Douglas-Williams* recognised that there are no charges at an inquest and a coroner must decide the scope of inquiry which is appropriate and the witnesses to be summoned: 'He therefore must, at least indirectly, have a greater say as to what verdict the jury should consider than a judge at an adversarial trial'.

Nevertheless the Court of Appeal in *Douglas-Williams* qualified its endorsement of *Galbraith* within the context of the coronial process. Lord Woolf added:

> The strength of the evidence is not the only consideration and, in relation to wider issues, the coroner has a broader discretion. If it appears there are circumstances, which, in a particular situation, mean in the judgement of the coroner, acting reasonably and fairly, it is not in the interests of justice that a particular verdict should be left to the jury, he need not leave that verdict. He, for example, need not leave all possible verdicts just because there is technically evidence to support them. It is sufficient if he leaves those verdicts which realistically reflect the thrust of the evidence as a whole. To leave all possible verdicts could in some situations merely confuse and over burden the jury and if that is the Coroner's conclusion he cannot be criticised if he does not leave a particular verdict.[32]

The thrust of *Douglas-Williams* is that Coroners will, in their discretion, decide that certain verdicts, though technically available to the jury, would not be left to them. This contrasts with the approach taken by the criminal courts to the principles of *Galbraith*. In the criminal jurisdiction, any verdict technically available to the jury will be left for the jury to decide.[33]

The Particularities of a Verdict

11.5 The court, whether it sits with or without the jury is required to deliver a verdict and certify that verdict in an inquisition.[34]

Guidance as to the form the inquisition will take at the verdict stage of the hearing can be obtained from the Coroners Rules1984, Form 22. Five questions required to be answered:

1. The name of the deceased (if known);
2. The injury or disease causing death;
3. The time, place and circumstances at or in which injury was sustained;

---

[32] *ibid*, 349.

[33] See for example the case of *Lahaye (Dean John)* [2005] EWCA Crim 2847; [2006] 1 Cr App R 11, where a count of section 18 of the Offences Against the Person Act 1861 was before the jury. The whole trial was conducted on the basis of guilty of s 18 or not guilty, and neither the prosecution or defence had made representations to the jury on the alternative of s 20 wounding. The Court of Appeal upheld the trial judge's ruling at the Central Criminal Court, that s 20 of the Offences Against the Person Act 1861 should be left before the jury, as it was technically available as an alternative verdict regardless of whether it was any party's case that it should apply. The facts of that case record that the jury decided to convict the expellant of s 20.

[34] Coroners Act 1988 s 11(3)(a)–(4)(a).

4. The conclusion of the jury or the coroner as to the death;
5. The particulars for the time being required by the Registration Acts to be registered concerning the death.

The particulars referred to in (5) above refer to the date and place of death, the name and surname of the deceased, the sex of the deceased, the maiden surname of a woman who has married, the date and place of birth and the occupation and usual address.

Although it was anticipated that the Lord Chancellor would prescribe a Form of Inquisition to be completed at the verdict stage of the hearing, this has not been done and the guidance given in Form 22 of the Coroners Rules 1984 is no more than advice as to what should appear in such a document. The parameters of an inquest may differ from the strict outline contained within the Coroners Rules and it is permissible for the form of inquisition to vary in accordance with the variables of the inquest.[35]

Criminal and Civil Liability

11.6 Importantly the Coroners Rules 1984, rule 42 state:

No verdict will be framed in such a way as to appear to determine any question of –

(a) Criminal liability on the part of a named person, or
(b) Civil liability.

This was emphasised by Lord Bingham in *Middleton*[36] wherein he reaffirmed that there must be no finding of criminal liability on the part of any named person within the inquest. Furthermore a verdict must not appear to determine any question of civil liability. Acts or omissions maybe recorded, the Court of Appeal confirmed, but expressions suggesting of civil liability, should be avoided.

Neglect

11.7 The expression of neglect within the context of the inquest is different to that more generally used within the civil negligence arena.

In *Jamieson*,[37] Sir Thomas Bingham MR (as he then was) considered the death by suicide of a prisoner who hanged himself. The family of the bereaved pursued appeals against the Coroners decision to refuse to leave a neglect finding as an

---

[35] See the Coroners Rules 1984, r 60 in relation to Form 22, which appears within the Coroners Rules 1984 Sch 4.
[36] *R (Middleton) v HM Coroner for Western District of Somerset and another* [2004] 2 AC 182 (HL).
[37] *R v North Humberside & Scunthorpe Coroner, ex parte Jamieson* [1995] QB 1 (CA).

option for the jury, but ultimately Bingham MR ruled that neither neglect nor self-neglect should ever form any part of any verdict unless a clear and direct causal connection is established between the conduct so described and the cause of death.[38]

Bingham MR also articulated the difference between neglect as interpreted in the Coroner's Court as opposed to the civil courts. He stated:[39]

> Much of the difficulty to which verdicts of lack of care have given rise appear to be due to an almost inevitable confusion between this expression and the lack of care which is the foundation for a successful claim in common law negligence. Since many of those seeking that verdict do so as a stepping stone towards such a claim the boundary is bound to become blurred. But lack of care in the context of an inquest has been correctly described as the converse of self neglect. It is to be hoped that in future the expression 'lack of care' may for practical purposes be deleted from the lexicon of inquests and replaced by 'neglect'.

The Court in *Jamieson* went on to observe that neglect in the context of that case meant 'gross failure to provide adequate nourishment or liquid, or provide or procure basic medical attention or shelter or warmth for someone in a dependent position (because of youth, age, illness or incarceration) who cannot provide for himself'.

11.8 The Court went on to consider issues of self-neglect. Bingham stated:[40]

> As in the case of self-neglect, neglect can rarely, if ever, be an appropriate verdict on its own. It is difficult to think of facts on which there would not be a primary verdict other than neglect. But the notes that accompany Form 22 of the Coroners Rules of 1984, although in themselves of binding no force, are correct to recognise that neglect may contribute to a death of natural causes, industrial diseases or drug abuse. Forms of attention at birth, also mentioned in the notes, may itself be regarded as a form of neglect. A verdict that, for instance, 'the deceased died from natural causes (or industrial disease, or drug abuse) to which neglect contributed' would seem perhaps more apt than a verdict that 'the deceased died from natural causes (or industrial disease, or drug abuse) aggravated by neglect', since 'aggravated' in this context means 'made worse', and in truth the neglect probably did not make the fatal condition worse but sacrificed the opportunity to halt or cure it.

It is a matter for the Coroner's discretion whether to leave neglect before the jury as a possible finding.[41]

In *Douglas-Williams* the Court of Appeal made it clear that in the context of the deceased showing signs of distress and then becoming beyond assistance, a neglect verdict is only appropriate 'where there is a gross failure to provide, among other things, medical attention for a dependant person who is not in the position to provide it for himself'. On the facts of *Douglas-Williams*, the deceased who died in police

---

[38] *ibid*, para 12.
[39] *ibid*, para 8.
[40] *ibid*, para 10.
[41] See *R v Inner South London Coroner, ex parte Douglas-Williams* [1999] 1 All ER 344, 355.

custody did so in circumstances where there was no opportunity to provide that sort of help, and therefore there was no neglect. In coming to this finding the Court of Appeal in *Douglas-Williams* were following the ruling of Bingham MR in *Jamieson*.[42]

In any event there must be a clear and direct causal connection between the neglect or self-neglect and death.[43] As has been stated by Jervis[44] there must be some distinct act or omission closely and directly associated with the death as its cause or as one of its causes.

It should be emphasised that in accordance with the inability of the Coroner's Court to find any civil liability, causal connection is to be defined as 'the opportunity of rendering care'.[45]

If there is no opportunity of rendering care, as in the facts outlined in *Douglas-Williams*, whereby the deterioration of the prisoner in police custody was so swift as to make the rendering of care impossible, then there will be no finding of neglect available. Furthermore, if there is an opportunity which is not taken but nevertheless would not have prevented death,[46] or indeed other circumstances broke the chain of causation between the lost opportunity and death, then again there will be no finding of neglect.[47]

As stated in *R v Inner North London Coroner, ex parte Diesa Koto*[48] a significant number of cases of lack of care would be more of omission rather than commission.

European Jurisprudence

11.9 The State has a positive obligation to protect life in accordance with Article 2 and failure to take the appropriate preventative steps when, for instance, the prison authority is aware that the life of a detainee may be under threat, be it for external reasons or that the prisoner is, for instance, in a depressive or suicidal state will constitute a breach of Article 2.

The families of the deceased have a right to obtain a competent and official investigation into any death in custody. This right has often properly been prescribed to the provisions of Article 2, the absence of which will in itself be a breach.[49]

There is also a concurrent duty under Article 3. In *Timurtas v Turkey*,[50] the applicants father was aware that his son had been taken into custody but was never

---

[42] *Jamieson* [1994] 3 All ER 972, 990: [1995] QB 1, 25.

[43] See *R (Scott) v Inner West London Coroner* (2001) 165 JP 417, where the Court ruled that the jury were entitled to take a common sense approach to the expression 'clear and direct causal connection'.

[44] See *Jervis on Coroners*, 12th edn (Sweet and Maxwell, 2002) para 13-47.

[45] See *R v Coventry Coroner, ex parte Chief Constable of Staffordshire Police* (2000) 164 JP 665.

[46] See *R(Khan) v West Hertfordshire Coroner*, unreported, 7 March 2002, para 43.

[47] See *Nicholls v Liverpool Coroner*, unreported, 8 November 2001, paras 57–58.

[48] *R v Inner North London Coroner, ex parte Diesa Koto* (1993) 157 JP 857 (DC).

[49] See *McCann v United Kingdom* (1995) 21 EHRR 97; *Kaya v Turkey* (1998) 28 EHRR 1; *Assenov v Bulgaria* (1998) 28 EHRR 652; *Salman v Turkey* (2002) 34 EHRR 17.

[50] *Timurtas v Turkey* (2001) 33 EHRR 6.

able to get satisfactory information from the authorities, and no explanation was given as to why his son had not been seen since. His family brought an action claiming that the disappearance of his son by the Turkish authorities and the anguish this had caused him violated his rights under Articles 2, 3 and 5. The Court assumed that his son had died in custody and the lack of an explanation by the authorities meant that Turkey would be held responsible for his death in violation of Article 2. The Court were also of the view that the lack of an effective investigation into the prisoner's death further violated Article 2.

In *R (on the application of Wright) v Secretary of State for the Home Department*[51] Mr Justice Jackson articulated five propositions from the case law considered in argument:

(a) That Article 2 and Article 3 enshrine fundamental rights, and where it is arguable that a breach of either provision has occurred, the State must procure an effective and official investigation;

(b) Such investigations are required to maximise future compliance with the Convention;

(c) There is a prescribed form that an investigation must take. Whether or not it is sufficient to discharge the obligations under the Convention will depend on the facts of the case and the procedures of the investigation;

(d) Where there is an arguable breach of Article 2 or Article 3 the investigation must comply with the conditions set down in *Jordan v United Kindgom*;[52] in short, the next of kin must be involved in the procedure and the investigation must be independent, public, effective, prompt and reasonably expeditious;

(e) The holding of an inquest may or may not (depending on the facts of the case) satisfy the obligations inherent in Article 2 and Article 3.

In the case of *Wright* the Court rejected the Home Secretary's argument that the duty to investigate had been discharged by the inquest and Fatal Accidents Act proceedings. The judge emphasised that the inquest did not comply with the requirements set out in *Jordan* and could never have been an effective hearing because of the lack of disclosure of the medical officer's history, the failure to call a cell-mate to give evidence and the failure to call an independent medical expert. Furthermore, because of the absence of legal representation of family members, the family had no effective chance of participating in the investigation.

11.10 In *McShane v United Kingdom*[53] the Court again recognised that the obligation to protect human life (and by implication to protect against ill treatment), read in conjunction with the State's general duty under Article 1 to secure to everyone within its jurisdiction the rights and freedoms defined in the Convention, also required by implication that there should be some form of effective official investigation. One of the reasons for this was to secure the effective implementation of domestic laws and in those cases involving State Agents or Bodies, to ensure their accountability. In finding that there had been a number of shortcomings in

---

[51] *R (Wright) v Secretary of State for the Home Department* [2001] EWHC Admin 520.
[52] *Jordan v United Kindgom* (2001) 11 BHRC 1.
[53] *McShane v United Kingdom* (2002) 35 EHRR 593, *The Times*, 3 June 2002.

an investigation into the death of the applicant's husband, which had been caused during his attempted apprehension, the European Court of Human Rights isolated six failings. They were:

1. The police officers investigating the incident were not independent of the officers implicated in the incident;
2. The police investigation lacked expedition;
3. The soldier who drove the vehicle which fatally injured the applicant could not be required to attend the inquest as a witness;
4. The inquest procedure did not allow any verdict or findings which could have played an effective role in securing a prosecution should a criminal offence had been disclosed;
5. The non disclosure of witness statements and other irrelevant documents contributed to long adjournments in the proceedings;
6. The inquest proceedings were not started promptly.

11.11 The positive obligations incumbent upon the State to protect, for instance, those in custody, is much the same as the obligation required of the State in relation to those who have their liberty.[54]

In *Keenan*[55] the Court laid down the parameters of the obligation. The European Court of Human Rights stated:

Bearing in mind the difficulties in policing modern societies, the unpredictability of human conduct and the operational choices which must be made in terms of priorities and resources, the scope of the positive obligation must be interpreted in a way which does not impose an impossible or disproportionate burden on the authorities. For every claimed risk to life therefore can entail for the authorities a Convention requirement to take operational measure to prevent that risk from materialising. For a positive obligation to arise, it must be established that the authorities knew or ought to have known at the time of the existence of a real and immediate risk to life of an identified individual from the criminal acts of a third party and that they failed to take measures within the scope of their powers which, judged reasonably, might have been expected to avoid that risk. In this case, the court has had to consider to what extent this applies where the risk to a person derives from self harm.

In the context of prisoners, the court has had previous occasion to emphasise that persons in custody are in a vulnerable position and that the authorities are under a duty to protect them. It is incumbent on the State to account for any injuries suffered in custody, which obligation is particularly stringent where that individual dies. It maybe noted that this need for scrutiny is acknowledged in the domestic law in England and Wales, where inquests are automatically held concerning the deaths of persons in prison and where the domestic courts have imposed a duty of care on prison authorities in respect to those detained in their custody.[56]

---

[54] See *Osman v UK* (2000) 29 EHRR 245.
[55] *Keenan v United Kingdom* (2001) 33 EHRR 913.
[56] *ibid*, paras 89–90.

11.12 In *R (Amin) v Secretary of State for the Home Department* before the House of Lords,[57] Lord Hope of Craighead[58] confirmed the Court of Appeal's judgment that there was a procedural duty to investigate deaths in these circumstances and that it was an adjectival duty. Although this duty is not expressly provided by the Convention, it was the judgment of the House of Lords that it must be fashioned by rulings in domestic courts as to what in their jurisdiction is sensibly required to support and vindicate the substantive convention rights. The Court approved a flexible approach as to whether a finding of neglect was appropriate.

This flexible approach will apply to the spectrum of possible Article 2 violations, allegations of killing, or murder by servants of the State, killing by gross negligence, manslaughter by servants of the State and plain negligence by servants of the State, leading to a death or allowing it to happen.

The duty to investigate will be fashioned to support and make good these substantive Article 2 rights.

Substantially the procedural obligation to investigate any possible finding of neglect must have the primary aim of minimising the risk of future similar deaths, to bring the beginnings of justice to the bereaved and to assuage the anxieties of the public.[59]

The Difference Between Individual Neglect and Systemic Failure

11.13 To identify a right which is protected by the Convention it is important to identify defects in a system rather than individual acts of negligence. The rationale behind this is that the identification of defects in the system can result in it being changed so that, for instance, death in the future can be avoided. A finding of individual negligence would be unlikely to lead to that result. Bereaved families, in particular, may endeavour to establish systemic failure.

The words of the mother and father of Geoff Gray, one of the young soldiers who died at Deepcut Barracks in Surrey, emphasise the difference between concerns relating to individual negligence and those that may delve into systemic failure:

> The care and safety of this country's young soldiers whilst under the control of the armed forces is not only of paramount importance to soldiers themselves and their families, but to the public at large. Clearly, the public must have confidence in their Armed Services in order to trust that their loved ones are able to work well in good conditions and are valued for their contribution. The manner of Private Gray's death

---

[57] *R (Amin) v Secretary of State for the Home Department* [2003] UKHL 51; [2004] 1 AC 653.
[58] *ibid*, para 61.
[59] See the Court of Appeal judgment in *Amin* [2003] QB 581, para 62.

together with the manner in which it was investigated was of vital importance to the issue of trust in and the morale of our Armed Services.[60]

11.14 Should it be decided by the court that there maybe systemic failings, the court, and in particular the jury, may wish to express their verdict beyond the confines of Form 22.[61] In consequence of this the practice has developed in the courts of providing to the jury a questionnaire from which they may structure a narrative verdict. This has been found to assist the State and agencies connected with them in learning any lessons from the death. The extent of this questionnaire will be agreed between all interested parties at the hearing.

The Court of Appeal in *Amin* laid down the criteria by which the tribunal will decide whether any systemic failure has occurred, rather than an individual act of negligence. The Court observed:

A verdict of neglect can perform different functions. In particular, in the present context, it can identify a failure in the system adopted by the Prison Service to reduce the incidence of suicide by inmates. Alternatively it may do no more than identify a failure of an individual prison officer to perform his duties properly. We offer two illustrations, which demonstrate the distinction we have in mind. On the one hand, the system adopted by a prison maybe unsatisfactory in that it allows a prisoner who is a known suicide risk to occupy a cell by himself or does not require that prisoner to be kept under observation. On the other hand, the system may be perfectly satisfactory but the prison officer responsible for keeping observation may fall asleep on duty.

For the purpose of vindicating the right protected by Article 2 it is more important to identify defects in the system than individual acts of negligence. The identification of defects in the system can result in it being changed so that suicides in the future are avoided. A finding of individual negligence is unlikely to lead to that result. If the facts have been investigated at the inquest the evidence given for this purpose should usually enable the relatives to initiate civil proceedings against those responsible without the verdict identifying individuals by name. The shortcomings of civil proceedings in meeting the requirements of Article 2 do not in general prevent actions in the domestic courts for damages from providing an effective remedy in cases of alleged and lawful conduct or negligence by public authorities.

In contrast with the position where there is individual negligence, not to allow a jury to return a verdict of neglect in relation to a defect in the system could detract substantially from the salutary effect of the verdict. A finding of neglect can bring home to the relevant authority the need for action to be taken to change the system, and thus contribute to the avoidance of suicides in the future. The inability to bring in a verdict of neglect (without identifying any individual as being involved) in our judgment significantly detracts, in some cases, from the capacity of the investigation to meet the obligations arising under Article 2.[62]

---

[60] Statement issued to the *Review of Circumstances Surrounding the Deaths of Four Soldiers at Princess Royal Barracks, Deepcut, Between 1995 and 2002* ('The Blake Review') (2006) HC 795.

[61] Found in Sch 4 to the Coroners Rules 1984.

[62] See *Amin* [2002] EWCA Civ 390, paras 87–89.

The Coroners Rules 1984 rule 42, which directs that no verdict shall be framed in such a way as to appear to determine any question of criminal liability or civil liability, is not impugned by the law as laid out above.[63]

Unlawful Killing

11.15 The court can return a verdict of unlawful killing without naming the alleged perpetrator. Such a verdict would be appropriate for instance, in cases of murder, infanticide or certain driving offences which cause death. An unlawful killing verdict will also encompass manslaughter.

Such a verdict is only available if a court finds the facts proven to the criminal standard of proof, beyond reasonable doubt or to the extent that the court is satisfied so that it is sure.[64]

In cases of murder, it is highly unlikely that any inquest will be necessary if a defendant has been arrested and placed before the criminal courts. If, during the course of an inquest an individual is charged with murder, the inquest will most likely be adjourned indefinitely and it will be very unlikely that that inquest will be resumed. In that rare eventuality, the inquest verdict must not be inconsistent with the verdict of the Crown Court.[65]

11.16 Manslaughter can be divided into two separate parts, unlawful act manslaughter and gross negligence manslaughter.

Unlawful Manslaughter

Most usually the unlawful act will constitute an assault[66] or some other offence against a person such as administering a noxious substance under the Offences Against the Person Act 1861, section 23. The element of intent is necessary for a conviction in relation to unlawful act, manslaughter.[67]

The offence can be committed even if the action is not directed against any particular victim. For instance an offence of arson or criminal damage will be sufficient to meet the element of unlawfulness required.[68] The test as to whether any act is dangerous is objective. This was laid down by Mr Justice Edmund Davies in

---

[63] See *Amin* [2002] EWCA Civ 390, paras 86–93.

[64] See *R v Wolverhampton Coroner, ex parte McCurbin* [1990] 2 All ER 759, in which the Court held that Coroner's faced with a complex case would be wise to prepare, in advance of their summing up, a written statement of the matters which the law requires in relation to each possible verdict and hand to the jury that statement prior to commencing the summing up. If that is done it can, beforehand, be considered by any advocates attending the inquest and been a subject of submissions. In addition, baring in mind the limited number of verdicts open to a jury it should be possible for standard directions to be prepared.

[65] See the Coroners Act 1988 s 16(7).

[66] See *R v Larking* [1943] KB 174.

[67] See *R v Lamb* [1967] 2 QB 981.

[68] See *R v Goodfellow* (1986) 83 Cr App R 23; but see also *R v Carey* [2006] EWCA Crim 17.

R v Church:[69] '[T]he unlawful act must be such as all sober and reasonable people would inevitably recognise must subject the other person to, at least, the risk of some harm resulting their harm, of be it not serious harm'.[70]

In *Goodfellow*[71] Lord Lane CJ dealt with a case where the appellant had set fire to his council house in the hope that he would be re-housed. The fire spread out of control, further than the appellant had anticipated and his wife and child and another woman died in the fire. In upholding the conviction for manslaughter, the Court of Appeal stated:

> The questions which the jury have to decide on the charge of manslaughter of this nature [are] (1) was the act intentional? (2) was it lawful? (3) was it an act that any reasonable person would realise was bound to subject some other human being to the risk of physical harm, albeit not necessarily serious harm? (4) was that act the cause of death?

Manslaughter by Gross Negligence (Involuntary)

11.17 The principle requirements of gross negligence manslaughter were laid out by Lord Mackay in *R v Adomako*[72] in which he stated:

> [I]n my opinion the ordinary principles of the law of negligence apply to ascertain whether or not the defendant has been in breach of a duty of care towards the victim who has died. If such a breach of duty is established the next question is whether that breach of duty caused the death of the victim. If so, the jury must go on to consider whether that breach of duty should be characterised as gross negligence and therefore as a crime. This will depend on the seriousness of the breach of duty committed by the defendant in all the circumstances in which the defendant was placed and where it occurred . . . the essence of the matter which is supremely a jury question is whether, having regard to the risk of death involved, the conduct of the defendant was so bad in all the circumstances as to amount in their judgment to a criminal act or omission.

In *R v Evans*[73] Lord Judge CJ, observed that the question of whether there is a duty of care is a matter of law for the trial judge although it is for a jury to decide whether any contingent facts, which the trial judge will identify, are established.

Examples of risks that must be foreseeable in the context of gross negligence manslaughter have included risks to health and welfare, a risk of serious injury and a risk of death. In *R v Singh*[74] the Court limited the definition of risk of death to 'the circumstances must be such that a reasonably prudent person would have foreseen a serious and obvious risk not merely of injury, even serious injury, but of death'. This approach was confirmed in the Court of Appeal in *R v Misra*[75] and added that the approach was in line with Lord Mackay's judgment in *Adomako*.

---

[69] *R v Church* [1966] 1 QB 59, 70.
[70] *Newbury* [1977] AC 500 confirmed the proposition in the House of Lords.
[71] *Goodfellow* (1986) 83 Cr App R 23 (CA).
[72] *R v Adomako* [1995] 1 AC 171 (HL) 187.
[73] *R v Evans* [2009] EWCA Crim 650.
[74] *R v Singh* [1999] Crim LR 582.
[75] *R v Misra* [2005] 1 Cr App R 328.

The courts are clear that a foreseeable risk of death is required to activate liability under this category of manslaughter and that the formulation of gross negligence manslaughter did not offend the principles of legal certainty as outlined in the European Convention on Human Rights Article 7.

Lord Chief Justice Judge clarified:

> In short, the offence required gross negligence in circumstances where what is at risk is the life of an individual to whom the defendant owes a duty of care. As such it serves to protect his or her right to life.[76]

Steps to a Verdict of Unlawful Act Manslaughter

11.18 There must be evidence upon which a jury, properly directed, could have concluded that:

1. One or more of the individuals committed an unlawful act
2. It was the act which caused the deceased's death, and
3. All sensible people would have realised that that act would have subjected the deceased to the risk of at least some physical harm, though not necessarily serious harm, resulting from it.

Steps to Reaching a Verdict of Gross Negligence Manslaughter

11.19 There must be evidence upon which a jury, properly directed, could have concluded that:

(a) Individuals owed a duty of care to the deceased in the management of him
(b) One or more of those individuals was in breach of that duty in that the standard of their care of the deceased fell below that which could reasonably have been expected of reasonably competent individuals (for instance police officers) in the same situation
(c) By their breach of duty they caused the deceased's death
(d) Their breach of duty was so serious that they should held to be criminal liable.

Corporate Manslaughter

11.20 The Corporate Manslaughter and Corporate Homicide Act was given Royal Assent on 26 July 2007. The Act came into force on 6 April 2008 and is referred to as Corporate Manslaughter in England, Wales and Northern Ireland and Corporate Homicide in Scotland. Provisions in the Act which relate to the management of custody[77] are expected to be implemented in between three and five years.

---

[76] See *R v Evans* (n 73 above) para 52.
[77] Corporate Manslaughter and Corporate Homicide Act 2007 ss 2(1)(d) and 2(2).

By virtue of the Corporate Manslaughter and Corporate Homicide Act 2007, Section 1, an organisation maybe guilty of an offence in the way its activities are managed or organised if it causes death and that that amounts to a gross breach of a relevant duty of care owed by the organisation to the deceased. Organisations to which the Act applies include a corporation, the police, or a partnership or trade union or employers association that is an employer.[78] Relevant duties of care, defined in the Act[79] exclude, for instance, military activities,[80] policing and law enforcement,[81] responses to emergency situations[82] and child protection and probation functions.[83]

Nevertheless these exclusions are nuanced particularly with reference to emergency service situations where, for example, emergency services will not be liable to those being rescued or bystanders for the way it responds to an emergency but liability may lie to its own employees for breach of its duties towards them or to visitors for breach of its duty as an occupier of premises.

In respect of policing and law enforcement functions, some operations are excluded such as those dealing with terrorism, civil unrest or serious disorder and officers come under attack or threat of attack or violent resistance. Any other activities may give rise to the relevant duty of care but under the provisions of employer/occupier as laid down in section 2(1)(a) or (b) of the 2007 Act.

There are broader exclusions to the protections offered by the 2007 Act, which continued to severely limit its impact. Section 3(1) excludes

> any duty of care owed by a public authority in respect of a decision as to matters of public policy (including in particular the allocation of public resources or the weighing of competing public interests).

This seems to exclude culpability under the 2007 Act if the deceased died as a result of a government decision not to allocate necessary resources to a particular service carried out by a public authority.

Section 3(2) is an exclusion to culpability that will benefit institutions such as the prison service. The provision excludes things done 'in the exercise of an exclusively public function'. The expression 'exclusively public function' is defined in Section 3(4) of the Act and describes a function which falls under the crown prerogative or functions exercisable with authority confirmed by the exercise of the prerogative or by or under a statutory provision. The exclusion will avail public authorities as well as private sector organisations which are given statutory powers, such as those who are tasked to run prisons.

Section 8 of the 2007 Act deals with Gross Breach Corporate Manslaughter and directs that where it is established that an organisation owed a relevant duty of care to a person, the jury must consider whether the evidence shows that the organisa-

---

[78] *ibid*, s 1(2).
[79] *ibid*, s 2.
[80] *ibid*, s 4.
[81] *ibid*, s 5.
[82] *ibid*, s 6.
[83] *ibid*, s 7.

tion failed to comply with any health and safety legislation that relates to the alleged breach, and if so, how serious that failure was and how much of a risk of death it posed.[84]

The Jury may also consider the extent to which the evidence shows that there were attitudes, policies, systems or accepted practices within the organisation that were likely to have encouraged any such failure as is mentioned within the legislation, or to have produced tolerance of it. The jury may have regard to any health and safety guidance, which relates to the alleged breach.[85]

The first corporate manslaughter trial started on 23 February 2010 in which a company was charged with gross negligence manslaughter over the death of an employee.[86]

The Act is not retrospective and will only apply to deaths, which occur on or after 6 April 2008. Deaths, which occurred before 6 April 2008, will continue to be covered by the previous law on corporate manslaughter.

Despite all the exclusions within the Act the new legislation will also apply in the case of deaths in custody which result from gross negligence either in the prison service or from those controlling police cells.

In short, the crime of corporate manslaughter is committed where an organisation owes a duty to take reasonable care for a persons safety and in the way its activities have been managed or organised they have perpetrated a gross breach of that duty which causes death. To convict a company or other organisation, the prosecution must prove that the failure came substantially from 'senior management'. Senior managers are defined as people who play a significant role in the management of the whole or a substantial part of the organisations activities. Furthermore the management failure must amount to a 'gross breach' of the duty of care.

Apart from the Act which is heavy laden with exclusions there are further restrictions within the legislation concerning the 'senior manager' test, which some commentators suspect will encourage companies to delegate health and safety responsibilities to non-senior managers so as to protect themselves from any criminal charges. Should this be done, however, there is a strong argument that that in itself might amount to gross negligence in respect to health and safety issues.

In its Regulatory Impact Assessment for the legislation, the government estimated that the new offence would result in only 10–13 additional prosecutions for corporate manslaughter each year, although as Professor Gary Slapper observed: 'The silent aim of the law is to stop corporate manslaughter'.[87]

The concept of 'relevant duty of care' is defined as meaning 'a duty owed under the law of negligence by the organisation.'[88] This formulation is drawn from

---

[84] *ibid*, s 8(1)–(2).

[85] *ibid*, s 8(3)(a)–(b).

[86] The company, Cotswold Geotechnical Holdings, faced the allegations arising from the death of an employee who worked as a junior geologist for the firm and died when a trench collapsed upon him as he collected soil samples. The case has been adjourned until October 2010.

[87] See *The Times Online*, 18 July 2007.

[88] See s 2(1) of the Corporate Manslaughter and Corporate Homicide Act 2007.

Adomako[89] and the test applied in that case for gross negligence manslaughter under which the defendant must owe a duty of care to the deceased. When this requirement was laid down by *Adomako*, it was considered that the formula would be appropriate on the basis that everyone owes a duty to others not to kill them and so the requirement was only meaningful in cases of omission where there will be liability only if a duty of care under criminal law principles is established. These assumptions were challenged in the case of *R v Wacker*[90] where it was argued on behalf of a lorry driver that he did not owe a duty of care to 58 illegal immigrants that he killed while illegally smuggling them into the country because of the tortious doctrine of *Ex Turpi Causa non Oritur Actio*. Although this argument was rejected in the Court of Appeal, the Court stated that the law of tort and criminal law have different objectives and so concepts such as duty of care need to be adapted to the different areas of law in which they are being applied.[91]

As was pointed out by Professor Clarkson,[92]

> the danger . . . [with this] and its explicit reference to 'the law of negligence is that it would open the door to similar arguments all over again'. The Law Commission recommendations contained no such requirement were superior. All that was required was that the management failure by the corporation be one of the causes of death.

Natural Causes

11.21 There is no definition of 'natural causes' but commonsense and understanding of the expression will suggest that death resulting from natural causes would be as a result of a normal progression of a natural illness or event without the intervention of human action. The final cause of death is usually failure of the vital centres which govern the beating of the heart and the act of breathing, the practical question relates to the disease or injury which leads to this failure.

One of the most common causes of death is Ischemic heart disease, followed closely by Malignant diseases. Respiratory disease and Cerebrovascular are also significant causes of death which most probably will be categorised as natural causes. Following these most prevalent diseases, motor vehicle accidents and other accidental falls or events are the most common causes of death followed then by suicide and self inflicted injury.[93]

The standard of proof required to establish a verdict of natural causes is the civil standard on the balance of probabilities. A natural death may cross the threshold into an unnatural event if there is an intervening act. The Court of Appeal articulated

---

[89] *R v Adomako* [1994] 3 WLR 288.
[90] *R v Wacker* [2002] EWCA Crim 1944; [2003] 1 Cr App R 22.
[91] Endorsed in *R v Willoughby* [2004] EWCA Crim 3365.
[92] 'Corporate Manslaughter: Yet More Government Proposals' [2005] Crim LR 677, 683.
[93] See William AR Thomson (ed), *Black's Medical Dictionary* 33rd edn (Adam and Charles Black, 1981) 243.

the position in *R v Poplar Coroner, ex parte Thomas*[94] when it considered the death of a woman as a result of an asthma attack who might have been saved if the ambulance had attended when it was first called rather than being delayed for forty minutes. Like many cases relating to natural deaths, Thomas is primarily an authority upon whether or not a coroner should hold an inquest. The case nonetheless provides helpful guidance as to the threshold between natural and unnatural events.

Lord Justice Simon Brown stated: 'It seems to me necessary to recognise that cases may well arise in which human fault can and probably should be found to turn what would otherwise be a natural death into an unnatural one'.[95]

Industrial Diseases

11.22 There is no definitive list of industrial diseases and it will be for the court to assess whether a condition falls within that category.[96] Guidance maybe obtained from the list of industrial industries which attract disablement benefit provided by the Department of Work and Pensions.[97] This includes leukaemia, Pneumiconiosis and Byssinosis, which substantially covers cancerous conditions as a result of working near cotton or flax.

Suicide

11.23 A finding of suicide requires specific intent and is defined as:

> 'Voluntarily doing an act for the purpose of destroying one's life while one is conscious of what one is doing. In order to arrive at a verdict of suicide there must be evidence that the deceased intended the consequence of his act.'[98]

For this verdict the standard of proof required is the criminal standard, that of beyond reasonable doubt or satisfied so that you are sure.[99]

The circumstances surrounding a potential suicide are complex and a court will be expected to take particular care when considering whether a verdict of suicide is appropriate. For instance, a significant number of psychiatrists are of the view that immediately prior to the taking of their life, an individual suffering from a condition which may lead to suicide is often euphoric, relaxed and happy in the company of people that he or she may meet. Those considering the mental state of

---

[94] *R v Poplar Coroner, ex parte Thomas* [1993] QB 610.
[95] See also *R v Birmingham Coroner, ex parte Benton* [1997] 8 Med LR 362, which gives further guidance on natural and unnatural deaths, with particular reference to medical treatment.
[96] See *R v South Glamorgan Coroner, ex parte BP Chemicals* (1987) 151 JP 799.
[97] See Appendix 1–3.
[98] See *R v Cardiff Coroner, ex parte Thomas* [1970] 3 All ER 469.
[99] *ibid.*

people about to commit suicide consider this to be a symptom of having firmly taken a decision to terminate their life and relieve themselves of the circumstances and situations which have hitherto caused them unhappiness.

This was particularly raised during the inquest of James Collinson, one of the young recruits who died at Deepcut Barracks. It was suggested by expert psychiatric evidence during that inquest that the happy and relaxed demeanour of Private Collinson days and hours before his death could not be taken as a reliable indicator that he had not settled upon taking his life.[100]

Suicide cannot be presumed and must be proved on the evidence.[101]

11.24 It is important to establish whether the death of an individual was deliberately at their own hands or was accidental.[102] The court will take into account all the surrounding circumstances of the fatality so as to exclude the possibility of accident. The axis of the investigation may change, for instance if the deceased is found hanging and no third party is implicated.[103]

Sometimes the courts must grapple with the possibility that the deceased had been indulging in self-harm which was not intended to cause death. Again the Coroner's Court is obliged to undertake a full and detailed investigation into the cause of death, hearing in mind the complex psychological and psychiatric features that will inevitably be part of an analysis as to the state of the deceased is mind at the time of death.

11.25 An example of the complexity of these matters can be seen in the context of death of members of the Armed Forces. The criteria and considerations taken into account here will apply equally to other situations where individuals are put in demanding conditions, such as those in prison or detained in other institutions.

In 1996 the *Walton Report*[104] began a study into suicide rates in the British Army. In Part Two of the report published in April 1997, Walton found that most cases of suicide that he examined were not 'spur of the moment' decisions but were premeditated. He noted:

> c. that an 'at risk' person may not apparently be 'at risk' through the objective eyes of a third party. What is important is the 'at risk' person's subjective view of their own personal circumstances and problems.

> d. that for those who know what to look for, indicators of an impending [suicide] are almost always present. In only one death of the period 1990–1996 (June) was there a total absence of any identified cognitive or behavioural correlate of [suicide].[105]

---

[100] The inquest jury nonetheless despite hearing the coroner sum up and deal with the appropriateness of a suicide verdict, delivered an open verdict.

[101] See *R v Northampton Coroner, ex parte Walker* (1988) 151 JP 773; *Re Davis (decd)* [1968] 1 QB 72; *R v City of London Coroner, ex parte Barber* [1975] 1 WLR 1310.

[102] *R v Essex Coroner, ex parte Hopper* [1988] COD 7.

[103] See *R v Newbury Coroner, ex parte John* (1992) 156 JP 456.

[104] A five part study of 'Suicide in the British Army' written by Dr Walton, a senior psychologist working for the Ministry of Defence.

[105] Walton Report, p 62.

In Part Four of Dr Walton's study,[106] he recommended that various matters would be of assistance in risk evaluation, they were rank, age, marital status, gender, previous self-harm attempts, health, alcohol use, relationship problems, and financial difficulties.[107]

The completion of Dr Walton's report was followed in October 1998 by a study of attempted suicide in the army conducted by Lieutenant Colonel Hawley.[108] He found that attempted suicide was associated with alcohol but not specifically with psychiatric illness.[109] He went on:

> Most authorities are agreed that there is usually a background of long term problems concerning marriage or partners, children, work and health. Specifically, the agreed factors which are associated with increased rates of attempted suicide include the following: socio-economic status, social deprivation, single or divorced, unemployment, family discord, early parental loss, physical and/or sexual abuse as a child, and physical illness of disability (particularly epilepsy). Underlining most of these factors is a failure or inability to interact successfully with others.[110]

Factual considerations to be added will include whether there maybe any evidence of bullying, intimidation, oppressive behaviour, or any other threatening attitudes towards the deceased.[111] In the case of the Armed Forces, there are further considerations which should be taken into account, including age as a risk factor for self-harm. The Walton Report[112] found that single young people were a statistically vulnerable group when it came to risks of self-harm in military service. The Hawley Report also identified a number of factors connected with the experience of living away from home in a strange environment that could put army personnel at risk.[113]

The Deepcut Review[114] acknowledges the correlation between risk factors relating to army personnel and those who are detained in custody. It states:

> This Review notes the persistent problem of adolescent self-harm and suicide within the penal system and in young offenders institutions. Voluntary service in Her Majesty's Armed Forces cannot be equated with a sentence of loss of liberty in one of Her Majesty's penal institutions. However, the extensive literature on self-harm by young people in prison indicates that there are points of comparison: social disadvantage, poor self-esteem, a sense of despair, fear of complaining about abuse, poor staff ratios and,

---

[106] May 1998.

[107] Walton Report, p 19.

[108] Lt Col Hawley, 'A Study of Attempted Suicide in the Army: Ten Years of Experience 1987–1996'.

[109] *ibid*, p 17.

[110] *ibid*, p 15.

[111] See the *Review of Circumstances Surrounding the Deaths of Four Soldiers at Princess Royal Barracks, Deepcut, Between 1995 and 2002* ('The Blake Review'): (2006) HC 795, para 9.32 (p 283).

[112] Walton, 'Suicide in the British Army', Part 1: 'Prevalence and Methods', December 1996.

[113] Lt Col Hawley, 'A Study of Attempted Suicide in the Army: Ten Years of Experience 1987–1996', p 15 of the Report where 'the shock and stress of joining a new organisation which is different from all prior experience', was seen as a warning factor as to risk. This is also relevant for any new situation in which an individual is placed, including prison or detention in lawful custody.

[114] Blake Review, para 9.34 (p 284).

consequently poor supervision. In the opinion of the Review, being young, under or about eighteen, and living 24/7 within the disciplined regime of an institution such as the Army is, itself, a significant factor indicative or risk.[115]

In *Middleton*[116] Lord Bingham, who delivered the single judgment giving the opinion of the Appellate Committee, recognised that suicide in prison was a matter of national concern, as rates of suicide amongst young prisoners were rising while suicide in society at large was falling. He stated:

> Unhappily, it is not a rare event. The statistics given in recent publications, (notably 'Suicide is Everyone's Concern, A Thematic Review by HM Chief Inspector of Prisons for England and Wales' (May 1999), the Annual Report of HM Chief Inspector of Prisons for England and Wales 2002-2003, and Evidence given to the House of Lords and the House of Commons Joint Committee on Human Rights (HL Paper 12, HC134, January 2004) make grim reading. While the suicide rate among the population as a whole is falling, the rate among prisoners is rising. In the fourteen years 1990–2003 there were 947 self-inflicted deaths in prison, 177 of which were of detainees aged 21 or under. Currently, almost 2 people kill themselves in prison each week. Over a third have been convicted of no offence. 1 in 5 is a woman (a proportion far in excess of the female prison population). 1 in 5 deaths occurs in a prison hospital or segregation unit. 40% of self-inflicted deaths occur within the first month of custody. It must of course be remembered that many of those in prison are vulnerable, inadequate or mentally disturbed; many have drug problems; and imprisonment is inevitably, for some, a very traumatic experience. These statistics, grim though they are, do not of themselves point towards any dereliction of duty on the part of the authorities or any individual official. But they do highlight the need for an investigative regime, which will not only expose any past violation of the State's substantive obligations already referred to but also, within the bounds of what is practicable, promote measures to prevent or minimise the risk of future violations. The death of any person involuntarily in the custody of the State, otherwise than from natural causes, can never be other than a ground for concern. This appeal is concerned with the death of a long-term convicted prisoner but the same principles must apply to the death of any person in the custody of the prison service or the police.[117]

If there is doubt as to the cause of death, and particularly if the jury could not be satisfied so that they are sure – the criminal standard – that the deceased committed suicide, then the proper verdict is an open verdict.[118]

---

[115] In 1999, Her Majesty's Chief Inspector of Prisons, Sir David Ramsbothom, was commission to prepare a Report on 'suicide and self-harm in the prison service 1999'. See also Barry Goldson and Deborah Coles, *In the Care of the State: Child Deaths in Penal Custody in England and Wales* (Inquest, 2005), that quotes extensively from the work of the subsequent Chief Inspector of Prisons, Anne Owers.

[116] *Middleton* [2004] UKHL 10; [2004] 2 AC 182.

[117] *ibid*, para 5.

[118] *R v Northampton Coroner, ex parte Walker* (1988) 151 JP 773.

Accidental Death

11.26 In *R (on the application of Touche) v Inner North London Coroner*[119] an unnatural death was described as 'where it was wholly unexpected and it would not have occurred but for some culpable human failing'.

Earlier in *R v Birmingham Coroner, ex parte Benton*[120] the Court considered the difference between what would be held as an accident or what could be death as a result of natural causes. This case was dealing with the particularity of a case where a child had died during medical intervention. On the facts of the case the treatment, which the child was receiving, was on the face of it, routine. During this treatment the child died. It was held that if at the time of the unsuccessful treatment the deceased was in an irrevocable life threatening position, regardless of the treatment, then the proper verdict would be natural causes, regardless of the quality of the medical treatment. If the deceased had not been in such a life threatening position, then the medical intervention, which resulted in death, could be interpreted by the courts as having caused death. In those circumstances the correct verdict would be one of accidental death. If any criminal behaviour could be established, then the potential verdict falls within the manslaughter categories.

Generally a finding of accidental death (also referred to as misadventure) is a matter for the jury.[121]

Dependent or Non-dependent Abuse of Drugs

11.27 Such a verdict should be reached with considerable care, taking into account the stigma which may be attached as a result of such a verdict to the memory of the deceased. The primary purpose of such a verdict is to alert the public to the

---

[119] *R (on the application of Touche) v Inner North London Coroner* [2001] QB 1206.

[120] *R v Birmingham Coroner, ex parte Benton* (1997) 8 Med LR 362.

[121] In *R v Portsmouth Coroners Court, ex parte Anderson* [1987] 1 WLR 1640, the Divisional Court stated (obiter) that the distinction between accident and misadventure was 'without purpose or effect', although in Benton, the Divisional Court, noting the above observation in Anderson, referred to the possibility of a verdict of 'death by accident/misadventure'. Christopher Dorries in his book *Coroners' Courts: A Guide to Law and Practice* (John Wiley and Sons, 1999) 215, argues that on balance, there remains a logical distinction between accident and misadventure and that it is right to differentiate a small number of cases as misadventure, even if only to preserve integrity in the phrase 'accidental death'. Dorries argues that if any logical distinction does exist, misadventure might be applied where a person deliberately undertakes a task which then goes wrong, causing death. He cites Gavin Thurston (1980), Coronership, (Barry Rose Publishers), as giving a clear example of the approach when an adverse drug reaction causes death, 'accident' might imply that the wrong drug or dose was given whilst 'misadventure' suggests the drug was given intentionally but that misfortune supervened. It is similarly been suggested that where a boxer hits an opponent intentionally with fatal results, the blow was not accidental but the outcome was not intended. See Burton, Chambers and Gill, *Coroners Inquiries* (Kluwer Law, 1985).

specific dangers of drugs which, in the view of the court, justifies departure from the policy of not stigmatising the deceased.[122]

Open Verdict

11.28 Form 22 of the Coroners Rules 1984, defines an open verdict as arising 'when the evidence did not fully or further disclose the means whereby the cause of death arose'.

In *R v HM Coroner for the City of London, ex parte Barber*[123] it was stated:

> I would impress upon Coroners (or juries) that if they find themselves compelled to return an open verdict, that is not in any sense a reflection upon them. It does not suggest that they are not doing their job properly or insufficiently perceptive. There are many, many cases where there is real doubt as to the cause of death, where an open verdict is right and anything else is unjust to the family of the deceased.

These observations, made as far back as 1975, still hold true. It should not be considered that the returning of an open verdict is indicative of the court failing to reach any decision. An open verdict is not analogous with a hung jury in a criminal trial, where the jury is hopelessly divided as to the appropriate verdict to bring.[124]

Article 2

11.29 A coroner is entitled to find a breach of Article 2 where a failure has increased the risk of death to a material extent[125] this is so even if the failure did not cause the particular death being investigated.[126]

In the House of Lords in *Van Colle*[127] the Court confirmed that the violation of a fundamental Convention right is a serious matter and since the Human Rights Act 1998, a cause of action arises in domestic law.

---

[122] See *R v Southwark Coroner Ex Parte Kendall* [1988] 1 WLR 1186 (Simon Brown LJ).

[123] *R v HM Coroner for the City of London, ex parte Barber* [1975] 1 WLR 1310, 1313 (Lord Widgery CJ).

[124] Freckelton and Ranson in their book, *Death Investigation and a Coroners Inquest* (Oxford University Press, 2006) 630, observe that an open verdict functions as a last resort where there is inadequate evidence to satisfy the criteria of any other verdict.

[125] Van Colle v Chief Constable of Hertfordshire [2007] EWCA Civ 325, paras 78–83.

[126] *R v HM Coroner for Coventry Ex Parte Chief Constable for Staffordshire* (2000) 164 JP 665.

[127] *Chief Constable of Hertfordshire Police v Van Colle and another* (2008) UKHL 50, para 139.

Determinations and Findings by the Jury

11.30 The jury will initially be directed by the Coroner to reach a unanimous verdict or finding. If the coroner considers that the jury have deliberated for a reasonable time without reaching a unanimous verdict, then the Coroner may expect a determination or finding on which the minority consists of no more than two people. Furthermore the jury spokesperson should announce publicly how many agreed. If the required number of jurors does not agree, then the coroner may discharge the jury and summon a completely new jury and the case will be heard again.[128]

The Coroners Court will follow the guidance of authorities in criminal cases as to how long the jury must deliberate for before being given a majority direction.[129] A majority verdict will not be accepted unless the jury have been considering their verdict for such period that the court considers as reasonable having regard to the nature and complexity of the case, in any event, the period must not be less than two hours.[130]

In practice more time than two hours will be allowed before a majority direction is given. Time spent not in actual deliberation, for example where the jury make their way to the jury room or elect a foreman is dealt with in the context of criminal trials by the Consolidated Criminal Practice Direction[131] which lays down that the jury should be allowed at least two hours and 10 minutes for deliberation before a majority direction may be given.

When a majority direction is appropriate will be a matter ultimately for the Coroner's discretion, based on the facts, complexities and issues of the case. Appropriate practice dictates that before such a direction is given, the advocates, representatives and interested parties will be consulted and argument heard before the final decision is taken. Good practice also dictates that the jury, where being informed that a majority direction is available to them, be urged to attempt, nevertheless, to reach a unanimous decision.

There is little authority in the context of inquests, as to the consequences of failing to observe the law in relation to the practice of taking verdicts. Assistance maybe obtained from the criminal law arena where the effect of non-compliance with procedures depends upon whether the non-compliance amounts to a breach of the Juries Act 1974 or is merely a breach of the Consolidated Criminal Practice Direction. In the case of the 1974 Act, since the courts power to accept a majority verdict depends entirely upon the statutory provision any conviction must be quashed.[132]

---

[128] Section 9(1)–(3) of the 2009 Act.
[129] *R v West Yorkshire Coroner Ex Parte Clements* (1993) 158 JP 17.
[130] Juries Act 1974 s 17(4).
[131] Consolidated Criminal Practice Direction, para IV 46.3.
[132] *R v Barry* [1975] 1 WLR 1190; *R v Pigg* [1983] 1 WLR 6.

If there has been merely a failure to comply with the practice direction then the conviction, if it be so, may stand since the direction is directory and not mandatory.[133] From this it can be anticipated that any majority direction that is given before two hours will render the inquest verdict flawed.

Coroner's Reports and Recommendations

Determination and Findings at the Hearing Following the 2009 Act

11.31 Section 10 of the 2009 Act deals with the communication of outcomes and determinations at the end of the inquest. Section 10(1)(a) requires the Senior Coroner (or the jury, if there is one), to make a determination at the end of the inquest as to who the deceased was, and how, when, where the deceased came by his or her death. This is broadly equivalent to the requirements under section 11(3)(a) and (4)(a) of the 1988 Act and rule 36 of the Coroners Rules 1984. Where there has been an investigation as to whether Article 2 of the Convention is engaged, the Coroner must also include a determination, or direct a jury to include a determination, as to the circumstances of the death.

Section 10(1)(b) also requires the coroner (or the jury where there is one) to make a finding at the end of the inquest about the details required for the registration of the death, as was required by Section 11(3)(b) and (4)(b) of the 1988 Act. This will, in normal circumstances, be a short finding such as accident or misadventure, suicide, industrial disease, natural causes, drug related or, where no clear cause of death has been established, the finding will be an open verdict.

The practice has recently increased of coroner's using narrative verdicts, in which he will sum up how the person came to die. Some of these narrative verdicts can be detailed, particularly in the case of controversial deaths. In recent case law there has been challenge as to the terminology used by coroner's in such verdicts.[134]

In 2008 the Defence Secretary, Des Browne, initiated a High Court challenge to comments made by the Assistant Deputy Coroner for Oxfordshire, Andrew Walker, during the inquest into the death of Private Jason Smith, who died of heat stroke in 2003 while serving as a Territorial Army officer in Iraq. Walker commented at the inquest in November 2006 that Smith's death was caused 'by a serious failure to recognise and take appropriate steps to address the difficulty that he had in adjusting to the climate'. It was argued in the High Court by those representing the Defence Secretary that the coroner should not have used, in his narrative verdict, the phrase 'serious failure'. Counsel for the Government argued that

[133] *R v Wright* (1974) 58 Cr App R 444; *R v Shields* [1997] Crim LR 758.

[134] Section 10(2) of the 2009 Act makes it clear that a determination may not be worded in such a way as to appear to determine any question of criminal liability of any named person or to determine any question of civil liability. See also, the High Court report in *R (Catherine Smith) v Assistant Deputy Coroner for Oxfordshire and Secretary of State for Defence* [2006] EWHC 694 (Admin).

the phrase could be seen as deciding civil liability for Private Smith's death, which was not permitted under rule 42 of the 1984 Coroners Rules.

At the time, the challenge by the Government was seen to be an attempt to stop the Ministry of Defence being exposed to civil actions, which used, as evidence, observations in narrative verdicts by coroners. At the time, David Masters, the Wiltshire coroner, who has conducted various inquests concerning deaths of British servicemen, observed:

> I do not consider that this will deflect coroners from conducting full, frank and fearless enquiries into the deaths that they are entrusted to investigate- those of people serving their country when they are killed abroad. If something needs to be said, I'll say it.[135]

The challenge in the High Court crystallised the competing concerns around the narrative verdict. Many of those representing the bereaved feel that the coroner cannot go far enough in the narrative verdict, both for the family and for society at large, as the court cannot properly determine any issue of criminal or civil liability. The campaign group 'Inquest' argue that the coroner should be free to say what happened, and what acts or omissions there were, without having to concern himself about liability. The counter argument against allowing the coroner further discretion in expression within the narrative verdict, is that a freer narrative would pave the way for more civil and criminal liability claims.

In *R(Catherine Smith) v Coroner and Defence Secretary* in the High Court.[136] Mr Justice Collins stated:

> 41. While there was a somewhat faint argument that the word 'failure' was undesirable, the real attack by (counsel for the Secretary of State for Defence) was directed at the adjective 'serious'. It is obvious that there is some tension between the prohibition contained in rule 42(b) and the need for an Article 2 inquest to identify those responsible and shortcomings so that they can be remedied for the future to avoid similar deaths. Section 8(3)(d) of the 1988 Act, which requires a jury if the continuance or possible recurrence of the circumstances in which the death occurred is prejudicial to the health or safety of members of the public, creates its own tension since their must be examination of and findings in relation to any shortcomings which led to the death and which may need to be addressed.

11.32 The Court refers to *R(Hurst) v London Northern District Coroner*[137] and *R(Jordan)* where the House of Lords confirmed that the prohibition in rule 42(b) of the Coroners Rules 1984 must be honoured.[138] This position had been laid down in *Middleton*[139] where Lord Bingham identified the correct approach to rule 42 as:

> The prohibition in rule 36(2) of the expression of opinion on matters not comprised within sub-rule 1 must continue to be respected. But it must be read with reference to the broader interpretation of 'how' in Section 11(5)(b)(ii) and rule 36(1) and does not

---

[135] *The Times*, 18 March 2008.
[136] *Smith* [2006] EWHC 694 (Admin).
[137] *R(Hurst) v London Northern District Coroner* [2007] 2 WLR 726.
[138] See *Jordan v Lord Chancellor*, [2007] 2 WLR 754, para 35.
[139] *R(Middleton) v HM Coroner for Western District of Somerset* [2004] 1 AC 182, para 37.

preclude conclusions of fact as opposed to expressions of opinion. However the juries factual consideration is conveyed, Rule 42 should not be infringed. Thus there must be no finding of criminal liability on the part of a named person. Nor must the verdict appear to determine any question of civil liability. Facts or omissions maybe recorded, but expressions suggestive of civil liability, in particular 'neglect' or 'carelessness' and related expressions, should be avoided. Self-neglect and neglect should continue to be treated as terms of art. A verdict such as that suggested in paragraph 45 below ('the deceased took his own life, in part because the risk of his doing so was not recognised and appropriate precautions were not taken to prevent him doing so') embodies a judgmental conclusion of a factual nature, directly relating to the circumstances of the death. It does not identify any individual nor does it address any issue of criminal or civil liability. It does not therefore infringe either Rule 36(2) or Rule 42.

In *Jamieson*[140] the Court of Appeal considered the scope of rule 42 in the context of a verdict of recording neglect or lack of care. The Court noted the prohibition in Rule 42 was fortified by consideration of fairness since an individual or body who might be identified as being liable was not afforded the safeguards to enable them to meet any such conclusion. For instance there was no right to call evidence or to address the coroner or jury on fact nor was there any right to receive disclosure of material evidence. *Jamieson* makes it clear that the coroner (and a jury if one is appointed) must explore facts bearing on criminal and civil liability and a coroner must ensure that the relevant facts are fully, fairly and fearlessly investigated.[141] Mr Justice Collins, in the High Court in *Smith* emphasised that factual conclusions not only may but must, if crucial, be recorded, but in a way that does not infringe rule 42.[142] He went on to state that anything to the contrary would not be capable of complying with the procedural obligation under Article 2.

In *Jordan v Lord Chancellor*[143] Lord Bingham stated:[144]

> I also agree with the Northern Irish courts . . . that nothing in the 1959 Act or the 1963 Rules prevents a jury finding facts directly relevant to the cause of death which may point very strongly towards a conclusion that criminal liability exists or does not exist.

The above observation by Lord Bingham will be considered just as applicable to findings which may point to civil liability.[145]

11.33 A coroner's decision not to allow an inquest jury to consider a verdict of unlawful killing or to leave a narrative verdict to the jury was considered improper in *R (on the application of Helen Cash) v HM Coroner for the County of Northamptonshire*.[146] A fresh inquest before a different coroner and a jury was ordered by the Court.

---

[140] *R v North Humberside & Scunthorpe Coroner, ex parte Jamieson* [1994] 3 All ER 972.
[141] See *Smith* in the High Court (n 134 above) para 43.
[142] *ibid.*
[143] *Jordan v Lord Chancellor* [2007] 2 WLR 754, an appeal from Northern Ireland to the House of Lords.
[144] *ibid*, para 39.
[145] See *Smith* (n 134 above) para 44.
[146] *R (on the application of Helen Cash) v HM Coroner for the County of Northamptonshire* [2007] EWHC 1354 (Admin), [2007] 4 All ER 903.

In that case the Court considered how the Coroner's Court should decide whether a verdict and in particular a verdict of unlawful killing should be left to the jury. The Court in *Cash* approved the observations of Lord Woolf MR in *R v HM Coroner for Exeter and East Devon, ex parte Palmer*:[147]

> In a difficult case, the coroner is carrying out an evaluation exercise. He is looking at the evidence before him as a whole and saying to himself, without deciding matters which are the province of the jury, 'Is this a case where it would be safe for the jury to come to the conclusion and there had been an unlawful killing?' If he reaches the conclusion that, because the evidence is so inherently weak, vague or inconsistent with other evidence, it would not be safe for a jury to come to the verdict, then he has to withdraw the issue from the jury. In most cases there will only be a single proper decision, which could be reached on any objective assessment of the evidence. Therefore one can either say that there is no scope for *Wednesbury* reasonableness or there is scope, but the only possible proper decision which a reasonable coroner would come to is either to leave the question to the jury or not, as the case maybe.
>
> However, as [was stated] in *Galbraith*, in these cases there will always be borderline situations where it is necessary for the coroner to exercise a discretion. It is only in such a situation that he has any discretion.

It was suggested in *Cash*[148] that the test of reasonableness is extremely limited.

Lord Woolf MR made it clear in *R v Inner South London Coroner, ex parte Douglas-Williams*[149] that the coroner should adopt the *Galbraith* approach in deciding whether to leave a particular verdict to a jury. His Lordship then made observations upon the limited discretion which the coroner enjoys in this area:

> The strength of the evidence is not the only consideration and, in relation to wider issues, the coroner has a broader discretion. If it appears there are circumstances which, in a particular situation, mean in the judgement of the coroner, acting reasonably and fairly, it is not in the interest of justice that a particular verdict should be left to the jury, he need not leave that verdict. For example, he need not leave all possible verdicts just because there is technically evidence to support them. It is sufficient if he leaves those verdicts which realistically reflect the thrust of the evidence as a whole. To leave all possible verdicts could in some situations merely confuse and overburden the jury and if that is the coroner's conclusion he cannot be criticised if he does not leave a particular verdict.

Mr Justice Leveson (as he then was) clarified Lord Woolf's judgment in *R (Sharman) v HM Coroner for Inner North London*:[150]

> Lord Woolf was doing no more than saying that the coroner should, within the spectrum of different verdicts open to the jury, decide which 'realistically reflected the thrust of the evidence' rather than be required to indulge in an analysis of each and every conceivable permutation.

[147] *R v HM Coroner for Exeter and East Devon, ex parte Palmer* [1997] EWCA Civ 2951, [2000] Inquest LR 78.

[148] *Cash* (above n 146) para 23.

[149] *R v Inner South London Coroner, ex parte Douglas-Williams* [1999] 1 All ER 344, 349 A–C.

[150] *R (Sharman) v HM Coroner for Inner North London* [2005] EWHC 850 (Admin), [2005] 1 Inquest LR 77, para 9, on appeal *Sharman v HM Coroner for Inner North London and Stanley* [2005] EWCA Civ 967.

Once a verdict has been left to the jury, the narrative must add information or significance relating to the circumstances of the death.

The facts of *Cash* related to an individual being knocked to the ground and pinned there by the police. Whilst he was in that position, he suffered myocardial insufficiency and died. In such circumstances the narrative should deal with the core factual questions which an inquest of this nature would address: whether the police had needed to restrain the deceased at all; if so, whether it would have been sufficient for the police officers to hold the deceased's arms without taking him to the ground; and if not, whether the degree of force used to restrain him while he was on the ground was excessive.[151] It was held in the circumstances of *Cash* (the death of an individual under police restraint), that it is open to the jury, depending upon their view of the evidence, to reach conclusions which are adverse to the police on all the above matters, even if the jury would not have returned a verdict of unlawful killing, for example because they did not think the force used on the deceased would have harmed him.

In some circumstances it is permissible for the coroner to suggest a particular form of words for the jury to use, which embodies a judgmental conclusion on the core factual issues which the inquest has addressed.[152]

11.34 In accordance with rule 43 of the Coroners Rules 1984, a coroner who believes that action should be taken to prevent the recurrence of fatalities similar to that in respect of which the inquest is being held may announce at the inquest that he is reporting the matter in writing to the person or authority who may have power to take such action.

The coroner may, at the end of an inquest which has revealed shortcomings which have or may have resulted in death, issue recommendations to prevent death in the future. The body to whom such recommendations under rule 43 are sent is obliged to respond within a certain time period.

An example of this can be seen in the case of Gareth Myatt and Adam Rickwood,[153] two young people aged 15 and 14 respectively, who died in secure training centres. A number of issues relating to the safety of these two young people arose during the inquest and the coroner made a number of recommendations. As a result of this the government produced an 'action plan' detailing responses to the recommendations, and showing an update as to the progress made since the action plan was first published. These are designed to ensure, so far as possible, that similar tragedies in custody are prevented in the future.[154]

There should, however be a nexus between the recommendations made by the coroner and the circumstances surrounding the death into which the coroner enquires.

---

[151] See *Cash* (above n 146) para 49.
[152] See *Cash* (above n 146) para 52.
[153] See *Inquest Magazine*, December 2009.
[154] See www.justice.gov.uk/publications/docs/response-Coroners-inquests-dec-08.pdf.

On this, Commonwealth authority is instructive. In *Matthews v Hunter*[155] Heron J stated:

> In going about his function the coroner must recognise the damage to reputations and the aggravation of personal suffering such comments may bring. In making general recommendations and comments about matters not the direct cause of death in the circumstances, care should be taken to make that clear.[156]

More recently, in this jurisdiction, the case of *R(Lewis) v HM Coroner for Mid and North Division of Shropshire*,[157] in the Court of Appeal, considered the issues relating to a prisoner who committed suicide in his prison cell. During the course of the inquest the coroner identified six substantive issues to be addressed and in due course, quite properly, gave the jury a written questionnaire. What was omitted from the questionnaire was the action taken after the deceased was found hanging in his cell. In consequence the jury was not given an opportunity to express a view on it. It was the contention, in the Court of Appeal, on behalf of the applicant's family that this was an unlawful omission. Lord Justice Sedley certainly saw the force of the proposition on behalf of the applicant that the circumstances of death were not limited to its probable causes; they extended as a matter of plain English to the surrounding facts. Furthermore it could intelligibly be said that, in a jurisdiction which was not concerned with the allocation of blame, potentially causative circumstances could be just as relevant as actual causative ones. The Court of Appeal observed that all of that spoke strongly in favour of a power to take the jury's verdict on such questions. Despite this the Court of Appeal were unable to find a reason of principle for making it a duty.

Interestingly, the Court went on to state that it would be quite different if rule 43 of the Coroners Rules 1984 did not exist, which made provision for a coroner to announce at an inquest that he was reporting the matter in writing to the person in authority where he believed that action should be taken to prevent the recurrence of fatalities in such circumstances. The present legislative allocation of functions between the coroner and the jury fulfilled the functions which were required by Article 2 of the Convention, which bound all public authorities and laid down that everyone's right to life should be protected by law. The Court of Appeal concluded that it was well established that that required the State not only to abstain from taking life, but to investigate impartially and diligently any death that occurred at or in its hands. This latter finding is surprising, given the imperative of thoroughly investigating and rectifying systemic failures that may lead to a risk of futures loss of life. *Opuz v Turkey*[158] has established that breaches of Article 2 include failures to put protections in place that have a real prospect of avoiding death. As such the judgment in *Lewis* seems restrictive and is presently subject to appeal.

---

[155] *Matthews v Hunter* [1993] 2 NZLR 683.
[156] *ibid*, 687–8.
[157] *R(Lewis) v HM Coroner for Mid and North Division of Shropshire* [2009] EWCA Civ 1403.
[158] *Opuz v Turkey* (Application No 33401/02), 3rd Section, judgment of 9 June 2009.

In Future Inquests will Identify the Possible Causes of a Death

11.35 In *R (on the application of Keith Lewis) v HM Coroner for the Mid and North Division of the County of Shropshire (Secretary of State for Justice as an interested party)*[159] the coroner declined to exercise his discretion pursuant to rule 43 of the Coroners Rules 1984, to alert the appropriate authorities to systemic failings identified with regard to the suicide of an 18-year-old detainee at a Young Offenders Institution. It was submitted in the Court of Appeal that the purposes of an Article 2 investigation include bringing to light, as far as possible, the full facts surrounding the circumstances of the death and the exposure of culpable and discreditable conduct with a view to rectification of dangerous practices and procedures.[160]

Furthermore it was argued at appeal that the object of an Article 2 investigation is not limited to ascertaining whether or not there has been a breach of duty, but covers the identification of lessons for the future and identifying shortcomings in the regulatory framework.[161]

The Court of Appeal in *Lewis* observed that the requirements of an Article 2 compliant investigation extend to the identification of lessons and the search for improvements. Lord Justice Sedley concluded that the Coroner's failure to include within his rule 43 report the 'lessons learnt' aspects of his discretion with regard to the events after the deceased had been found hanging amounted to a breach of duty. Lord Justice Sedley stated that:[162]

> The want of equipment, training and effective procedure which the undisputed evidence revealed was so eloquent of action that needed to be taken to prevent similar fatalities that the Coroner cannot have believed otherwise . . . In such a situation the permissive power – 'may report' – could only be properly exercised in one way if the purpose of Article 2 were to be respected, and that was by making a report on the issue.

Lord Justice Sedley observed that the requirement to take measures which 'could have had a real prospect of altering the outcome' was also relevant.[163] The Coroners and Justice Act 2009[164] makes it mandatory for a Coroner to report and there be an official response, where, in the Coroner's opinion, action should be taken to prevent similar future fatalities.[165]

Where facts are disputed or uncertain, 'a finding by verdict is a desirable or even a necessary foundation of any Rule 43 report', and the Court of Appeal went on

---

[159] *R(Lewis) v HM Coroner for Mid and North Division of Shropshire* [2009] EWCA Civ 1403.

[160] See Lord Bingham in *Amin* [2003] UKHL 51, para 31.

[161] See *Oneryiodiz v Turkey* (2005) 41 EHRR 20 and *R (Sacker) v West Yorkshire Coroner* [2004] UKHL 11.

[162] *Lewis* [2009] EWCA Civ 1403, para 16.

[163] See *E v United Kingdom* (2002) 36 EHRR 519.

[164] Coroners and Justice Act 2009, Sch 5, para 7.

[165] This does not come into force until April 2012, although the Court of Appeal in *Lewis* confirmed that such procedure would be Article 2 compliant.

that in hearings which concern themselves with the learning of lessons, 'potentially causative circumstances can be just as relevant as actually causative ones.' Although *Lewis* does not impose a duty upon Coroners to leave factual disputes relating to non-causative matters to the jury, the import of the case is that Coroners have such a discretion and are encouraged to rely upon it where a case does raise the issue of learning lessons and where the jury could assist in resolving disputed or uncertain facts.[166]

Whether the Coroner should Rule on the Legality of Force?

11.36 In *R (on the application of Carol Pounder) v HM Coroner for the North and South Districts of Durham and Darlington*[167] the Administrative Court considered judicial review of a Coroner's decision not to leave this matter before a jury. The case analysed the circumstances of the youngest person to die in a British penal establishment, at least in modern times. The young person was 14 at the time of his death when he strangled himself using a shoelace. The Coroner decided that it was unnecessary and undesirable for him to rule on the legality of any restraints used upon the deceased at the time of his death. The Coroner's approach was that all that mattered were the primary facts including the question whether any staff using restraint at the time honestly considered that they had power to do so.

It was accepted that the inquest engaged the investigative obligations inherent under Article 2 as enshrined in *Middleton*.[168] Reference was also made to *Amin*[169] in relation to the importance of public investigation before an independent tribunal giving the opportunity for relatives of the deceased to participate. It was emphasised in accordance with *Amin* that the purposes of the investigation are to ensure so far as possible that the full facts are brought to light, that culpable and discreditable conduct is exposed and brought to public notice, that suspicion of deliberate wrong doing (if unjustified) is allayed, that dangerous practices and procedures are rectified and that those who have lost their relative may at least have the satisfaction of knowing that lessons learnt from his or her death may save the lives of others.[170]

Although the Administrative Court had some sympathy with the Coroner they were of the view[171] that it is impossible for an inquiry to be made into whether the

---

[166] As a result of *Lewis* it is clear that the Coroner's duty to report, including matters in respect of non-causative issues will be amenable to judicial review.

[167] *R (on the application of Carol Pounder) v HM Coroner for the North and South Districts of Durham and Darlington* [2009] EWHC 76 Admin.

[168] *Middleton* [2004] UKHL 10.

[169] *Amin* [2003] UKHL 51.

[170] *ibid*, para 31.

[171] *Pounder* [2009] EWHC 76 (Admin), para 61.

force used on the deceased was appropriate or proportionate without a ruling or clear guidance to the jury on whether it was lawful. The Court observed that physical restraint is prima facie trespass to the person. Such a trespass may be justified if there is a power to use restraint and the power is exercised reasonably or proportionately.

In *Pounder* the Coroner had decided, without any dispute from the parties, that the propriety and proportionality of the force used on the deceased was an issue for the inquest. The Court decided that the jury at that inquest were in effect left to form their own policy on how children in detention should be treated, without any of the relevant principles being explained to them as a result of the Coroner's ruling. The Administrative Court explained its position in this way:

> 63. In my judgment, if the inquest was going to explore a matter that may have contributed to [the deceased's] death, it needed to do so properly. The fact that examination of the legality of the restraint used may have led to witnesses being warned of their right not to answer questions that may incriminate them, and thus potentially depriving the inquest jury of the benefit of the answer, could and should not drive the proper scope of the ambit of the investigation that needs to be made. There are many cases where juries may be considering possible verdicts of unlawful killing in one form or another, where warnings may have to be given to individuals but that does not prevent or deter inquiry into the legality of the force used in all the circumstances of the case. It is to be noted that such a verdict is not a breach of Rule 42 of the Coroners Rules because no criminal liability of an individual is attributed and such a verdict does not determine or purport to state any question of civil liability.

12

Remedies and Appeals of
Inquest Decisions

12.1 A separate chapter of this book deals with the forthcoming reforms contained within the 2009 Act in relation to a comprehensive appeals process which was anticipated within the coronial regime. This was designed to achieve consistency and predictability of decision making at the inquest and to present a more unified approach to proceedings within the Coroner's Court.

Of course, the role of the Chief Coroner in the appeals process was abolished, although there is no expressed intention to discard the appeal procedure.

Existing alongside this inherent procedure are more established processes, fundamental of which is judicial review.

Judicial Review

12.2 Any claim for judicial review must be filed with the court promptly and in any event not later than three months after the grounds to make the claim first arose.[1]

The court does have a discretion under the Civil Procedure Rules, rule 3.1(2)(a) to allow a late claim but this will only be used in exceptional circumstances.

The Administrative Court, upon application, can consider whether the Coroners decision was legal or *ultra vires*; whether there was an error of law; whether the decision was perverse;[2] whether relevant factors were ignored or irrelevant factors were given undue weight; whether natural justice was breached and whether the claimants rights under the Human Rights Act 1998 were ignored or inadequately considered.

By virtue of the Civil Procedure Rules rule 54.2, the Administrative Court can, if it feels it appropriate: quash the result; order a particular course of action; issue an injunction or order a stay; make a declaration as to the parties' rights; or award damages.

---

[1] See the Civil Procedure Rules rule 54.5(1).
[2] See *Associated Provincial Picture Houses Limited v Wednesbury Corporation* [1947] 2 All ER 680.

12.3 There is a strict Pre-action Protocol for Judicial Review.[3]

Before making a claim, the claimant is expected to send a letter to the defendant. The purpose of this letter is to identify the issues in dispute and establish whether a Judicial Review can be avoided.

The standard format for the letter is outlined at Annexe A on the Ministry of Justices pre-action protocol document. Essentially it should set out clearly the matter being challenged, especially if there has been more than one decision. The letter should also contain the issue that maybe subject to judicial review, setting out the date and details of the decision or act or omission being challenged and a brief summary of the facts and why it is contended to be wrong.

The letter should also include details of the action that the defendant is expected to take, specifying the remedy sort by the claimant. It is important also to include within the letter details of any interested parties who should receive a copy of the letter being sent.

It is also important to request in the letter a full explanation of the reasons for the decision being challenged so that the parties and the Court if need be are able to focus upon the contentious issues. Details of any documents that are considered relevant should also be referred to in the letter including any policy documentation and if appropriate legal authorities.

It will be a matter between the parties as to any time constraints given for a reply to the pre-action protocol letter although 14 days is considered by the Ministry of Justice to be a reasonable time to allow in most circumstances.

Any documentation and in particular the pre-action protocol letter should be directed to the address where the coroner is most likely to receive it. The lack of resources and even office space afforded to Coroners makes communication difficult. Practitioners should ascertain the correct address for all correspondence to be sent although it is most likely that the local authority or county council responsible for the particular coroner will be the correct recipient.

The pre-action letter is important within the Judicial Review procedure and failure to send it can result in costs implications at any eventual hearing.[4] The response to a letter before claim should set out a fuller explanation of the decision where it is considered appropriate. Furthermore it should clarify whether any issue in question is conceded in part or in full or will be contested. Where it is not proposed to disclose any information that has been requested, the respondent should explain the reason for this. When an interim reply is being sent and there is a realistic prospect of compromise, details of this should be included. The respondent coroner should also identify any other parties who they consider have an interest or who have not already been sent a letter by the claimant.

---

[3] This can be obtained on the Ministry of Justice's website: www.justice.gov.uk/civil/procrules_fin/contents/protocols/prot_jrv.htm.

[4] See *R v Horsham District Council, ex parte Wenman* [1995] 1 WLR 680, 709 E–H.

12.4 The first phase of the formal judicial review procedure involves obtaining permission from the High Court.[5]

This is done by completing and lodging a claim form which will contain the grounds of the application and witness statements or supporting documentation which will be filed in the Administrative Court.

In addition to specifying the precise decision that is being complained of, the time and place it was made and the remedies sort, the claim form should also establish whether the hearing is urgent and include reasons for any delay in making the application.

Documentation should also include copies of the pre-action protocol letter and any response received. If this procedure has not been undertaken the claimant will be required to explain why in their application for permission for Judicial Review.

The claimant will be expected in the permission documents to be precise as to the relief sought, whether they require the decision to be quashed, injoined or other action taken.

It should be borne in mind that the document will be used at the full hearing if permission is granted and therefore it is prudent to formulate the permission document in the style of a skeleton written argument.

Four copies of the permission document need to be stamped at the Administrative Court, with one being sent to the defendant containing the accompanying documentation, statement of grounds, and facts.

There is a fee of £50 to be paid upon issue.

A copy of the claim form must be served on the defendant within seven days after the date of issue. Copies of all documents relied upon should also be served within this time frame.

The defendant is required to file and serve an acknowledgement of service within 21 days after the service of the claim form.

12.5 Following the filing of the above documentation, the Administrative Court may grant the permission on the papers. Alternatively the Court may order an oral hearing for developed argument on the issues.

The single judge's response in indicating that permission will be granted may contain within it advice and guidance to a defendant as to how the complaint may be remedied. This can encourage a defendant to review and reassess their approach and attempt to correct the decision-making process, subject to potential judicial review, so as to avoid the need for a hearing.

If, of course, a defendant refuses to do this or inadequately corrects their position then this will weigh against them at any future full judicial review hearing.[6]

---

[5] Civil Procedure Rules, r 54.4.

[6] There is an overriding duty within the Civil Procedural Rules, rule 1.1(2)(a)–(c) to act reasonably in exchanging information and documentation in relation to the claim and attempting to avoid any unnecessary proceedings. See also the Pre-Action Protocol, para 4.

Should permission be granted the defendant will have 35 days to file and serve detailed grounds contesting the issue, together with any written evidence.[7]

Upon the receipt of further documentation from the defendant, there remains a duty upon the claimant to consider whether any compromise or agreement can be reached between the parties to avoid the necessity of judicial review proceedings, continuing the arbitration orientated approach within this jurisdiction.

12.6 Ultimately and if necessary, the matter will come before the Administrative Court for an adjudication.

Public funding for the legal costs in judicial review are available in accordance with the normal legal aid means testing regime.

The award of costs at the end of any judicial review hearing is at the court's discretion.[8]

Although the general approach is that costs will follow the event and that the losing party pays the costs of the winning party, there remains a discretion to depart from this rule.[9] It is at this stage that the conduct of the parties leading up to Judicial Review will be taken into account. Failure to adhere to pre-action protocols may result in adverse costs awards against that party.

Furthermore the court will assess whether a particular party have been wholly or partially successful in their application and again, this maybe reflected in the consequent costs order.

Significantly, if any party has made a reasonable offer to compromise or settle the issue in advance of the judicial review which has in the view of the court, been unreasonably refused, again costs may reflect this.

In any event, a party applying for costs maybe asked by the Administrative Court to immediately quantify that figure and it will be prudent for practitioners to have a detailed cost assessment in advance of the hearing to enable them to assist the Court if called upon to do so.

Should any party against whom an adverse costs border has been made, be of the view that the claim of the successful party is excessive they should bring that to the Court's attention immediately. The Court is not bound to accept any costs figure given to them.

The coroner is in no different position to any other litigant who may fail in court proceedings. He will be as vulnerable to an adverse costs order as any other party.[10]

12.7 Judicial review is available across the sphere of the Coroner's decision making.

Challenge at Judicial Review may arise right at the start of the process if it is considered that a coroner unreasonably refuses to hold an inquest[11] and will

---

[7] Civil Procedure Rules, r 54.14.

[8] See Civil Procedure Rules, r 44 3(1).

[9] *ibid*, r 44.3(2).

[10] See *R v HM Coroner for Inner North London, ex parte Touche* [2001] QB 1206, paras 50–59.

[11] *R (on the application of Touche) v Inner North London Coroner* [2001] QB 1206.

include challenges to a Coroner's decision not to empanel a jury,[12] issues relating to disclosure[13] and matters relating to the *verdict*.

In relation to this latter consideration, the Administrative Court has expressed its reluctance to overturn a Coroner's decision which is primarily based upon his hearing evidence which the Administrative Court will not have done.[14]

Ultimately, when considering whether a decision of the coroner during the inquest process, which includes the pre-inquest hearing process, is susceptible to judicial review the fundamental principles of *Wednesbury* unreasonableness will apply. The fairness under scrutiny is the fairness to the applicant in the conduct of the inquest process. Furthermore intervention by the High Court in the inquest process is likely to be comparatively rare.[15]

A finding of *Wednesbury* unreasonableness is not straightforward. De Smith states:[16]

> The issue under this ground of review is not whether the decision maker strayed outside the terms or authorised purposes of the governing statute '(the test of illegality)'. It is whether the power under which the decision maker acts, a power normally conferring a broad discretion, has been improperly exercised or insufficiently justified. The court therefore engages in the review of the substance of the decision or its justification.

De Smith goes on to recognise that the critical question to ask is whether the decision falls 'within the range of reasonable responses open to the decision maker'. He further recognises that where a broad discretionary power has been conferred on the decision maker there is a presumption that the decision is within the range of that discretion and the burden is therefore on the claimant to demonstrate the contrary.[17]

In short, judges will not likely interfere with the Coroners decision on this ground.

In R v Secretary of State for the Home Department ex parte Daily[18] Lord Cooke articulated the recent rationalisation of the *Wednesbury* Principals and noted that the test '. . . is being increasingly rephrased to a decision which is 'within the range of reasonable responses''.

De Smith concludes:[19]

> 'A decision is a irrational in the strict sense of that term if it is unreasoned; if it is lacking of sensible logic or comprehensible justification . . . less extreme examples of the irrational decision include those in which there is an absence of logical connection between the evidence and the ostensible reasons for the decision, where the reasons display no adequate justification for the decision, or where there is absence of evidence in support of the decision.'

---

[12] *R v Hammersmith Coroner, ex parte Peach* [1980] QB 211, a refusal to call witnesses. *Siberry's application (No 2)* [2008] NIQB 147 a case involving judicial review of a Coroner's decision not to call the Prisons and Probations Ombudsman.

[13] See *R (on the application of Bentley) v HM Coroner District of Avon* [2001] EWHC Admin 170

[14] See *R (on the application of Khan) v HM Coroner for West Hertfordshire* [2002] EWHC Admin 302, para 45.

[15] *Siberry's application* (No 2) [2008] NIQB 147, para 57 (McCloskey J).

[16] De Smith, *Judicial Review*, 6th edn (Sweet & Maxwell, 2009), para 11-003.

[17] *ibid*, para 11-006.

[18] [2001] 2AC 532 at paragraph 32.

[19] At paragraph 11-024.

Any potential applicant for judicial review of a matter within the inquest, must therefore be realistic as to the difficulty of achieving the overturn of the Coroners decision. Put simply, what may not seem right, or indeed appear inequitable, may not be susceptible to judicial review and for this reason the expectation of the lay client should be managed.

The Attorney-General's Fiat by Virtue of the Coroners Act 1988 Section 13

12.8 Tactically, if a party is considering initiating judicial review proceedings, they should not engage in the procedure under section 13 of the 1988 Act. In short, if the Attorney-General refuses a fiat, the difficulty in persuading the Administrative Court, given the hurdles of establishing *Wednesbury's* unreasonableness will be even more acute if the Attorney-General, by refusal, has bolstered the Coroners decision.

Under section 13 of the Coroners Act 1988 an appeal can be lodge by or on behalf of the Attorney-General against a coroner either if he refuses or neglects to hold an inquest or where an inquest has been held by him it is necessary or desirable in the interest of justice that another inquest should be held.[20]

If successful, the Attorney-General will refer the matter to the High Court who can order that an inquest or a further inquest be initiated or that the result of any inquest held by quashed. The coroner may also be ordered to pay costs.[21]

The Attorney-General is not susceptible to judicial review should he refuse to refer the matter to the High Court.[22]

Any application for the Attorney-General's fiat should be made to the Attorney-General's office and is done by way of a letter with the appropriate documentation annexed to it. This will include details of the inquisition, relevant correspondence and transcripts and notes of evidence.

If the Attorney-General's fiat is granted it is the responsibility of the applicant to draft an originating motion. This document will set out the grounds of the application, which will be accompanied by the Attorney-General's fiat.

The notice of motion will be lodged at the Administrative court and all interested parties will receive service of it within six weeks following the grant of the fiat. In appropriate circumstances the court may grant an extension of time for service.

As with judicial review all interested parties including the coroner will be given the opportunity to make responses in the form of a written statement or affidavit.

---

[20] See section 13(1)(a)–(b).
[21] See section 13(2)(a)–(c).
[22] See *R v Attorney-General ex parte Ferrante* [1995]COD 18.

The ambit of the Attorney-General's fiat is restricted to circumstances where there has either been no inquest held or where an inquest has taken place there should be a further inquest.

In the first category of cases, where there has been no inquest, a close analysis of the provisions in section 8 of the Coroners Act 1988 will be appropriate, outlining where the coroner has a duty to hold an inquest. Reference will also be made to the new provisions contained in the 2009 Act which appear at section 1 of that legislation.

The second limb of the section 13 challenge designates particular grounds under which proceedings can be taken. The areas listed under section 13(1)(b) cover fraud, retraction of evidence, irregularity of proceedings, insufficiency of inquiry and the discovery of new facts or evidence.

An example of insufficiency of inquiry can be seen in *R v Coventry Coroner ex parte O'Reilly*[23] which criticised the coroner for failing to examine relevant documentation. In that case he relied purely on oral evidence.

The category of challenge resulting from discovery of new facts or evidence can include information and material heard at subsequent inquests relating to the deaths of other individuals as well as entirely new witnesses or other expert evidence.

In accordance with section 13(3) there is an overriding duty upon the Attorney-General to be satisfied that any decision to order an inquest or a further inquest must be done if it is necessary in the interest of justice.

The requirements contained within Article 2 of the Convention for a thorough and expeditious investigation into death will provide the imperative for an inquest or a further inquest into the circumstances of an individuals death.

The interests of justice criteria was considered in *R v Inner South London Coroner ex parte Douglas-Williams*[24] where the court of appeal stated that although they were dealing with a case of judicial review, the same principals as to what was in the interest of justice would apply to any section 13 application.[25]

Lord Woolf cited *R v Divine ex parte Walton*:[26]

'The court is not to attend to mere informalities, nor to criticise minutely the summing up, or the nature of the evidence or of the procedure. But if the inquest has been so conducted, or the circumstances attending it are such, that there is a real risk that justice has not been done, and a real impairment of the security which right procedure provides that justice is done and is seen to be done, the court ought not to allow the inquisition to stand.'

Lord Woolf emphasised the discretion of the coroner when it comes to what verdicts to leave to a jury and the Coroners unique position of having heard the evidence. The court further observed that the misdirections complained of in

---

[23] (1996) 160JP 749.
[24] [1999] 1 All ER 344.
[25] Per Lord Woolf MR at page 348.
[26] [1930] 2KB 29 at 37.

Douglas-Williams would not have affected the outcome of the inquest and the coroner had been perfectly entitled to take the view that in the circumstances of that case, neglect would be an inappropriate verdict for the jury to consider on the evidence. Moreover, it was held that it was most unlikely that a fresh inquest would come to any other verdict and that the inquest had performed in an exemplary manner its purpose of investigating the facts, and little more could be achieved by subjecting all concerned to the considerable expense and stress of a further inquest. For those reasons the Court of Appeal were not minded that judicial review was appropriate.

It will not be in the interests of justice to set aside an inquest on the basis of a misdirection if the misdirection would not have effected the outcome.[27]

Civil Actions Following an Inquest Verdict

12.9 Often, material gathered during the course of an inquest will not only be potential material in relation to a criminal prosecution but may also found a civil action against some or all of the interested parties.

Remarks made in any narrative verdict by the coroner which may assist in any future civil proceedings can be utilised in later civil drafting.

The scathing remarks of coroners following numerous inquests into the deaths of service personnel in the theatre of war were influential, not only in the formulation of civil proceedings but also in the ultimate settlement of the claims of bereaved families against the Ministry of Defence.[28] A finding at the inquest relating to systemic failure will be particularly powerful in any future civil claim.

In practice, if it is anticipated that bereaved families or any other interested parties, may, at some future date, be formulating a civil claim, advocates should prepare questions designed to facilitate any future action.

In short claims will arise from such issues as negligence in the workplace, failure to protect those in State custody or like institutions and claims under Article 2 and Article 3 of the European Convention on Human Rights.

Attention should be paid to the limitation period for actions which may mean that a civil action should be issued before an inquest has concluded. Special care should be taken in relation to the time limits regarding human rights actions. Cases against public bodies alleging a breach of the Convention must be brought within one year of the date on which the relevant act took place.[29] Although this time limit maybe extended where the court considers it equitable to do so, in practice, the courts are loath to extend that period.

The one year limitation period will begin from the date that the act complained of took place.

---

[27] See *R v Wolverhampton Coroner ex parte McCurbin* [1990] 2 All ER 759 at 767; [1990] 1 WLR 719 at 730.

[28] See the mitigation in relation to the Nimrod, Hercules and Puma fatalities.

[29] Human Rights Act 1998 Section 7(5).

If there is a continuing act, such as maltreatment in a place of custody, it is probable that the date on which the act complained of took place can be construed as meaning the date when the continuing act ceased, and not when it began.[30]

Any applicant under section 7(5) of the Human Rights Act 1988 who seeks to extend time must identify a fact or circumstance which makes it equitable to displace the general rule.[31]

In establishing whether it is equitable to extend time under section 7(5) of the 1998 Act the court will take into account the time it has taken to obtain legal aid or to exercise functions in relation to treasure.[32]

In *Jeffrey v Secretary of State for Transport*[33] time was extended for over the 12-month period under section 7(5)(b) in a case in which the claimants lawyers had forgotten about the time limitation provision under the Human Rights Act.

Furthermore the court will consider the proportionality of the claim and in particular if the claim is substantially one designed to recover money, rather than for a vindication of Human Rights. The court will also consider the length of the delay and the reasons given for it.

Another important criteria will be whether there has been any prejudice caused to another litigant as a result of the delay. If no such prejudice has been caused then there is a better chance that an extension will be granted.[34]

---

[30] *Sommerville v Scottish Ministers* [2007] 1 WLR 2734.
[31] Section 7(5)(b) of the 1998 Act.
[32] See section 11 of the Treasure Act 1996.
[33] *Jeffrey v Secretary of State for Transport* [2004] EWHC 2772 (Ch).
[34] See *R v Commissioner for Local Administration, ex parte Croydon London Borough Council* [1989] 1 All ER 1033, 1046.

13

Funding

13.1 Lord Bach, the Parliamentary Undersecretary of State, stated in a letter to Lord Thomas of Gresford QC[1] that there were approximately 800 inquests a year where a public authority chose to be represented. He added: 'Using the same average figure the cost to the Legal Aid budget of providing funding for the family in these inquests would be £6.4 million per annum, a significant sum'.[2]

What Lord Bach fails to point out in his letter is that the sum of money incurred by the public authorities who choose to be legally represented is paid by the taxpayer.

Ministers responsible for public funding have consistently argued that as a matter of general practice, proceedings in the Coroners' Courts should not attract public funding on the grounds that their procedures are of an inquisitorial nature. This argument does not bare close analysis. On the Continent the inquisitorial system in its various guises is well established, and public funding is available to the interested parties to participate in it. Furthermore although the coronial process is, strictly, inquisitorial, the modern day inquest can involve controversial and contested issues.

Routinely, interested parties at such inquests, including governmental departments, the police or the Armed Forces, are comprehensively and often expensively legally represented at the tax payer's expense. It is against this backdrop that the absence of public funding, save in exceptional circumstances, for bereaved families gives the appearance of unfairness.

A second explanation for the lack of automatic public funding at an inquest is that the coroner can represent the position and look after the interests of bereaved families. Again this does not bare analysis particularly as the coroner has another function, that of maintaining the independence of the tribunal. The coroner, furthermore, will have duties as to disclosure, some of which involve controversial decisions as to whether to give bereaved families access to documentation or whether such documentation should be redacted. It will be difficult for a coroner to represent the interests of bereaved families and decide that they should not receive full disclosure, often at the submission of government departments. Such a situation will be liable to place the coroner in a conflict of interest dilemma.

---

[1] Letter dated 13 July 2009.

[2] The letter dated 13 July 2009 from Lord Bach to Lord Thomas is available in the library of the House of Lords.

Additionally, however much the coroner seeks to represent the interests of the parties he is not in a position to have conferences with bereaved families or supply the important support that is required during difficult and traumatic inquests. In short, the coroner cannot replace or substitute the services of a properly instructed advocate on behalf of the bereaved families at inquests.

It follows from the above that the public funding regime which applies to the representation of bereaved families and some other interested parties is driven more by the availability of resources rather than a black-letter approach to fairness and equality of arms.

13.2 Public funding or legal aid for representation at an inquest was specifically excluded from the public funding regime by the Access to Justice Act 1999, Schedule 2.

Nevertheless, funding was available by way of a grant of exceptional funding under Section 6(8)(b) of the 1999 Act.

Section 6(8)(b) provides that the Lord Chancellor may authorise the Legal Services Commission or any other body that supersedes it, to fund the provision of specified services.

In practice the procedure prior to the 2009 Act was that funding was recommended or refused by the Minister responsible for legal aid. In *R(on the application of Main) v Minister for Legal Aid*[3] Mr Justice Owen allowed an application for judicial review of the Minister's decision not to fund advocacy at an inquest, holding that she had been wrong not to take the view that representation would serve the wider public interest and would be necessary in order to ensure an effective investigation for the purposes of the European Convention on Human Rights, Article 2.

13.3 To succeed in persuading the Minister that the exceptional funding criteria applies, the applicant must demonstrate that there are exceptional factual or legal issues which indicate that legal representation is required at the inquest in order to ensure an effective investigation.[4]

In refusing judicial review of the minister's decision in *R(on the application of Andrew Jones) v Legal Services Commission*[5] the Administrative Court held that the ultimate question before them upon judicial review was whether the decision to refuse funding was irrational. The Court concluded that the following analysis by the Minister was not irrational:

> Whilst there maybe unusual legal aspects to the inquest, there is no indication of complex expert evidence to be considered. Although the coroner has stated that the family should be represented, I am not satisfied that it is necessary to enable the coroner to carry out an affective investigation into the facts of this case. In particular, whilst your

[3] *R(on the application of Main) v Minister for Legal Aid* [2007] EWHC 742 (Admin).
[4] See *R(on the application of Andrew Jones) v Legal Services Commission* [2007] EWHC 2106 (Admin).
[5] *ibid*, paras 35–36.

clients may wish that particular legal submissions are made in order to direct the course of the inquest, these are matters that are in principle within the coroner's remit. Alternatively, written submissions on such legal issues could be provided by you under the Legal Help Scheme.

13.4 Over a period of time the government have developed principles upon which the discretion to grant exceptional public funding will be exercised.

In 2001, the Lord Chancellor issued guidance to indicate the types of cases that he would consider appropriate for exceptional funding.[6] Before approving an application the Lord Chancellor would expect the relevant funding authority

> to be satisfied that either
>
> There is a significant wider public interest . . . in the applicant being legally represented at the inquest; or
>
> Funded representation for the family of the deceased is likely to be necessary to enable the coroner to carry out an effective investigation into the death as required by Article 2 of [the Convention].

The inherent reluctance of government departments to grant public funding to bereaved families can be seen from the tone of the Lord Chancellor's guidelines in 2001, issued before the Court of Appeal's decision in *R(Khan) v Secretary of State for the Department of Health*,[7] in which it was observed[8] that for most inquests where the Article 2 obligation arises, the coroner will be able to carry out an effective investigation into the death without the need for advocacy. In considering whether funded representation maybe necessary to comply with the Article 2 obligations, the guidance stated that the nature and seriousness of any allegations which are likely to be raised at the inquest, including in particular any allegations against public authorities or other agencies of the State, would be taken into account. Furthermore the guidance observes that particular attention will be paid to whether the families have participated in any other form of investigation or whether there will be any other form of investigation in addition to the inquest.

It was considered that in most cases a family should be able to participate effectively at an inquest without the need for advocacy on their behalf. This approach was taken literally at the inquest into the death of Geoff Gray, one of the trainee soldiers who died at Deepcut Barracks. At the start of that inquest, the bereaved family was not legally represented and was not encouraged to obtain representation. The inquest lasted half a day. Conversely a later inquest into the death of another Deepcut trainee, James Collinson, whose family did have legal representation, lasted some three weeks and revealed significant failings at Deepcut Barracks, which were not the subject of investigation in the half-day hearing in relation to the death of Geoff Gray.

---

[6] Lord Chancellor's Guidance on Exceptional Funding, 1 November 2001. Legal Services Commission, *The Funding Code: Decision Making Guidance (Part C)*, Section 27.2, para 8.

[7] *R(Khan) v Secretary of State for the Health* [2003] EWCA Civ 1129.

[8] *ibid*, para 9.

Clearly the approach of Ministers toward funding needed to be changed as a result of *Khan*. This case dealt with the criteria that would apply to the funding of inquests and compliance with Article 2 investigative obligations. The case held that the State had a duty to fund the claimant's legal expenses in the context of an Article 2 inquiry.[9]

From an analysis of the combination of cases referred to above and the Lord Chancellor's guidelines, the situation, prior to the 2009 Coroners and Justice Act in relation to public funding is that the minister will pay attention to the nature and seriousness of the allegations and whether any allegations are to be made against public authorities or other agencies of the State as an important indicator as to whether public funding should be available. Furthermore if there are suggestions or maybe suggestions of closely related or multiple and avoidable deaths or systemic failings at the same institutions, suggestion that evidence or the facts may have been inappropriately concealed or interfered with, or if there is any potential for criminality, then all these factors will indicate that public funding maybe available.

The Lord Chancellor's guidance in 2001 states that those making a decision as to public funding must pay attention as to whether there is any alternative means to examine the evidence and involve family in the investigation.

Most importantly will be the particular nature of the inquest and whether the complexities or controversies anticipated within the hearing can be dealt with by the bereaved family unassisted or whether legal assistance is required so that the may fully participate at the hearing.

In the High Court in *R(Catherine Smith)v Assistant Deputy Coroner for Oxfordshire and Secretary of State for Defence*[10] Mr Justice Collins found in the case of an inquest into the death of a soldier who died of heat exhaustion in Iraq, that he had no doubt that 'a failure to provide legal aid for the family in this case would be likely to breach their rights'.

Waiver of Financial Eligibility Limits

13.5 A general rule of any application for public funding at inquests is that applicants must satisfy the financial eligibility limits for legal representation.

In relation to procedures at the Coroners' Courts the Legal Services Commission (or any body assuming their functions) may request the Lord Chancellor to exercise his discretion to waive financial eligibility limits for claimants.[11]

Waiver will be considered if it would not be reasonable to expect the family to bear the full costs of representation at the inquest. Factors such as the background

---

[9] It should be noted that Art 2 does not require equality of Arms between the State and the bereaved family: See the observations of Mr Justice Silver at first instance in the High Court in *Khan*.

[10] *R(Catherine Smith) v Assistant Deputy Coroner for Oxfordshire and Secretary of State for Defence* [2006] EWHC 694 (Admin), para 33.

[11] Community Legal Service (Financial) Regulations 2000 (SI 2000/516), as amended, reg 5C(2).

and circumstances of the case, the seriousness of the allegations that maybe raised, the applicants' assessed disposable income and capital, other financial resources of the family and the estimated costs of providing representation will be taken into account.

Contributions to legal funding may also be waived in whole or in part.[12] Any assessment of a contribution that is deemed payable will depend upon the claimant's disposable income and disposable capital and in practice, in total, will normally quantify as one month's assessed income contribution, and a proportion of the assessed capital contribution.[13]

The Lord Chancellor also has a discretion to waive the upper financial eligibility limits with regard to the provision of legal advice and assistance towards the preparation for an inquest which will include disbursements such as experts' fees.[14]

Applications for Exceptional Funding

13.6 There is no set form for applications for exceptional funding. In practice, reference should be made to all the criteria listed above as to whether funding should be available.

Applications should be made at the earliest possible opportunity and in any event early in the proceedings. There can be a protracted period of time before the application is dealt with. Often this period covers a matter of months whilst the Legal Services Commission, or any other organisation tasked with the duty of assessing the application, considers the issues involved. A delay is particularly exacerbated by the length of time it takes for a Minister to consider any recommendations made by the Legal Services Commission. Again, as a matter of practical experience, the application may sit upon the Minister's desk for weeks if not months before it is dealt with.

Unfortunately, it is not unusual for timely applications only to be granted only within a matter of weeks of an inquest and therefore it is the common experience of practitioners that much work done in preparation for the inquest is performed without any guarantee of remuneration.

Even if authority is granted for public funding, the Legal Services Commission will require a detailed breakdown of the hours required to be authorised for the inquest preparation and appearance.

Practitioners will be expected to prepare documentation for submission to the Legal Services Commission which includes precise hours and minutes that the advocate anticipates he requires to deal with the case. This time assessment will need to be cross-referred to the papers and documentation already in possession

---

[12] See *ibid*, reg 38(8A) and (9).

[13] See the comprehensive opinion provided by Fiona Murphy to the Blake Review at annexe C.

[14] See Community Legal Service (Financial) Regulations 2000, reg 38(8A)(9), as amended on 25 July 2005.

of the advocate with references to the pages and precise times required to consider that information. Furthermore a precise submission as to hours and minutes required for conferences will also be expected by the Legal Services Commission.

This procedure is not unusual for criminal practitioners who perform contracted work within the 'Very High Cost Case' regime and will reflect the precision and detail demanded within that jurisdiction.

Once that detailed assessment is received and agreed by the Legal Services Commission, any further work and preparation required in addition will need a supplementary document, itself outlining a full analysis of the work required, to be approved for funding.

Every aspect of preparation and representation should be covered within this documentation and practitioners should not hesitate to contact the Legal Services Commission immediately should there be any change of requirement as the preparation and representation at the inquest develops. Prior approval is essential.

Amendments by the 2009 Act

13.7 The 2009 Act will amend the Access to Justice Act 1999.

The Access to Justice Act 1999 at paragraph 2 of Schedule 2 states that the Legal Services Commission (or any other organisation subsuming its role) may not fund advocacy, except in the circumstances listed in that paragraph and paragraph 3.

Section 51(2) and (3) of the 2009 Act amends that list by adding that advocacy may be made available in inquests into the death of British Service Personnel who die while on active service and inquests into the death of persons who die while in the custody of the State, or those who die in the course of a police action or arrest (paragraphs 2(5) and 4 of the 1999 Act).

Furthermore the Legal Services Commission will be authorised to fund advocacy for family members to be represented at such inquests subject to the funding criteria in the Funding Code of the Access to Justice Act 1999 being met.[15]

Funding will continue to be subject to the means test.

In the context of active service, the expression covers those engaged in an action or operation against an enemy, an operation outside the British Isles for the protection of life or property or the military occupation of a foreign country or territory.[16]

'Custodial institution' means a prison, young offender institution, a secure training centre or a remand centre. The provisions also include those detained under the Mental Health Act 1983 and those governed under section 156 of the Immigration and Asylum Act 1999.[17]

---

[15] See s 8 of the Access to Justice Act 1999. Legal Services Commission, *The Funding Code* (n 6 above).
[16] Access to Justice Act 1999 Sch 2, para 4(5)(a)–(c).
[17] See Access to Justice Act 1999 Sch 2, para 4(5).

Costs of Representation Recoverable in Subsequent Civil Proceedings

13.8 The costs of attendance at an inquest are capable of being recovered as costs incidental to subsequent civil proceedings.

In *Re Gibson's Settlement Trusts*[18] the Court laid down the principles as to whether costs of work done prior to the commencement of civil proceedings can be recoverable. They are:

- Relevance to an issue:
- Whether attributable to the paying party's conduct.

Costs of attendance at an inquest are capable of being recovered as costs incidental to subsequent civil proceedings.[19]

The matter was revisited in the High Court in the case of Craig Roach.[20] The deceased was a heroin addict and detained in prison. He committed suicide by hanging himself from his bed using his sheets as a ligature. As a result of evidence heard at the inquest the family of the deceased pursued a civil claim for compensation for breaches of Article 2, Article 3 and Article 8 of the Convention. The parents of the deceased entered into a conditional fee agreement to fund the civil claim, as they were not eligible for public funding.

In due course the action against the Home Office was settled for £10,000 plus costs. Ninety per cent of the costs related to the cost of representation of the family at the inquest. The defendant Home Office argued that for the purpose of the civil claim, the claimant should only be entitled to the costs of briefing a local junior barrister and a noting brief at the inquest. At the costs assessment before the costs judge the Court ruled that the deceased's parents were only entitled to recover 50 per cent of the inquest costs from the defendant.

On appeal from this decision the defendant Home Office changed its position and contended that none of the inquest costs were now recoverable.

The High Court ruled that inquest costs were recoverable in subsequent civil proceedings subject to relevance and the general principles of reasonableness and proportionality.[21] The Home Office submission that Parliament had decided that there should be no costs in the Coroner's proceedings and therefore, such costs could not be recovered in subsequent proceedings as that would defeat Parliament's purpose was rejected by the High Court. Mr Justice Davis ruled that Parliament had only decided that Coroners had no power to award the costs of an inquest, not

---

[18] *Re Gibson's Settlement Trusts* [1981] 1 Ch 179.
[19] See *The Bowbelle* [1997] 2 Lloyds Rep 196; *King v Milton Keynes General NHS Trust* 13/5/04 SCCO AGS 04000350.
[20] *Gerald Laurence Roach and Jean Roach v Home Office; Francis Matthews v Home Office* [2009] EWHC 312 (QB)
[21] Davis J.

that costs could not be recovered in subsequent proceedings. Additionally the Court ruled that section 51 of the Supreme Court Act 1981 allows the Court to order the costs of and incidental to civil proceedings, which can include inquest costs.

The High Court specifically rejected the analysis of the costs judge that costs should be divided on a 50-50 basis because in the view of the costs judge, the role of legal representatives at an Article 2 inquest had two purposes, first to assist the coroner and secondly to gather evidence necessary for a civil claim. Mr Justice Davis found that a party's purpose in attending an inquest could not be decisive of the question of whether costs are recoverable.

The High Court in *Roach* also ruled that the manner in which the inquest was funded had no bearing on the recoverability of the costs relating to the inquest and costs of and incidental to the civil proceedings. In *Roach*, the bereaved were provided with exceptional funding from the Legal Services Commission.[22]

Following the appeal in the High Court, *Roach* was referred back to the Senior Costs Judge, who concluded that it was not justified or necessary to have a fee earner sitting behind counsel every day of the inquest. Master Hurst observed: 'Any counsel worth their salt . . . would have a sufficient memory of his cross-examination to be able to make a comprehensive note at the end of the day'. Master Hurst decided that the costs applied for by the claimant were disproportionate, having regard to the level of damages (£10,000) received.

Master Hurst did, however, accept that there would be occasions when counsel were asking questions throughout the whole of the day to have 'somebody sitting behind counsel on such a day'.

It should be noted that Master Hurst was not specific as to who should sit behind counsel and although the precedent of a Senior Costs Judge may be of limited value, it is indicative of the difficulty in claiming properly incurred expenses.

Any advocate requiring the assistance of a legal representative or agent behind them will therefore be required, as a matter of prudence, to outline in writing the reasons why this is necessary, with particular reference to the anticipated time that counsel will literally be asking questions, the complexity of the evidence, the volume of documentation, and the nature of the witnesses.

---

[22] The case of *Roach* was heard alongside the appeal in *Matthews v Home Office*, which was also a death in custody case in which the costs of the inquest were claimed in the subsequent civil proceedings. Here the claimants were not precluded from recovering costs of their representation at the inquest as part of civil proceedings and the fact that the claimants had been publicly funded did not alter that.

14

Military Inquests

14.1 Inquest hearings cover a wide range of factual circumstances which result in death. This will require those participating in the inquest analysing particular details, which relate to such circumstances. For instance death in police custody and in prison will require particular appreciation of police and prison regulations and an understanding of the psychological and psychiatric issues which may impact upon those held in State custody, some of which have been dealt with earlier in this book.[1] But in each of these particular circumstances, the fundamentals of coronial procedure will remain the same, albeit, with a particular emphasis upon legislation and regulation which relate to the death under investigation.

Inquests involving the death of those serving in the Armed Forces have particular and special complexity, not only in relation to the documentation which will be required for a proper and thorough hearing, but also in respect of the procedure and manner in which evidence is heard, sometimes in situations of considerable sensitivity. It is for these reasons and the emergence of the Military inquest within the coronial system, that this book considers that a special treatment of inquests involving the death of those in the Armed Forces is both necessary and timely.

14.2 The full Geneva Conventions of 1949 and their predecessors the Hague Conventions of 1907 attempt to protect, the wounded and sick on land; the wounded, sick and shipwrecked at sea; prisoners of war; and civilians, who are referred to as non-combatants. In accordance with the Geneva Conventions, to be considered soldiers, individuals should be in a chain of command, wear identifiable insignia, carry their weapons openly, and act in accordance with the laws of war.

Soldiers or members of the Armed Forces should be distinguished from mercenaries – people who fight solely for financial gain. This maybe important in the future as a result of the increasing use of private contractors by the US military, in some cases near or in combat zones.

Journalists are considered to be civilians even when 'embedded' within army units, provided that they do not themselves take up arms.[2]

---

[1] See chapter 11 (The Verdict); Suicide (paras 11.23–11.25).
[2] For a comprehensive analysis of the law of war see Michael Byers, *War Law* (Atlantic Books, 2005).

Territorial Jurisdiction

14.3 A soldier who dies on a UK base abroad, dies within the jurisdiction of the United Kingdom within the meaning of Article 1 of the European Convention on Human Rights, which provides that the contracting parties to the Convention

> shall secure to everyone within their jurisdiction the rights and freedoms defined in Section I of [the] Convention.

Such rights and freedoms include Article 2, the Right to Life.

The position is established by *R(Al-Skeini) v Secretary of State for Defence*[3] where the House of Lords observed that section 6(1) of the Human Rights Act 1998 provides that it is unlawful for a public authority to act in a way which is incompatible with a Convention Right. Furthermore the Court was clear that a public authority must be a UK public authority and that the British Army is a public authority within the meaning of section 6 of the 1998 Act.

Furthermore although Article 1 of the Convention is not scheduled to the Human Rights Act 1998, the jurisdictional scope of the Human Rights Act is identical to that of the Convention.[4]

A UK base or hospital overseas is within the jurisdiction of the United Kingdom.[5]

In *Bankovic v Belgium*[6] the applicants and their deceased relatives were citizens of the Federal Republic of Yugoslavia (FRY), which was not a Contracting State. The deceased in that case was killed when NATO bombed the radio and television station (RTS) in Belgrade. The respondent States were Belgium and 16 other Contracting States who were members of NATO. The European Court of Human Rights[7] observed:

> The exercise of 'jurisdiction' therefore involves the assertion or exercise of legal authority, actual or purported, over persons owing some form of Allegiance to that State or who have been brought within the State's control. They [ie the respondent states] also suggest that the term 'jurisdiction' generally entails some form of structured relationship normally existing over a period of time.[8]

In *Al-Skeini*[9] Lord Brown propounded the central principles:

> (1) Article 1 [of the Convention] reflects an 'essentially territorial notion of jurisdiction' (a phrase repeated several times in the Court's judgment [in *Bancovic*]), 'other bases of jurisdiction being exceptional and requiring special justification in the particular circumstances of each case' . . . The Convention operates, subject to article 56, 'in an essentially regional context and notably in the legal space . . . of the contracting states' (ie within the area of the Council of Europe countries).

---

[3] *R(Al-Skeini) v Secretary of State for Defence* [2007] UKHL 26, [2008] 1 AC 153, [2007] 3 WLR 33.
[4] See *Al-Skeini*: Lord Rodger at paras 57–9; Baroness Hale at para 88; and Lord Brown at para 150.
[5] See again *Al-Skeini* and *Bankovic v Belgium* (2001) 11 BHRC 435.
[6] See n 5 above.
[7] *Bankovic v Belgium* (2001) 11 BHRC 435, para 19 and para 36.
[8] See also *Drozd and Janousek v France and Spain* (1992) 14 EHRR 745.
[9] *R(Al-Skeini) v Secretary of State for Defence* [2007] UKHL 26, para 109.

(2) The Court recognises article 1 jurisdiction to avoid 'a vacuum in human rights' protection' when the territory 'would normally be covered by the Convention' . . . (ie in a Council of Europe country) where otherwise (as in Northern Cyprus) the inhabitants 'would have found themselves excluded from the benefits of the Convention safeguards and system which they had previously enjoyed' . . .

(3) The rights and freedoms defined in the Convention cannot be 'divided and tailored' . . .

(4) The circumstances in which the Court has exceptionally recognised the extra-territorial exercise of jurisdiction by a state include . . .

> Where the state 'through the effective control of the relevant territory and its inhabitants abroad as a consequence of military occupation or through the consent, invitation or acquiescence of the government of that country, exercises all or some of the public powers normally to be exercised by [the government of that territory]' . . .

The important case of *Al-Skeini* in the House of Lords held[10] that in appropriate circumstances, the Human Rights Act extended to the acts of UK public authorities such as the Armed Forces undertaken abroad as well as in the United Kingdom.

Al-Skeini observed that establishment of victim status under section 7 of the Human Rights Act required the claimant to show that the deceased was within the jurisdiction of the Convention as stated in Article 1.[11]

In *Smith*, the Court of Appeal concluded jurisdiction of the United Kingdom over the deceased when he was in Iraq, not only when he was at a base or hospital but also when he was not.[12]

Unlike in *Al-Skeini*, the deceased was a member of the British Armed Forces. In *Al-Skeini* the claimants were the relatives of six deceased Iraqis who had been killed by or in the course of action taken by British troops in Iraq. The first five cases of *Al-Skeini* dealt with those who had been shot in separate armed incidents involving British troops. In the sixth case, that of Daoud Mousa, the deceased had been arrested by British troops and taken into custody at a British military base, where he died allegedly as a result of torture carried out at that base.

14.4 The Court in *Smith* concluded that the position of the soldier, Private Smith, could be contrasted with that of the five Iraqis whose claims failed in *Al-Skeini*. In *Al-Skeini* Lord Rodger focused on the importance of the status of the victim and his relationship with the Contracting State and the Court in *Smith* stressed the importance of focus upon the position of the victim, because Article 1 itself expressly provides that the State

> shall secure to everyone within [its] jurisdiction the rights and freedoms defined in . . . [the] Convention.

---

[10] By a majority, Lord Bingham dissenting.

[11] Lord Rodger at paras 55 and 56: Baroness Hale at paras 86, 90 and 91; and Lord Carswell at paras 96–8.

[12] *Secretary of State for Defence v R(Catherine Smith), HM Deputy Coroner for Oxford shire and Equality and Human Rights Commission* [2009] EWCA Civ 441.

The question posited by Lord Rodger in *Al-Skeini* was whether the victim is within the jurisdiction. On this point Lord Rodger said:[13]

> It is important therefore to recognise that, when considering the question of jurisdiction under the Convention, the focus has shifted to the victim or, more precisely, to the link between the victim and the contracting state. For the purposes of the extra-territorial effects of section 6 of the 1998 Act, the key question was whether a public authority – in this case the army in Iraq – was within Parliament's legislative grasp when acting outside the United Kingdom. By contrast, for the purposes of deciding whether the Convention applies outside a territory of the United Kingdom, the key question is whether the deceased were linked to the United Kingdom when they were killed. However reprehensible, however contrary to any common understanding of respect for 'human rights', the alleged conduct of the British forces might have been, it had no legal consequences under the Convention, unless there was that link that the deceased were within the jurisdiction of the United Kingdom at the time. For, only then would the United Kingdom have owed them any obligation in international law to secure their rights under article 2 of the Convention and only then would the relatives have had any rights under the 1998 Act.

In short, if the deceased is linked to the United Kingdom when they were killed, (or some other relevant time), then the deceased is within the jurisdiction of the United Kingdom within the meaning of Article 1 of the Convention.[14]

In *Smith* the Court was clear that even though the deceased died outside a UK base or hospital, there was sufficient link between the deceased and the United Kingdom when he died. The Court of Appeal observed that there was 'a degree of artificiality in saying that soldier is protected so long as he remains in the base or military hospital but that he is not protected as soon as he steps outside'.[15]

Gentle Distinguished[16]

In the case of Gordon Gentle, the claimants were the mothers of two soldiers who were killed while serving with the British Armed Forces in Iraq. The claimants sought judicial review of a refusal by the Government to hold an independent inquiry (as distinct from an inquest) into the question whether the government had taken reasonable steps to be satisfied that the invasion of Iraq was lawful under international law. It was held by the House of Lords, dismissing an appeal from the Court of Appeal, that the implied procedural duty under Article 2 of the Convention to investigate whether a death which has occurred involved a breach of the substantive duty to protect life imposed by Article 2, was parasitic upon the substantive duty and did not exist independently of it. Consequently, the claimants had to

---

[13] *Al-Skeini* [2007] UKHL 26, para 64.
[14] On the facts of *Al-Skeini* it was only Daoud Mousa who had the necessary link.
[15] *R(Smith) v Oxfordshire Assistant Deputy Coroner* [2009] EWCA Civ 441.
[16] *R(Gentle) v Prime Minister* [2008] UKHL 20, [2008] 1 AC 1356; see in particular para 8 and the judgment of Lord Bingham.

show at least an arguable case that the substantive duty arose on the facts of the case. In *Gentle*, the Court held that they could not do so.

The House of Lords in *Gentle* came to their conclusion because, as Lord Bingham said,[17] there was no warrant for reading Article 2 as a generalised provision protective of life, irrespective of any specific death or threat. The right and duty alleged by the claimants did not depend upon their sons' deaths. If they existed, they would have arisen before either was killed and would have existed even if they had survived the conflict. This was, his Lordship reasoned, because the case against the Government arose from an alleged failure to take reasonable steps before the deceased left England. Central to this conclusion was that the claimants in *Gentle* conceded that they were not seeking an inquiry into the question whether the invasion of Iraq was lawful or unlawful and, moreover, that the question would indeed be outside the remit of an inquiry under Article 2.[18]

Lord Hoffmann also observed[19] that there was no independent duty to use reasonable care to ascertain whether war would be contrary to the United Nations Charter or not. The House of Lords considered that it was too simplistic to suggest that any lack of diligence in investigating the legality of the war could be a relevant cause of death. As Baroness Hale put it in *Gentle*,[20] the point of taking reasonable care is to discover what you can and cannot do, and if you do not owe a duty to individual soldiers not to send them off to fight in an unlawful war, it makes no difference whether or not you take reasonable care to discover whether or not it was unlawful. You could have them sent anyway. She concluded[21] that it is not a breach of the substantive duty under Article 2 to send troops to fight in an unlawful war; hence the duty to investigate does not arise.

14.5 The critical observation of Lord Bingham which caused the Court in *Smith* some concern appears in paragraph 8 of his judgment in *Gentle*. Here he stated that it maybe significant that Article 2 has never been held to apply to a process of deciding on the lawfulness of a resort to arms, despite the number of occasions on which Member States have made that decision over the past half century and despite the fact such a decision almost inevitably exposes military personnel to the risk of fatalities. Lord Bingham then gave three main reasons for that view. It was his third reason that caused further analysis in *Smith*. It demands citation:

> (3) The obligation of member states under article 1 of the Convention is to secure 'to everyone within their jurisdiction' the rights and freedoms of the Convention. Subject to limited exceptions and specific extensions, the application of the Convention is territorial: The rights and freedoms are ordinarily to be secured to those within the borders of the state and not outside. Here, the deaths of Fusilier Gentle and Trooper Clarke occurred in

[17] *ibid*, para 7.
[18] *ibid*, Lord Bingham at para 2, Lord Hoffmann at para 13, Lord Hope at para 22, Lord Rodger at paras 34–9, Baroness Hale at paras 56–8, Lord Carswell at paras 63–4, Lord Brown at para 69 and Lord Mance at paras 72–3.
[19] *ibid*, para 16.
[20] *ibid*, para 59.
[21] *ibid*, para 60.

Iraq and although they were subject to the authority of the respondents they were clearly not within the jurisdiction of the UK as that expression in the Convention has been interpreted . . . The appellants seek to overcome that problem in reliance on authorities such as *Soering v United Kingdom* (1989) 11 EHRR 439, by stressing that their complaint relates to the decision-making process (or lack of it) which occurred here, even though the ill-effects were felt abroad. There is, I think, an obvious distinction between the present case and *Soering*, and such later cases as *Chahal v United Kingdom* (1996) 23 EHRR 413 and *D v United Kingdom* (1997) 24 EHRR 423, in each of which, action relating to an individual in the UK was likely to have an immediate and direct impact on that individual elsewhere. But I think there is a more fundamental objection: that the appellants' argument, necessary to meet the objection of extra-territoriality, highlights the remoteness of their complaints from the purview of article 2.

The Court of Appeal in *Smith* made clear distinction between the case before them and *Gentle*.[22]

In *Gentle* Lord Bingham was not considering any distinction between the position of the alleged victims in *Al-Skeini* and Private Smith. None of the deceased relatives of the first five claimants in *Al-Skeini* were even arguably within the jurisdiction of the United Kingdom. The claimants' argument had been that jurisdiction was conferred by the fact that their relatives were killed by British troops, which the House of Lords held was not sustainable in the light of *Bancovic*.[23] The sixth claimant's relative, Mousa, was only within the jurisdiction because he was allegedly mistreated whilst within a British detention facility. In short, the House of Lords and in particular Lord Bingham was not considering the position of a victim such as Private Smith.

The Court in *Smith* concluded:[24]

In these circumstances we do not think that Lord Bingham intended to decide the issue which arises in this appeal as part of the *ratio* of his decision. Moreover, we are of the opinion that a consideration of the other speeches leads to the same conclusion. Lord Hoffmann set out his own reasoning which did not refer to the jurisdiction question. He then said at [16] that for those reasons he would dismiss the appeal and added that he also agreed with the reasons given by Lord Bingham.

It follows through all this that the Court in *Smith* did not feel that they were bound by the decision in *Gentle*, which would hold that Private Smith was outside the jurisdiction.[25]

Catherine Smith in the Supreme Court

14.6 The case finally came before the Supreme Court which overturned the decision of the courts below that the Human Rights Act applied to British troops

---

[22] See *Smith* [2009] EWCA Civ 441, para 48.
[23] *Gentle* [2008] UKHL 20.
[24] *Smith* [2009] EWCA Civ 441, para 54.
[25] *ibid*, para 60.

serving abroad but outside of British bases. Essentially this means that whilst the Ministry of Defence has a legal obligation to properly safeguard the life and wellbeing of members of the Armed Forces on British bases, they have no such obligation outside of the base.[26]

The Supreme Court held that British soldiers on active service abroad were not within the jurisdiction of the United Kingdom within the meaning of Article 1 of the Human Rights Convention and were accordingly not protected by the Convention Rights scheduled to the Human Rights Act 1998. The Supreme Court followed the guidance in *Bankovic v Belgium*[27] which was applied by the majority of the Houses of Lords in *Al-Skeini*[28] for the principle that Article 1 of the Convention reflected the territorial concept of jurisdiction, other bases being exceptional and requiring special justification.[29]

Exceptional circumstances which were contemplated in *Bankovic* will depend upon the exercise by one State abroad of State power and authority over individuals, particularly nationals of that State by consent, invitation or acquiescence of the other foreign State.[30]

The Supreme Court also ruled in *Catherine Smith* that an Article 2 inquest was not automatically required whenever a member of the Armed Forces dies on active service. Lord Phillips specifically stated that the investigative obligation only arose where there was ground for suspicion that the State might have breached a substantive obligation under Article 2. As such, the death of a soldier on active service did not, of itself, raise a presumption of such a breach and therefore did not give rise automatically to an obligation to hold an investigation which complied with Article 2. In the particular facts of *Catherine Smith*, the Supreme Court nevertheless held that there was evidence before the Coroner in the first inquest which raised the possibility of systemic failure by the Military Authorities to protect soldiers from the risk posed by the extreme temperatures in which they had to serve. The Supreme Court ruled that it was therefore an arguable breach of a substantive obligation under Article 2 that was revealed at that inquest which was sufficient to trigger the need for a verdict which complied with the requirements of that Article.

In coming to this judgment the Supreme Court overturned both the decisions in the High Court and the Court of Appeal and it is anticipated that the jurisdictional decision will ultimately be decided in Strasbourg, although not as a result of *Smith* which is unlikely to be taken to Europe, but as part of a ruling relating to

---

[26] *R (on the application of Smith) (FC) (Respondent) v Secretary of State for Defence (Appellant) and another* [2010] UKSC 29.

[27] (2001) 11 BHRC 435.

[28] [2008] AC 153.

[29] *R (on the application of Gentle) v Prime Minister* [2008] UKHL 20, [2008] 1 AC 1356 and *Al-Saadoon v UK* (Admissibility) [2009] EWCA Civ 7 ECHR considered.

[30] Per Lord Mance. (dissenting) his Lordship stated that in circumstances where the United Kingdom was an occupying power recognised as such under International law, there was an irresistible case for treating its jurisdiction over its Armed Forces as extending to soldiers serving in Iraq for the purposes of Article 1. He added that to distinguish fundamentally between the existence of protective duties on the part of the UK to its soldiers at home and abroad appeared as unrealistic under the Convention as it was at common law.

the deaths of various Iraqi civilians, which will be considered in due course in Strasbourg.[31]

The 'Custody Principles' and Members of the Armed Forces

14.7 The Court of Appeal in *Smith* concluded that the general custody principles do apply to serving soldiers. Furthermore, on the basis of Strasbourg jurisprudence, there is no distinction between a regular soldier who is not a conscript and a member of the Territorial Army when in active service. 'When in active service both regular soldiers and members of the Territorial Army are subject to army orders, instructions and discipline in the same way'. There is no distinction between them.[32]

The Court went on:[33]

> The question is therefore whether the principles applied to active service in Iraq. We conclude that they do. They are under the control of and subject to army discipline. They must do what the army requires them to do. If the army sends them out into the desert they must go. In this respect they are in the same position as a conscript. Once they have signed up for a particular period they can no more disobey an order than a conscript can. The army owes them the same duty of care at common law. We recognise that they may not be quite as vulnerable as conscripts but they may well be vulnerable in much the same way, both in stressful situations caused by conflict and in stressful situations caused, as in Private Smith's case, by extreme heat. We see no reason why they should not have the same protection as is afforded by article 2 by a conscript.

An analysis of the investigation in *Takoushis*,[34] which involved a death in hospital, is instructive. There it was stated[35] that where an individual dies in hospital, arguably as a result of medical negligence by a National Health Service institution, the State must have a system which provides for the practical and effective investigation of the facts and for the determination of civil liability. As with deaths in custody questions will arise as to the system as a whole including both any investigation initiated by the State and the possibility of civil and criminal proceedings and of a disciplinary process, satisfying the requirements of Article 2.[36]

---

[31] The decision taken in the Supreme Court was by a 6-3 majority with Lady Hale, Lord Mance and Lord Kerr dissenting. Lord Mance observed that the United Kingdom under International law had 'an almost absolute power of the safety of its forces.' The European Commission have also referred to members of the Armed Forces as 'citizens in uniform'. The Supreme Court judgment seems to go against these observations.

[32] *ibid*, para 104.

[33] *ibid*, para 105.

[34] *R (on the application of Takoushis) v HM Coroner for Inner North London* [2005] EWCA Civ 1440.

[35] *ibid*, paras 105–7.

[36] It is important to stress that the custody principles were rejected on the ground that Takoushis would have been detained under the Mental Health Act 1983 s 3 if the hospital had been made aware that he was about to leave. The Court expressed the opinion that there was an important difference between those who are detained and those who, like Takoushis, were not.

In the case of *R(JL) v Secretary of State for Justice*[37] Lord Rodger noted[38] that Convention jurisprudence draws a distinction between prisoners and individuals who are at liberty.

The essential basis for this is that 'persons in custody are in a vulnerable position'.[39]

Lord Rodger in *JL*[40] ruled that Article 2 goes further than requiring the prison authorities not to harm those in custody. In particular, they must proceed on the footing that prisoners are a class who present a particular risk of suicide. For this reason the prison authorities must take systemic measures and precautions to diminish the opportunities for prisoners to harm themselves, without infringing their personal autonomy. Lord Rodger noted[41] that the authorities are also under an 'operational' obligation in well-defined circumstances, namely where there is a real and immediate risk that the prisoner will commit suicide, to take reasonable steps to prevent it.[42]

JL is further authority for the proposition that whenever a prisoner kills himself, it is at least possible that the prison authorities, who are responsible for the prisoner, have failed, either in their obligation to take general measures to diminish the opportunities for prisoners to harm themselves, or in their operational obligation to try to prevent the particular prisoner from committing suicide. Lord Rodger went on:[43]

> Given the closed nature of the prison world, without an independent investigation you might never know. So there must be an investigation of that kind to find out whether something did indeed go wrong. In this respect a suicide is like any other violent death in custody. In affirming the need for an effective form of investigation in a case involving the suicide of a man in police custody, the European Court held that such an investigation should be held 'when a resort to force has resulted in a person's death'.[44]

In such circumstances an Article 2 investigation is appropriate.[45]

---

[37] *R(JL) v Secretary of State for Justice* [2008] UKHL 68, [2008] 3 WLR 1325.

[38] *ibid*, paras 54–6.

[39] See *Edwards v United Kingdom* (2002) 35 EHRR 487 (a case of the killing of a prisoner by his cellmate.)

[40] *R(JL) v Secretary of State for Justice* [2008] UKHL 68, para 55.

[41] *ibid*, para 57.

[42] See *Osman v United Kingdom* (1998) 23 EHRR 245 and *Van Colle v Chief Constable of the Hertfordshire Police* [2008] UKHL 50, [2008] 3 WLR 593.

[43] *R(L) v Secretary of State for Justice* [2008] UKHL 68, para 59.

[44] See *Akdogau v Turkey (Application No 46747/99)* [2005] ECHR 932, para 52.

[45] In *Savage v South Essex Partnership NHS Foundation Trust* [2008] UKHL 74, [2009] 2 WLR 115 the House of Lords considered a case in which the allegation was that the death of a mental patient who was detained under the Mental Health Act 1983 was caused by a breach of the operational obligation of the UK under Article 2 of the Convention. The House of Lords held that the questions for decision at a trial were whether there was a real and immediate risk that Savage would commit suicide and, if so, whether all reasonable steps were taken to prevent it. See also a short analysis of this case in the (2010) 160 *New Law Journal* 655, following the award of damages in compensation in [2010] EWHC 865 (QB).

Suicide in the Armed Forces

14.8 It flows from the above, that many of the principles relating to suicide of individuals in State custody or in, for example, NHS hospitals, apply to those in military service.

Although suicide has not been a crime since 1961, a high standard of proof is required to reach the conclusion of suicide. It is the same standard of proof required to reach a conclusion of unlawful killing.

Like unlawful killing, suicide must never be presumed, and a verdict of suicide can only be reached where there is evidence of suicidal intent or any other reasonable possibility has been excluded.[46] The difficulty of returning a suicide verdict, even in the face of what seems to be the most compelling evidence, is demonstrated by a brief analysis of the facts in *R v Essex Coroner, ex parte Hopper*.[47] In this case a young man of 19 years of age, with no apparent problems or concerns, was found dead at his home as a result of gunshot wounds inflicted by a weapon in close proximity to his head whilst his family were away on holiday. The coroner, sitting without a jury, returned a verdict that the deceased had taken his own life (suicide) but the verdict was quashed on appeal because, as Mr Justice Pill (as he then was) put it,

> [t]he facts and circumstances in this case did not, in my judgment, point irresistibly to the existence to a suicidal intent. The possibility that the discharge of the gun was accidental could not be excluded as a reasonable possibility.

In the context of deaths during military service, particular care is required, especially when one takes into account the close proximity of any deceased to weaponry.

In his report into the deaths of four young soldiers at Deepcut Barracks, Nicholas Blake QC[48] considered that the four deceased were in a special category of cases imposing particular investigative obligations.

The Deepcut Review was particularly conscious of the young ages of the deceased (who were either under 18 years of age or had just reached their 18th birthday) and the fact that they were supplied with lethal weapons. In *Kilinc v Turkey*[49] a conscript who died from gunshot wounds while assigned to guard duty was in such a position after doubts had been raised as to his fitness to do so. The European Court of Human Rights found Turkey in violation of obligations to take all reasonable steps to protect the life of the trainee under Article 2 of the Convention. The Court was required to establish whether the military knew, or ought to have known, that there was a real and immediate risk to the life of the individual concerned and, if so, whether the

---

[46] *R v City of London Coroner Ex Parte Barber* [1975] 1 WLR 1310.
[47] *R v Essex Coroner, ex parte Hopper*, unreported, 13 May 1988 (Divisional Court).
[48] See *A Review of the Circumstances Surrounding the Deaths of Four Soldiers at Princess Royal Barracks, Deepcut Between 1995 and 2002* (Blake Review); HC 795, para 2.66.
[49] *Kilinc v Turkey* (Application No 40145/98) ECtHR, 7 June 2005 (unreported).

authorities had done everything in their power to prevent that risk materialising.[50] The European Court observed that the Commandant had seen no problem in sending the deceased back to his garrison, despite the medical examination previously ordered not having taken place and furthermore the Commandant had given the deceased a weapon and assigned him to guard duty. In doing so it was held that the Commandant had failed to appreciate that the deceased had still not undergone any decisive diagnosis and there was therefore no reason to believe that the deceased would be able to handle a solitary mission or that he would not take advantage of such a situation to commit suicide.[51]

The European Court considered that the only explanation for this outcome was the absence in Turkish legislation of clear provisions concerning those whose fitness for military service was in doubt, or, more importantly, the duties and responsibilities of their superiors towards those with mental illness such as the deceased.[52]

Therefore, in the view of the European Court, the regulatory framework contained weaknesses as regards to procedure to establish and monitor the psychiatric ability of the deceased before and after his conscription. Moreover, that situation created uncertainty regarding the nature of activities that could be assigned to him. In this way, it played a decisive role in the causation of the suicide, as the authorities had not done everything in their power to protect the deceased from the danger he posed to himself, which was as well known as it was avoidable.[53]

14.9 The Deepcut Review, controversially, concluded on the balance of probabilities, that the deaths of three of the young soldiers, Benton, James and Gray were self-inflicted.[54]

A short analysis of the evidence in relation to these three soldiers provides guidance as to how a court may interpret behavioural patterns of deceased, particularly those in military service who die in circumstances where suicide becomes a question within the proceedings.

According to the Deepcut Review, Sean Benton was known to have become emotionally distressed and had engaged in at least two attempts of self-harm in the months before he died. The squadron had previously taken measures to deny Private Benton access to a weapon on guard duty. The Review considered that the opportunity for self-harm was created when the deceased acquired a weapon from another trainee on false pretences and took the chance to be by himself.

In the case of Cheryl James, the deceased was not known by anybody in authority in the army to have been unhappy or to have had a predisposition to self-harm. There was no evidence of bullying being a factor in her death. It was observed by Blake QC that there were 'unresolved complications in her private life, at a time when she may have been vulnerable and lacking self-esteem'.[55]

---

[50] *ibid*, para 43.
[51] *ibid*, para 54.
[52] *ibid*, para 55.
[53] *ibid*, para 56.
[54] See Blake Review (above n 42), para 12.2.
[55] *ibid*, para 12.8.

In the case of Geoff Gray, there was nothing in his past to suggest to anyone that he posed a risk of self-harm or that he might misuse his weapon. There was nothing in his conduct or treatment by the army to suggest he was a risk of self-harm. Furthermore there was no reason to believe bullying was a factor in his death.

In the cases of Cheryl James and Geoff Gray the Review found frequent armed guard duties at remote locations unsupervised, afforded them the opportunity to self-harm.[56]

In the case of James Collinson, evidence was given at his inquest that he had informed soldiers of his intention to self-harm if he had access to a weapon, although there was no clear evidence of any motive to self-harm. The jury returned an open verdict in his case on 10 March 2006. There was further evidence during the course of Collinson's inquest that he was happy and content in the hours shortly before his death.

In relation to all four young soldiers the Blake Review considered that low morale was an issue in relation to the deaths. According to evidence presented to the Review[57] reasons for low morale included: the quality of the accommodation blocks and particularly the sanitary and washing facilities there; the delicate balance between effective security denying unauthorised access to the dormitories and the ability of responsible adults to lead a private life; the limited range of recreational activities provided on site; and the practical ability to leave the barracks in off-duty hours. The extended configuration of the camp and the additional demands it imposed for guard duty were also another issue which the Review considered attributed to the low morale of those who were forced to live and train there.

In addition to the physical environment there was a psychological element, referred to in the Review[58] described as the indeterminate and unpredictable length of training at Deepcut.

All these matters, coupled with the propensity for unsupervised access to weapons, and a regime of bullying, referred to by various witnesses, led to a cocktail of circumstances at the barracks which caused young people, many under the age of 18, to be at risk.

Although a significant amount of these factual circumstances can equally apply to detainees in custody or in other State institutions, the combination of all these risks in one environment is unique to the military.

As such the Deepcut Review presented a series of conclusions and recommendations at Chapter 12 of the document.[59] These include, a review of the training environment for those under 18, a screening of recruits to reveal any medical or social background which may put them at risk in a training or military environment and strict guidance, training and requirements of those tasked to supervise potentially

---

[56] *ibid*, para 12.13.
[57] *ibid*, para 12.15.
[58] *ibid*, para 12.16.
[59] *ibid*, ch 12 (pp 379 et seq).

vulnerable recruits, including at recommendation 18,[60] 'failure to report any sign of abuse of power should itself be a matter for disciplinary sanction'.

14.10 A case which takes its facts from a non-military perspective, provides further guidance as to how the risk of self-harm should be dealt with in the military context.

Savage v South Essex Partnership NHS Foundation Trust[61] established that there were two stages in defining the duty of the State under Article 2 to take steps to prevent persons killing themselves, in this case in the context of a detained patient in a mental hospital. The first was to decide whether the defendant had the requisite knowledge, actual or constructive, of a 'real and immediate risk to life' from self-harm. The second was whether the defendant failed to do all that could reasonably been expected of it to avoid or prevent that risk. The test depended not only on what the relevant authority had known but also what it ought to have known. The relevant knowledge was what they had known or ought to have known at the time, and the court should warn itself against the dangers of hindsight. The authorities were clear that there was a high threshold to be crossed before the test was satisfied. The threshold that any person would have to surmount was higher than the test in clinical negligence cases in domestic law. Once the test was triggered by the requisite knowledge on the part of the local authority, and consideration was focused on whether they had done all that could have reasonably been expected of them, then the question could only be answered in the light of all the circumstances of the particular case. At the second stage, the test for causation was not the English 'but for' test, but a looser one: The applicant did not have to show that had the trust acted appropriately there would probably have been no death, but merely that she had 'lost a substantial chance of that'.

Disclosure

The Board of Inquiry

14.11 A Board of Inquiry is, where practicable, to be composed of service personnel or a majority of service personnel, particularly where the report or opinions on questions of fact may lead to disciplinary action against, or financial consequences for, persons subject to military law.[62]

The Board of Inquiry process was established in the Army Act 1955. It is a wholly internal and domestic investigation by the Armed Forces into the death of personnel. One of the overriding complaints by bereaved families is that they have been, on the whole, excluded from these hearings and only received copies of the

---

[60] *ibid,* ch 12 (p 396).

[61] *Savage v South Essex Partnership NHS Foundation Trust* [2010] EWHC 865 (QB), [2010] All ER (D) 196 (April).

[62] See Queen's Regulations for the Army 1975, Chapter 5, Annexe A, paras 35–6.

Board of Inquiry's conclusions sometime after that inquiry had happened and then only in an edited state.

Although the exclusion of families from Board of Inquiry hearings continues, exceptionally families of the deceased are allowed access to some or part of the hearings and it is important for the families to press their claims to be in attendance from the outset.

Annexe A to Chapter 5 of the Queen's Regulations for the Army (the annexe) sets out the administrative instructions in respect of Boards of Inquiry. The Board of Inquiry remit is:

> To address itself in particular to the following and, if possible, to adduce and record evidence thereon:
>
> - whether any lack of training or supervision, which should be rectified, was a contributory factor;
> - whether the deceased was on authorised leave of absence at the time death occurred;
> - the medical cause of death as shown in the death certificate or as given in evidence;
> - the circumstance which was instrumental in bringing about the death, eg a traffic accident, drowning or a fire; and
> - whether the death was linked to any procedural or equipment faults or any other military failings that may require rectification to avoid a recurrence.

The Board of Inquiry report must be made available to the next of kin on request, subject to the minimum security and/or disclosure requirements.[63] Despite this, neither the public nor family members are automatically permitted to be present at the inquiry proceedings, and there is no provision for consultation with regards to the terms of reference. Furthermore, the record of the proceedings remains confidential, although the final report is to be made available on request. Board of Inquiry reports and any subsequent reports, and any subsequent comments by the Authority or his Superior Commander are not explicitly to attribute blame or negligence.[64]

Similarly with regard to Board of Inquiry recommendations, an inquiry is to record the steps which have been taken or should be undertaken to prevent a recurrence of the matter and to make any recommendations it thinks fit to this end, but again is to refrain absolutely from making recommendations regarding disciplinary action.[65]

In practice the attitude of the Board of Inquiry is dictated by the approach of its President. It is also informed by the level of controversy and public interest in the events leading to the deaths of personnel.

It is vital that as much information as possibleis obtained from the Board of Inquiry by parties to any inquest involving the death of military personnel. It will reveal, at least as a starting point for an inquest's investigation, areas which the Board of Inquiry have found significant in relation to the deaths of personnel.

---

[63] *ibid*, para 15(a) of the Annexe.
[64] *ibid*, para 15(a)(5) of the Annexe.
[65] *ibid*, para 64 of the Annexe.

Indeed those who have given evidence at the Board of Inquiry will also, conceivably, be giving evidence at the inquest and the document is a highly valuable tool for use in asking further probing questions of participants (although, strictly, cross-examination is not permitted in style).

Again as a matter of practice, the President of the Board of Inquiry will sit in the Coroner's Court throughout the inquest, and take a leading role in assisting the coroner and all parties concerned with the evidence and procedure that will be heard. Often the President of the Board of Inquiry will sit next to counsel representing the Ministry of Defence and effectively act as an instructing solicitor.

The role of the President in the inquest cannot be underestimated and many coroners rely heavily upon their interpretation of events. It will not be unusual, in a military inquest, where there is a point of evidence which is either contradictory, unclear or controversial, for the coroner to defer to the view of the President of the Board of Inquiry. Given this practical reality, advocates should be aware and be prepared to deal with any situation in an inquest where they consider that the views of the President of the Board of Inquiry are having too much emphasis placed upon them by the coroner.

It is right that it be observed that under probing questions in an inquest, the President can be shown to be not as reliable as the military authorities may have hoped for, and should not be granted status at an inquest which can position him more as another Coroner's Officer than an interested party. It is equally fair and appropriate to state that as a matter of style, members of the Armed Forces and particularly senior members of the Armed Forces, whether they have served on the Board of Inquiry or are giving evidence for the first time at the inquest, require particularly careful handling when being questioned. Many of these individuals are not used to being challenged, however courteously, and show a fierce loyalty to the Service they represent. The art of careful and prepared questioning, not only based upon a clear and precise understanding of the Board of Inquiry, but also other documentation, reports and research into pertinent issues, will be required of the advocate to get the best out of these witnesses.

Nicholas Blake QC in the Deepcut Review was critical of the approach of the Boards of Inquiry to bereaved families. He observed[66] that the systemic issues to be addressed by the Board of Inquiry are of concern to bereaved families and 'there seems little value or purpose in excluding the bereaved from the process'. Blake goes on to emphasise that in his view the quality and value of the Board of Inquiry would be significantly enhanced by the effective participation of the families.

What it is vital to understand about the Board of Inquiry is that there is little evidence of independent oversight of the process and they should not be treated necessarily, as impartial expert reports.

---

[66] Blake Review (above n 42) para 10.7.

Other Relevant Disclosure

14.12 The testing of evidence in inquests involving the deaths of members of the Armed Forces is often founded upon the provision of information and reports in respect of procedure, practice or research. They will include:

- Previous and historic research reports commissioned by the Ministry of Defence and or the Armed Forces or their agents.
- Internal Armed Forces documentation relating to reports by military personnel as to the functioning of equipment that they are provided with. There is, as with any branch of the Armed Forces an internal procedure as to the reporting of any faults or observations in relation to equipment. Often the observations are candid and provide an insight into the efficiency and safety of such equipment.
- Internal Forces correspondence, which may provide a paper trail as to maintenance and monitoring of equipment and procedure.
- Correspondence and documentation between the Armed Forces and the Ministry of Defence or other government departments, which may illuminate issues not only relating to maintenance and safety but also the procurement of equipment.
- Any reports or documentation created by the Coroner's Officer who may have had further meetings or interviews with Armed Forces personnel in preparation for the inquest. As has been laid out earlier in this book, the role of the Coroner's Officer can be wide ranging and one of the functions is to take statements or clarify matters with witnesses in advance of an inquest on the instruction of the coroner. This is not habitually reported to parties, but in any inquest, and particularly military inquests, it is prudent for practitioners to enquire of the coroner as to whether any such meetings have taken place and if so seek disclosure of documentation generated as a result of those meetings.
- There may be police reports that have been made as a result of the fatality. This will be particularly appropriate in the case of deaths within the United Kingdom upon premises owned, occupied or under control of the Ministry of Defence. In such circumstances the civilian police will have primacy in deciding whether a Board of Inquiry can continue and whether it should be adjourned to avoid impeding or tainting the police investigation. Furthermore paragraph 4.2 of the Protocol published by the Ministry of Defence in September 2005 states that the police will retain primacy throughout, including, in respect of the presentation of case papers to the coroner.[67]
- Any internal Ministry of Defence or Armed Forces Protocols in relation to practice, procedure, maintenance and safety upon premises owned, occupied or under control of the Ministry of Defence.

---

[67] This can cause complex issues of conflict of interest when the police who have investigated and who have the primary responsibility to present case papers to the coroner, are also potentially interested parties and to be criticised as a result of their investigation. (As was the case in the inquest into the death of James Collinson, a trainee soldier who died at Deepcut Barracks.)

- Transcripts and recordings of communications made by radio or in other electronic forms at or around about the time of the incident under investigation.
- Previous reports or notifications of events in and around (often weeks before) the incident under investigation, which may inform the court as to what steps were or should have been taken to reduce risks which caused the death or deaths being considered at the instant inquest.
- In relation to deaths which involve the coalition of Armed Forces for instance in Iraq or Afghanistan, practitioners should seek disclosure of evidence, often witness statements made by United States Armed Forces personnel. As a matter of practice this evidence will be difficult to obtain and the United States are under no obligation to assist in providing this evidence to Coroners' Courts. In real terms, experience reveals that the United Kingdom Armed Forces are less reticent in disclosing information and assisting the United States and it is often a point of considerable frustration to coroners in the United Kingdom that the United States presents an uncooperative and at times obstructive attitude to the disclosure of evidence which may assist a coroner and provide information to bereaved families as to how the deceased lost their life.
- Photographs and filmed material will also be in existence. The photographs can depict the scene of the fatalities taken contemporaneously or provide reconstructions of what may have caused the fatalities.
- Disciplinary records of witnesses.
- Information and evidence relating to personnel who were subject to the Board of Inquiry investigation. Although the Board of Inquiry does not address itself specifically to disciplinary matters, often personnel have received demotion or other disciplinary action after the Board of Inquiry and prior to the inquest. This information should be sought for disclosure.
- Disclosure of reports and documentation generated by any Special Investigations Branch of the Royal Military Police.
- Any statements provided to the Board of Inquiry, the Special Investigations Branch of the Military Police or any law enforcement authority.
- Any medical reports or notes which maybe in existence and particularly those provided to the Board of Inquiry.[68]

Redactions

14.13 Even if documents and materials are supplied by the Ministry of Defence or other government agencies in military inquests, they are often heavily redacted. As a matter of practice the initial redactions are both comprehensive and extensive, and any practitioner receiving such documentation should not accept them as a final document.

---

[68] In *R(Catherine Smith) v Assistant Deputy Coroner for Oxfordshire and Secretary of State for Defence* in the High Court [2006] EWHC 694 (Admin), para 34, Collins J observed that some of the medical notes had gone missing and expressed profound concerned that this had occurred.

It follows that unless the party has seen what the redaction initially was, which somewhat undermines the purpose of the redaction, it is difficult to be specific as to whether any objection can be taken. To some degree the situation, in practice, can be remedied in two ways. First, the coroner should be asked to consider any unredacted documents and to assess whether they are properly redacted in accordance with the law. Secondly, a procedure commonly used in military inquests which involves redactions is that parties, whether they be legal practitioners or unrepresented interested parties, are allowed to look at the less sensitive, unredacted documentation in strict conditions, often a locked room with the Coroner's Officer invigilating, much the way as an invigilator would in an exam room. This, of course, only caters for redactions which are not in the most serious category of purported national security, but at least gives the parties an opportunity to consider and challenge the redactions. This is often important for bereaved families, who require the hearing to be as public as possible and the full information to be within the public domain.

14.14 National security does not mean avoiding political embarrassment, and as a matter of practice those seeking redactions often exclude passages which are more akin to avoiding political loss of face than national security. It is important to understand precisely what national security is. Substantially it is an issue for the court, but practice in the field dictates that if representations are made to the Ministry of Defence or government departments by parties that certain material should be unredacted on the basis that it is not national security, then often concessions are immediately forthcoming from the government which leads to the assumption that when practitioners are faced with issues of redaction on the basis of national security they should challenge the basis of the withholding of information.

When national security is raised there will be a certificate of the Secretary of State in relation to the matter. The coroner is not obliged to accept what is contained within it although he will inevitably be influenced by it.

14.15 Mr Justice Collins in the High Court in *Smith*[69] was particularly critical of the redaction process in military inquests. The inquest into the death of Private Smith as a result of heat-stroke in Iraq is a particular example of inadequate disclosure and overzealous redaction, which often is a feature of military inquests.

Following the death of Private Smith the Board of Inquiry was convened. There was also an investigation by the Special Investigations branch of the Royal Military Police but these reports were not disclosed to the deceased's family. The Board of Inquiry undertook a supplementary report following the conclusion of the first inquiry. That supplementary report was the only one provided to the coroner and it was not until the last day of the inquest that the existence of the first report was made known when the President of the Board of Inquiry gave evidence confirming its existence. Despite this, during the inquest the parties and the coroner had been assured that the entire report had been produced.

[69] *ibid.*

Furthermore the medical notes of the deceased which covered a crucial part of the period in Iraq had been lost or, as Mr Justice Collins put it in the High Court, 'certainly they have not been produced'.

As to redactions in the Smith inquest the Ministry of Defence insisted that there be redaction of parts of the various reports and statements, and the coroner had not been prepared to disclose anything further when the applicant objected to the Ministry of Defence's stance.

Furthermore the deceased's family had no advance disclosure of statements of witnesses to be called. This is, again, a particular feature of military inquests when often as a result of operational commitments, members of the Armed Forces cannot be precise as to when they will be giving evidence.

Mr Justice Collins refers at para 34 of his judgment to the Ministry of Defence's practice in relation to disclosure of the Board of Inquiry and Special Investigation Branch reports. The Ministry of Defence rely on the fact that the Board of Inquiry is a fact-finding exercise and does not seek to proportion blame. Mr Justice Collins went on:

> This, it is said helps to ensure that 'people are prepared to provide complete and open statements'. It is suggested that if they were aware that the statements and reports could be disclosed to interested parties, such as families of the deceased, there might not be the same willingness to provide such statements. Since most witnesses will be serving members of the armed forces, I find that suggestion unpersuasive. It is also said that the MOD's obligations under the Data Protection Act 1998 and at common law mean that the identity of the witnesses should be protected and so not disclosed.
>
> All statements and documents produced routinely redact the names of any person. This makes it very difficult and sometimes impossible for interested parties to make preparations to deal with the evidence of a particular witness or to understand how that witness fits into the whole picture. This redaction is taken to absurd lengths: thus the names have been redacted from correspondence which had been sent to the family or their representatives. In addition, all material which is said to be irrelevant is also redacted.
>
> While I gather that the full material is sent to the coroner together with redacted versions, it seems to me that there is no justification for the practice adopted. Naturally, any specific claim, that a witness's identity should not be disclosed, because, for example, he or she might be put at risk of harm or because there was a particular request and need for confidentiality, can be made and should be considered by the coroner. Equally, any claim that material should not be disclosed on national security grounds must be considered by the coroner. His is an inquisitorial, not an adversarial process. He must have all of the information, but he must, bear in mind the requirements of the procedural obligation which include enabling the family to play a proper and effective part in the process.[70]

Generally, there must be a presumption in favour of as much disclosure as possible.[71]

---

[70] *ibid*, paras 34–6.

[71] See *R(Bentley) v HM Coroner for Avon* (2001) EWHC (Admin) 170; 74 BMCRI (Sullivan J): See also *R v Lincoln Coroner, ex parte Hay* [2000] Lloyds Rep Med 204: advance disclosure should not be obligatory but it was for an individual coroner to decide 'how best he should perform his onerous duties in a way that is as fair as possible to everyone concerned' (Brooke LJ).

14.16 Disclosure in any case, but in particular military cases, is often met by the Ministry of Defence with complaints as to cost, especially if the inquest is complex and voluminous. Mr Justice Collins in the High Court in *Smith* met this problem with the observation that costs could be dealt with by a requirement that those who seek disclosure must pay all reasonable copying charges and it may be that all that is needed in some cases is that the parties' representatives have access to the material and take copies only of that which is regarded as essential.[72] In any event, in an Article 2 inquest it will be difficult to justify any refusal to disclose relevant material.

14.17 In the case of sensitivity, any disclosure should be made, as a matter of good practice, subject to the recipient giving an undertaking not to use it other than for the purposes of the inquest and, if considered necessary, to return it when it has served its purpose. This, Mr Justice Collins observed,[73] will help to avoid intrusive media attention since the undertaking will prevent disclosure to any third parties.

The Home Office Circular issued on 5 June 2002[74] sets out policy in respect of general disclosure and has been dealt with elsewhere in this book. It, of course, applies equally to military inquests.

Deaths on Ministry of Defence Land within the United Kingdom – Police Primacy

14.18 In September 2005 the Ministry of Defence published an agreed protocol for the investigation of deaths on land or premises owned, occupied or under the control of the Ministry of Defence.[75]

In 2008 the Home Office also issued a protocol[76] relating to arrangements in England and Wales and associated territorial waters providing for an efficient and effective working relationship between the Ministry of Defence Police, the Service Police and Home Office Police forces and specifically addressing itself to areas of responsibility and accountability.

The primary responsibility for conducting investigations into all deaths rests with the Chief Officer of Police under whose jurisdiction the death occurs. Primacy in this context includes responsibility for the preparation of case papers for the coroner and the Crown Prosecution Service, and the police will liaise, where appropriate, with the Health and Safety Executive.

---

[72] See *Smith* [2006] EWHC 694 (Admin), para 37.

[73] *ibid*, para 38.

[74] Home Office Circular 31/2002: *Deaths in Custody: Guidance to the Police on Pre-inquest Disclosure.*

[75] MOD/ACPO Protocol on the Investigation of Deaths on Land or Premises Owned, Occupied or Under the Control of the Ministry of Defence at www.mod.uk/DefenceInternet/Home/.

[76] Home Office Circular 028-2008: A protocol between police forces and the Ministry of Defence Police.

The police should have unfettered access to all information and material, subject to legal advice in respect of any disclosure which has the potential to undermine security or prejudice national interests. The Ministry of Defence will retain responsibility for the pastoral aspect of family liaison and the police will have responsibility for engaging the family in the investigative process.

As a matter of practice, the Armed Services now instruct a designated individual to liaise with the families in the case of bereavement.

The Ministry of Defence must take responsibility for the initial scene preservation pending the arrival of the civilian police, who will then take primacy.

It seems from the reading of the protocol that the civilian police will have responsibility not only in respect of establishing the immediate facts and circumstances of the death but also in identifying issues of systemic failings which may have contributed to the death.[77]

In reality what primacy means in the context of military investigations is that the first police officer on the scene prevents movement of exhibits, evidence being obliterated, additional material being added and loss of evidence.[78]

---

[77] See the implicit suggestion in para 4.2 of the protocol.

[78] For a thorough analysis of the requirements of the police to investigate on military premises see Nicholas Blake QC's analysis in the Deepcut Review (above n 42) ch 13.

15

Notification, Certification and Registration of Death

15.1 The Shipman Inquiry published its Final Report on 27 January 2005 and was decommissioned at Easter 2005.

The background to the inquiry concerned the crimes of Doctor Harold Shipman, who was convicted at Preston Crown Court on 31 January 2000 of the murder of 15 of his patients while he was working as a general practitioner in Hyde. It was thought by the police that he may have murdered many more pensioners while he was a GP.

In February 2000, the Secretary of State for Health announced an independent inquiry into the circumstances relating to these crimes in an attempt to establish what changes to current systems could be made in order to safeguard patients in the future.

The Third Report of the Inquiry, which was published on 14 July 2003,[1] considered the existing system for death and cremation certification and for the investigation of deaths by coroners, together with the conduct of those who had operated those systems in the aftermath of the deaths of Shipman's victims. The Chair of the Inquiry, Dame Janet Smith, made certain recommendations for change.

The Third Report established that at the time of Shipman's crimes the systems for registration of death and medical certification for cause of death remained much the same as they were in 1927, when the Births and Deaths Registration Act 1926[2] prohibited the disposal of a body except following the receipt of a certificate of the Registrar or an order of the coroner. The 1926 Act required the certificate to be delivered by a medical practitioner to the Registrar. The duty to complete the certificate was imposed on the medical practitioner who had been in attendance during the deceased's last illness. Despite the recommendation of an 1893 House of Commons Select Committee, which was appointed 'to inquire into the sufficiency of the existing Law as to the Disposal of the Dead', that either the certifying practitioner should inspect the body after death, or the fact of death should be certified by two 'neighbours' of the deceased, the 1926 Act imposed no such requirements.

---

[1] The Shipman Inquiry: *Third Report – Death Certification and the Investigation of Deaths by Coroners* (July 2003) (Cm 5854, 2003).
[2] Births and Deaths Registration Act 1926 (16 & 17 Geo V c 48).

The 1926 Act should be read in conjunction with the Registration (Births, Stillbirths, Deaths and Marriages) Consolidated Regulations 1927.[3] They provided that a Registrar would be under a duty to report a death if it appeared that the certifying practitioner had either not seen the deceased within 14 days before death or seen the body after death. A doctor would be required to state whether he had seen the deceased after death and how long before death he had last seen the deceased alive. The Registrar would then be required to refer to the coroner any death in which the doctor had not seen the body after death or had not seen the deceased within a reasonably short period before death. At that time, the 'reasonably short period' within which the doctor was required to have seen the deceased had not been defined. In 1927, it was decided that the period should be 14 days. The effect of the rule was that, provided the doctor had seen the body after death, it did not matter how long before death the doctor had last seen the patient alive. In short, the provisions provided for in 1927 completely failed to ensure that doubtful cases, such as cases in which the doctor had not seen the patient for months before death, would be reported to the coroner. As was pointed out by Dame Janet Smith in the Third Report:[4]

> If the doctor took the trouble to see the body after death, it would not matter when he had last seen the patient alive. He might be in no good position to certify the cause of death, although he could be quite certain that life was extinct.

At the time of the Shipman Inquiry, registration was governed by the Births and Deaths Registration Act 1953. Section 15 required that

> the death of every person dying in England and Wales and the cause thereof shall be registered by the registrar of births and deaths for the sub-district in which the death occurred.

The Role of the Coroner in Relation to Death Registration

15.2 The Births and Deaths Registration Act 1836 required coroners to notify the Registrar of bodies 'found exposed' which were reported to them. The Act gave Coroners power to compel the attendance of a medical witness at an inquest and to order the witness to perform an autopsy, if the cause of death remained uncertain. This increased the potential for the detection of cases of murder.

In 1965 the Broderick Committee was established to consider the Coronial service. It reported in 1971 and envisaged the coroner becoming 'a principle agent in the certification of medical causes of death'. Unfortunately its recommendations were not implemented.

[3] Registration (Births, Stillbirths, Deaths and Marriages) Consolidated Regulations, 1927 (SR & O 1927 No 485).
[4] The Shipman Inquiry: *Third Report*, para 2.26.

Section 16(2) of the Births and Deaths Registration Act 1953 identified individuals who were qualified persons with a duty to notify the registrar of the district in relation to a death at home. These individuals include:

(a) any relative of the deceased present at the death or in attendance during his last illness;
(b) any other relative of the deceased residing or being in the sub-district where the death occurred;
(c) any person present at the death;
(d) the occupier of the house if he knew of the happening of the death;
(e) any inmate of the house who knew of the happening of the death; [or any]
(f) person causing the disposal of the body.

Section 41 of the 1953 Act states that a house can include 'a public institution' and therefore includes hospitals, mental health institutions or drug rehabilitation facilities.

Section 17 of the 1953 Act applies itself to information concerning fatalities which occur other than in a house or where the deceased is found and no information as to the place of death can be ascertained. In such circumstances, according to section 17(2), qualified persons will include:

(a) any relative of the deceased who has knowledge of any of the particulars required to be registered concerning the death;
(b) any person present at the death;
(c) any person finding or taking charge of the body; or
(d) any person causing the disposal of the body.

The Registrar must be provided within five days from the date of death, information to the best of any of these qualified persons' knowledge of details and particulars required concerning registration by virtue of sections 16(3) and 17(3) of the Act.

15.3 The whole notification and registration regime is significantly adjusted by the 2009 Act.

By virtue of section 18 of the Act,

the Lord Chancellor may make regulations requiring a registered medical practitioner, in prescribed cases or circumstances, to notify a senior coroner of a death of which the practitioner is aware.[5]

Hitherto there were no statutory obligations upon registered medical practitioners to report a death to a coroner.[6]

Section 20 of the 2009 Act enables the Secretary of State for Health to make regulations about the preparation, scrutiny and confirmation of medical

---

[5] Section 18(1) of the Coroners and Justice 2009 Act.
[6] This is distinct from the duty upon medical practitioners who attended during the last illness to report matters under s 22(1) of the Births and Deaths Registration Act 1953.

certificates of cause of death and about the way the confirmed certificate is notified and given to the registrar, or about how the death is referred to a Senior Coroner. Section 20 also enables regulations to be made about the payment of a fee for the service provided by a medical examiner.

15.4 The provisions within Section 20 of the 2009 Act arise directly from the considerations in the Shipman Inquiry, and the independent scrutiny and confirmation of medical certificates of cause of death is part of a wider process that begins with the preparation of the certificate by a registered medical practitioner who attended the deceased and ends with the certificate being returned to the medical examiner after it has been used by the Registrar to register the death. The new unified process is specifically intended to be simpler and more transparent then the previous one and requires specification of activities, responsibilities and alternative scenarios that are more suited to regulations than to provisions on the face of the Act.[7] Regulations made under Section 20(1)(a) will require a registered medical practitioner who attended the deceased prior to death to prepare a medical certificate stating the cause of death to the best of the practitioner's knowledge and belief.[8] The certificate compiled by the registered medical practitioner who attended the deceased prior to death will be prepared using first-hand knowledge of the deceased's condition prior to death together with information from medical notes and the patient's records.

If the registered medical practitioner attending the deceased prior to death is unable to establish the cause of death, or is unable to do so in a period of time prescribed by regulation, then the death must be referred to a Senior Coroner. If the practitioner is not contactable within a period of time after the death, to be prescribed by regulation, then again the death must be referred to a Senior Coroner. This is particularly relevant to deaths in the community which, even though they maybe apparently due to natural causes, occur at a time when the deceased's usual doctor is not contactable.

If there is no attending practitioner, for example where the deceased person was not receiving treatment for the condition that caused the death, then the provisions under section 20(1)(a) do not apply and the death must be notified to a Senior Coroner as prescribed by regulation that may be made under section 18.

15.5 Although regulations are yet to be made, the Explanatory Notes attached to the 2009 Act indicated that the legislature intended that the regulations will specify that an attending practitioner certificate will not be required when the death has been notified to a Senior Coroner in accordance with regulations made under section 18 and is envisaged by the Senior Coroner as specified in Section 1. This, it is stated, is a key change from the previous process and addresses a long-standing issue which, on a strict interpretation of the 1953 Act, requires an attending

---

[7] Section 20(1) provides the power to make the necessary regulations.
[8] This duty has been transferred and adapted from s 22 of the Births and Deaths Registration Act 1953.

practitioner to prepare a certificate even if he or she cannot establish the cause of death, and requires the registrar to refer this certificate to a coroner.[9]

Section 20(4) allows for regulations to provide for functions otherwise exercisable by medical practitioners, in the context of medical certification, to be carried out by registered medical practitioners who did not attend the deceased prior to death.

Medical Examiners

15.6 Primary Care Trusts in England and Local Health Boards in Wales will be required by section 19 of the 2009 Act to appoint Medical Examiners to discharge the functions given to them by the 2009 Act.

Enough Medical Examiners must be appointed, and make available sufficient funds and other resources (including Medical Examiner's officers), to enable the Medical Examiners to discharge their functions in the area served by the Primary Care Trust or the Local Health Board.[10] Although the Primary Care Trusts and Local Health Boards will be required to monitor the work of the Medical Examiners, they must take no role whatsoever in relation to the way the Examiners exercise their professional judgement as medical practitioners.[11] Only registered medical practitioners for the previous five years who are practising at the time of their appointment or practised within the previous five years will qualify to be a Medical Examiner.[12]

Regulations will be made to specify the terms of appointment of Medical Examiners and allow for their termination.[13] It is anticipated that Medical Examiners will have the power to request a fresh certificate from a medical practitioner who attended upon the deceased prior to death.[14] A fresh certificate maybe required if, during registration, the informant provides new information about the death which invalidates the cause of death previously confirmed by the Medical Examiner. This, in effect provides a statutory safety-net for the registrar to ensure that all appropriate deaths are reported to the Senior Coroner.

15.7 The Medical Examiner may also have deaths referred to him by the Senior Coroner.[15] It is anticipated that these fatalities encompass deaths that were originally notified to a Senior Coroner under section 18 of the 2009 Act or referred to a Senior Coroner in circumstances where the practitioner was unable to establish

---

[9] Section 1 of the Coroners and Justice Act 2009 Act relates to the duty of the coroner to investigate certain deaths.

[10] See s 19(2)(a) of the 2009 Act.

[11] *ibid*, s 19(2)(b).

[12] *ibid*, s 19(3).

[13] *ibid*, s 19(4).

[14] *ibid*, 20(1)(c).

[15] *ibid*, 20(1)(d).

the cause of death, by virtue of section 20(1)(a)(ii), but which the Senior Coroner has decided not to investigate. In these cases, the Senior Coroner will issue a form stating that he or she has no further interests in the death and will transmit this form to the Medical Examiner's office together with any relevant information about the death that he or she has used in coming to his or her decision. In some cases, this information may include advice provided by a Medical Examiner in response to a request from the Senior Coroner or Coroner's Officer.

15.8 If there is no attending practitioner prior to death or if the attending medical practitioner is not available within a prescribed period after Senior Coroner decides not to investigate, then the Medical Examiner will establish the cause of death and prepare a Medical Examiner's certificate as will be specified in regulations, stating the cause of death to the best of the examiner's knowledge.[16]

15.9 Medical Examiners may also be provided with the authority to make whatever enquiries appear necessary in order to confirm or establish the cause of death.[17] Medical Examiners have full access to medical notes and patient records as a result of amendments to the Access to Health Records Act 1990.[18] Medical Examiners will not be able to *require* any individual or organisations to respond to their enquires or provide information.

If a Medical Examiner is not able to obtain information required to confirm or establish the cause of death, then the death will be referred to Senior Coroner and the Senior Coroner will be able to require the information to be provided.

15.10 Upon receipt of the certificate of the medical practitioner who attended upon the deceased prior to death, at the medical examiner's office, there should also be appended relevant medical notes and/or patient records. Where these cannot be provided, arrangements may be made for a medical examiner to view them in situ. It is the duty of the Medical Examiner's Officer to ensure that the attending practitioner's certificate has been completed and that the associated notes and records have been provided or are available and then, if necessary, to contact the deceased person's next of kin, or other appropriate person or people, to obtain any further information required.

To ensure that the scrutiny carried out by the Medical Examiner is robust, proportionate and consistent, the legislature will produce a protocol that recognises different levels of risk depending on the setting, the stated cause of death and circumstances. The protocol will establish the minimum level of scrutiny for specific situations but this will not impinge upon the discretion of the Medical Examiner to use his professional judgement to determine the degree to which the scrutiny will be pursued.

---

[16] This aspect of the 2009 legislation is intended to reduce the continuing, though small number of uncertified deaths.

[17] Coroners and Justice Act 2009, s 20(1)(e).

[18] See para 29 of Sch 21 to the 2009 Act which refers in particular to s 3(1) of the Access to Health Records Act 1990.

15.11 During such scrutiny, the Medical Examiner may be unable to confirm the cause of death or may alternatively decide that it does not meet any of the criteria laid out in section 18 of the 2009 Act dealing with notification by medical practitioners to the Senior Coroner. In such circumstances the death must be referred to a Senior Coroner as will be specified in regulations.

The Medical Examiner will be required to give reasons for the referral and, where appropriate, suggest what type of post-mortem maybe necessary. If, in exceptional circumstances, the Senior Coroner decides not to investigate the death and cannot come to an agreement with the Medical Examiner about the cause of death then the matter will be subject to the appeals procedure set out in Part 1, Chapter 6 (Governance etc) of the 2009 Act.

If during the scrutiny the Medical Examiner is of the opinion that the cause of death stated on the medical practitioner's certificate, created by a medical practitioner who dealt with the deceased prior to death, is either insufficient or incorrect, but the death is not reportable to a Senior Coroner, then the Medical Examiner is required to discuss the death with the medical practitioner and invite him to prepare a fresh certificate.

If, in exceptional circumstances, the medical practitioner responsible for the deceased prior to death and the Medical Examiner are unable to agree on the cause of death, the Medical Examiner will be required to refer the case to a Senior Coroner.

When the scrutiny by the Medical Examiner has been completed, then the Medical Examiner or Medical Examiner's Officer must speak to the next of kin of the deceased or any other appropriate people to advise them as to the outcome of the scrutiny.[19]

Persons nominated as the informant for the purposes of registration will be required to confirm in writing that a Medical Examiner or someone acting on his behalf has explained the confirmed cause of death in accordance with section 20(1)(k).[20] The rationale behind this is to provide evidence that the cause of death has been explained to the informant or such other prescribed individuals, thereby lending transparency to the process in contrast to that which existed before the implementation of the 2009 Act.

The Medical Practitioner's Certificate

15.12 Regulations made under section 20(1)(a)(i) allow the practitioner attending upon the deceased prior to their death to prepare an attending practitioner's certificate.

The certificate will include information that the medical practitioner attending upon the deceased prior to death has seen, identified and externally examined the

---

[19] This contact will be required by regulations made under s 20(1)(k) of the 2009 Act.
[20] *ibid*, s 20(1)(l).

deceased's body after death. The purpose of this is to confirm that there are no injuries or other suspicious features which may indicate that the fatality was an unnatural death.

If, exceptionally, and in circumstances agreed with a Medical Examiner, the attending practitioner has not been able to see, identify and examine the body, then the Medical Examiner must arrange to do so during their scrutiny. The Medical Examiner will also need to see, identify and examine the body in the case of deaths that are referred to him by a Senior Coroner and which require a Medical Examiner's certificate as laid out in section 20(1)(d).

The Medical Examiner has the power to invite the medical practitioner to prepare a fresh certificate where, in the view of the Medical Examiner, the cause of death stated on the original certificate is either insufficient or incorrect, but the death is not reportable to a Senior Coroner.[21]

Authorisation by the Medical Examiner

15.13 Once the cause of death has been confirmed and the medical certificate of cause of death can be issued and used to register the death, and upon the completion of analysis of any issues raised by the next of kin or other appropriate people, the medical certificate of cause of death will be available to be collected from the hospital bereavement office, the general practitioner's surgery, or in the case of a certificate prepared by a Medical Examiner, from the Medical Examiner's office.

The authorisation will be sent to the relevant medical practitioner who attended upon the deceased prior to death and to the Registrar to notify them that the cause of death has been confirmed and that the certificate can be used and issued to register the death.

A copy of the authorisation will be sent to funeral directors to allow them to undertake their duties in relation to the deceased, especially where it may involve changing the body in a way which might render it unsuitable for a post-mortem.

Registrars must wait until they have received or can access a copy of the Medical Examiner's authorisation before they are able to accept or confirm acceptance of a request to register a death, a request to defer registration or a request to authorise disposal before registration.

---

[21] *ibid*, s 20(1)(c).

Periods of Emergency

15.14 The legislature may make regulations in relation to death registration which

provide for the functions that would otherwise be exercisable by a registered medical practitioner who attended the deceased before his or her death to be exercisable, during a period of emergency, by a registered medical practitioner who did not do so.[22]

For the purposes of the 2009 Act

'period of emergency' is a period certified as such by the Secretary of State on a basis that there is or has been, or is about to be, an event or situation involving or causing, or having the potential to cause, a substantial loss of human life throughout, or in any part of, England and Wales.[23]

The National Medical Examiner

15.15 The Act makes provision for the appointment by the Secretary of State of a National Medical Examiner.[24] The role of the examiner will be to issue guidance to Medical Examiners with a view to securing that they carry out their functions in an effective and proportionate manner. Medical Examiners will not be bound to follow these communications, which are not directive.

The National Medical Examiner must be a registered medical practitioner for the past five years and must practise as such or have done so within the previous five years.

Post-mortems

15.16 The term 'post-mortem examination' is not defined, but the Explanatory Notes associated with the 2009 Act indicate that it will include any examination made of the deceased including non-invasive examinations, for example, using Magnetic Resonance Imaging (MRI) scans.

The 2009 Act amends the previous legislation, which can be found at sections 19 and 20 of the Coroners Act 1988.

15.17 The Coroners Act 1988 made a distinction between post-mortem and 'special' examinations. Special examinations were a more specific version of the

---

[22] *ibid*, s 20(4).
[23] *ibid*, ss 19(7) and 20(7).
[24] See s 21(1).

post-mortem examination and would contain, for instance, toxicology tests to establish whether there was alcohol or drugs in the bloodstream of the deceased. The 2009 Act removes this discretion.

Section 14(1) of the 2009 Act gives the Senior Coroner power to ask a suitable practitioner to make a post-mortem examination of the deceased if the Senior Coroner is either responsible for conducting an investigation into the death or a post-mortem examination will enable the Senior Coroner to decide if he has a duty under section 1 of the 2009 Act to conduct an investigation. This could be particularly important where it is unclear whether a death has occurred as a result of a notifiable disease or whether a child was stillborn where, for example, an infant's body is found and it is not clear whether it ever had independent life. Where it is known or established that a child was stillborn, the Senior Coroner will have no further power to carry out an investigation.

The 'suitable practitioner' referred to in section 14(1), to make a post-mortem examination is so qualified if they are

(a) ... a registered medical practitioner, or
(b) in the case where a particular kind of examination is requested, a practitioner of a description designated by the Chief Coroner as suitable to make examinations of that kind.[25]

If, in the informant's opinion, the death was caused wholly or partly by the improper or negligent treatment of a registered medical practitioner or other person, that practitioner or other person must not make, or assist at an examination prescribed under section 14, of the body but nevertheless is entitled to be represented at such an examination.

The report of a post-mortem examination must be sent to the Senior Coroner in whatever form the coroner requires as soon as practicable.[26]

Exhumations

15.18 A coroner may order the exhumation of a body buried within his district

where it appears to him that it is necessary for the body to be examined—

(a) for the purpose of holding an inquest into that person's death or discharging any other function of [the coroner] in relation to the body or the death; or
(b) for the purposes of any criminal proceedings which have been instituted or are contemplated in respect of the death of that person or of some other person who came by his death in circumstances connected with the death of a person whose body is needed for examination.[27]

The power of exhumation is exercisable by the Coroner's warrant.

---

[25] *ibid*, s 14(3).
[26] *ibid*, s 14(5).
[27] See s 23(1) of the Coroners Act 1988.

As such the power of the coroner to order exhumation is limited to the conduct of the inquest before him. Once an inquest is completed, those seeking an exhumation must apply to the Home Office for a licence or to the Faculty of Clergy if the body lies in consecrated ground. The Faculty of Clergy will meet on prescribed occasions to resolve contentious issues or non-contentious issues, and is usually chaired by a practising barrister of relevant experience.

Representation at The Post-mortem

15.19 When a post-mortem takes place, the coroner will notify the people and organisations set out in rule 7(2)(a)–(g) of the Coroners Rules 1984 of the date, hour and place at which the examination will be made, unless it is impracticable to notify any such persons or organisations or unless to do so would cause the post-mortem to be unduly delayed.

Individuals such as relatives of the deceased, medical practitioners, hospital or law enforcement authorities, including any governmental department, may be represented at the post-mortem, as may any other interested party whom the coroner may designate as being an appropriate person or organisation to attend.[28]

Second Post-mortems

15.20 A second post-mortem maybe obtained, if the coroner gives his permission, by the bereaved family or other relevant interested party who is facing or maybe facing the risk of allegations that it caused the death of the deceased.

The cost of any second post-mortem will be borne by those seeking it.

A Home Office Circular[29] has set out guidelines as to time-tabling for second post-mortems. Essentially it lays down that if the coroner is informed by the Chief Officer of Police that no one is likely to be charged with murder the body can be released within 28 days, though a coroner can arrange for a second post-mortem to be conducted by a pathologist who is independent from the first pathologist.

The second coroner's post-mortem must take place as soon as possible but in any event no later than 28 days after the first examination. In certain circumstances a third post-mortem maybe required if there are significant discrepancies between the previous post-mortems. It will be for the coroner to decide when no further examination is necessary. As within the criminal jurisdiction, there is significant pressure upon parties to hearings, to finalise the requirements of post-mortems expeditiously. Family, relations and friends of the deceased will be anxious to resolve the burial or cremation of the deceased and coroners, in

---

[28] Coroners Rules 1984 r 7(4).
[29] Home Office Circular No 30/1999, Post-mortem Examinations and the Early Release of Bodies.

practice, will be particularly vigilant to ensure that the post-mortem process does not become unnecessarily lengthy. Consultations relating to secondary legislation indicate that the Ministry of Justice's purpose is to enable the release of the body within, a shorter period of time, although respondents to the consultation, including the Criminal Bar Association have criticised this as being too soon, given the problem of securing public funding for subsequent post-mortems.[30]

Removal of the Body

15.21 A Senior Coroner who is responsible for conducting an investigation into the death or who needs to request post-mortem examination in order to decide if he has a duty under section 1 of the 2009 Act to conduct an investigation may order that the body be moved to any suitable place.[31]

Previously under section 22(1) of the Coroners Act 1988 a body could only be moved within a Senior Coroners area or to an immediate adjoining area. This caused practical difficulties in major incidents where there were multiple deaths. The new power under section 15 of the 2009 Act will allow a Senior Coroner to make use of specialist equipment or skills which are available in different parts of the country and it is anticipated that this may mean that full post-mortems can be avoided.

The Senior Coroner may not order the removal of a body under section 15 to a place provided by a person who has not consented to its being removed there (an example given within the Explanatory Notes is a mortuary manager), except in the case of local authority premises.

Discontinuance of an Investigation

15.22 The coroner must discontinue an investigation if a post-mortem examination under section 14 reveals the cause of death and the coroner thinks that it is not necessary to continue the investigation.[32] This will arise, for example, if the death is shown to be due to natural causes and there are no other circumstances, such as State detention associated with the death, which would mean that the investigation needs to continue to the coronial process.

The coroner has no discretion to discontinue an investigation if he suspects the deceased died a violent or unnatural death or died while in State detention.[33]

---

[30] Consultation Paper CP06/10, *Reform of the Coroner System: Next Stage Planning for Implementation*, published 11 March 2010, ch 3 (p 28).

[31] See s 15 of the Coroners and Justice Act 2009.

[32] *ibid*, s 4.

[33] This is in line with s 19 of the Coroners Act 1988.

If the Senior Coroner does decide to discontinue an investigation under section 4 of the 2009 Act he is not permitted to go on to hold an inquest into the death or make any determination. Section 4 includes a new requirement for the coroner to explain why an investigation has been discontinued if requested to do so.[34] This request must be in writing by an interested person who in turn should receive as soon as practicably possible, a written explanation by the Senior Coroner as to the reasons for discontinuance.

Should new information be revealed about the death, there is provision for a fresh investigation to be conducted.[35]

---

[34] See the Coroners and Justice Act 2009 s 4(4).
[35] *ibid*, s 4(3).

16

Treasure

16.1 The law governing treasure, prior to the implementation of the provisions of the 2009 Act is contained in the Treasure Act 1996.

Section 1 of the Treasure Act 1996 defines treasure in four categories:

(a) Any object at least 300 years old when found and which accords with certain specifications laid out in section 1(1)(a)(i)–(iii).

(b) Any object at least 200 years old when found which the Secretary of State may designate to be an item of outstanding historical, archaeological or cultural importance.

(c) Any object which would have been treasure trove if found before the commencement of section 4 of the 1996 Act. As Jervis points out[1] this is likely only to be significant in relation to objects less than 300 years old, or less than 200 years old and not designated by the Secretary of State, because objects at least 300 years old or 200 years old and so designated will usually fall within other categories of treasure (the main exception being a single gold or silver coin).

(d) Any object which, when found, is part of the same find as an object within paragraphs (a), (b) or (c) above found at the same time or earlier, or an object found earlier which would be within paragraphs (a) or (b) above if it had been found at the same time.

The definition of treasure within the 1996 Act is complex, but by virtue of its construction it includes any object which would have been treasure trove if found before the commencement of the Act, and preserves the Medieval Law of Treasure.

This means that for property to be deemed treasure it must be:

(i)   made of gold or silver;
(ii) deliberately concealed by the owner with a view to later recovery; and
(iii) the owner or his present heirs or successors must be unknown.

Substantially the Crown has a prerogative right to treasure trove under the medieval construction of the law.[2] It follows from this that if the item is not considered treasure trove then it will usually belong to the original owner or their heirs. If the owner or heirs cannot be found the item will belong to the owner of

---

[1] *Jervis on Coroners* 6th edn (Sweet & Maxwell 2002) 372 at para 16-12.
[2] But see the peculiar position as to the Duchy of Lancaster and the Duchy of Cornwall.

land in which it is buried or attached.[3] If an object, which is later adjudicated not to be treasure trove, is found on unoccupied land or upon land occupied by an individual who does not manifest an intention to exercise control over it, then providing the finder is not a trespasser, the individual who first finds the object will be deemed to possess it.[4] A crucial amendment to the Medieval Law was made by the 1996 Act by removing the necessity of the owner of the find to be unknown in order for the object to constitute treasure trove. Treasure will automatically vest in Crown.

16.2 The Secretary of State must prepare a code of practice relating to treasure and keep the code under review and revise it when appropriate. It must in particular, set out the principles and practices to be followed by the Secretary of State when considering: to whom treasure should be offered; whether it should be, for instance, transferred to a museum and the value of that award.[5]

The code must include guidance for those who search for or find treasure and for museums and may be used at any time once the potential treasure has been reported to the coroner. In such circumstances the coroner will return the item to the finder, having given notification to the occupier and the landowner (if they are different individuals) that he intends to do so, not less than 28 days after the date of notification from the Secretary of State that a disclaimer will be issued.

As stated in paragraph 50 of the Code, the coroner does not have the power to make a legal determination as to title between the occupier, the landowner and the finder following disclaimer, and if necessary the issue will have to be resolved in the normal way in the civil courts.

Procedure in the Coroners' Courts

16.3 The coroner must hold an inquest on any finds that have been reported to him and that he has reasonable grounds for believing to be treasure, except where the Secretary of State has issued a disclaimer. General procedure within the Coroners' Courts will be the same as any other Coroner's hearing dealt with within this book, although since the Coroners Rules 1984 do not define an inquest as including a treasure trove inquest, Jervis is of the view that the Coroners Rules probably do not apply.[6]

The coroner is required to inform the national museum if he intends to hold an inquest.

---

[3] *Elwes v Brigg Gas Company* (1866) 33 ChD562: *South Staffordshire Water Company and Sharman* [1896] 2Q B 44 DC.
[4] *Armoury v Delamirie (1722) 5Stra.505.*
[5] Treasure Act 1996 s 11. See the *Treasure Act 1996 Code of Practice* (2nd Revision).
[6] See Coroners Rules 1984 r 2(1).

16.4 Specific analysis and expertise will be required to be presented to the coroner or the jury.

16.5 The object of the Act and the codes of practice was to simplify the task of Coroners in determining whether or not a find is treasure and included a new offence of non-declaration of treasure.[7]

If an object is part of the same find as another object, that is, if it's found in the same place or had previously been left together with the other object it will be for the Coroner's inquest to establish these facts and the circumstances will vary from case to case. The coroner may seek advice from the finder and also from the Finds Liaison Officer, the local archaeologist or museum curator or from a curator of a national museum (listed in the Code) as to whether the objects reported as treasure should be considered as coming from the same find.[8]

A number of objects found over a period of time may qualify as treasure, including those that would not have been treasure but for an earlier find of treasure. According to paragraph 16 of the Code, the find may consist of different classes of objects and it will not need to have been found at the same time or by the same person.

However, the 1996 Act does not have retrospective effect, for example, if a finder discovers first one coin on a particular site, which will not be treasure, and then subsequently discovers more coins on the same site, which will then qualify as treasure, the original discovery will not be considered as treasure. The Code advises that this will apply regardless of whether the earlier find was made before or after the commencement of the Act. The duty to report such finds will rest with the finder who will have a legal duty to report a find if he believes or has reasonable ground for believing it to be treasure.[9]

16.6 By section 8 of the Act any person who finds an object which he believes or has reasonable ground to believe is treasure must notify the coroner for the District in which the object was found before the end of the notice period which is 14 days beginning with the day after the find or, if later, the day on which the finder believes or has reason to believe the object is treasure.[10] It should be emphasised that the finder is only required to report treasure but not necessarily deliver it within that time frame. Failure to do so is a criminal offence punishable by a maximum term of imprisonment of three months or a fine not exceeding £5,000 or both.

16.7 Under section 6 of the 1996 Act the Secretary of State has power to disclaim at any time, objects that have been submitted as potential treasure. If this is so it will normally mean that a treasure inquest will not need to be held. If any scientific

---

[7] See also the Treasure (Designation) Order 2002.
[8] See ss 3(4) and 3(5): See also the Revised Code of Practice 2002 paragraph 14.
[9] See paras 23–26 of the Code.
[10] See para 23 of the Code in relation to s 8 of the 1996 Act.

analysis is required of the item, permission of the coroner for any invasive procedures should be obtained.[11]

16.8 It is the Coroners responsibility to notify the finder, the occupier and the landowner and any other interested parties as to where and when the inquest is to take place. These individuals may be given an opportunity to examine witnesses at the inquest and be treated as interested parties. In some cases the Crown or the National Museum or the local museum or a local archaeological officer may wish to be represented at the inquest. In accordance with normal procedure it will be for the coroner to decide whether they are designated as interested parties.[12] Coroners are advised in paragraph 58 of the Code to keep confidential the precise location of the find-spots and not give details of the finder, occupier or landowner at public hearing within the inquest. Any decision or verdict at the inquest will be subject, to Judicial Review or challenge under section 13 of the Coroners Act 1988.

The 2009 Act

16.9 The 2009 Act makes important changes to the former regime. Section 25 of the 2009 Act gives effect to Schedule 4 and provides for the appointment of a Coroner for Treasure and Assistant Coroners for Treasure.

Part 1 of Schedule 4 allows the Lord Chancellor to appoint a person as the Coroner for Treasure. This new appointment will have the duty to investigate all finds believed to be treasure or treasure trove from across England and Wales. Although it is expected that this individual will have an office in a particular location, the convenience of interested people, including the finder and the landowner, will be taken into account when considering the location for any inquest that maybe required as a result of a find.

Senior Coroners will be able to apply to become a Coroner for Treasure and qualification for the position is the same legal qualification as that used for Senior Coroners.[13]

One or more Assistant Coroners will be designated as Assistant Coroners for Treasure. In this case they will cease to be Assistant Coroners for Treasure if they cease to be Assistant Coroners.[14] An Assistant Coroner for Treasure will, by virtue of Part 3 Schedule 4, be able to undertake any of the functions of the Coroner for Treasure, should he be absent or unavailable or otherwise with the consent of the Coroner for Treasure.[15] Under this provision the Lord Chancellor will be able to appoint staff to carry out the administrative functions relating to treasure investigations.[16]

[11] See para 56 of the Code.
[12] See para 58 of the Code.
[13] Coroners and Justice Act 2009, Sch 4, part 1, para 2.
[14] *ibid*, Sch 4, part 2, para 9.
[15] *ibid*, Sch 4, part 3, para 11.
[16] *ibid*, Sch 4, part 3, para 12.

16.10 Any items reported to the Coroner for Treasure under section 8 of the 1996 Act will be investigated. An investigation may be appropriate in addition to this, if there is a suspicion about any object found but which has not been reported. This investigation will seek to establish whether or not the object is treasure or treasure trove, and if so, who found it, where and when it was found.[17]

16.11 It should be emphasised that Senior Coroners, Area Coroners and Assistant Coroners have no functions in relation to these objects, unless the Assistant Coroner has been designated as an Assistant Coroner for Treasure.[18] The effect of this is that there will be a single reporting point for all treasure across England and Wales, and a single point of investigation providing a uniform approach to this regime.

16.12 An inquest will be held without a jury to consider a find unless there is sufficient reason for one to be empanelled. Provision in relation to the number of jurors and guidance as to how they will arrive at their determination is identical to that which relates to death investigation.

When considering whether a jury will be required, the principles which apply in death investigation will also apply, as modified, to investigations into treasure or treasure trove. Given the complexity of some investigations into treasure or treasure trove, it is anticipated that argument upon complexity will be taken to avoid the empanelling of juries.

16.13 It will be for the coroner or a jury to determine whether or not the object in question is treasure or treasure trove, and if it is treasure or treasure trove, then who found it, where it was found and when it was found.[19]

16.14 Section 29 of the 2009 Act extends the circumstances in which the Crown or relevant franchisee may disclaim title to an object, to allow notice to be given to the Coroner for Treasure disclaiming the title before it is determined that the object is treasure. As the Explanatory Notes point out, the finder in these circumstances would not be compensated under the treasure evaluation system, but the object would be returned to the finder, for them to dispose of it as they see fit.[20]

16.15 There will be a duty on acquirers of objects which might be treasure to report them to the Coroner for Treasure. This duty is incorporated into the 1996 Act at section 8(1) by virtue of section 30 of the 2009 Act. In such circumstances the object will be investigated and the usual determinations made about it; that is, when, where and by whom it was found and indeed whether it is treasure. This provision is intended to cover situations where the acquirer may have bought the

---

[17] *ibid*, s 26.
[18] *ibid*, s 26(6).
[19] *ibid*, 26(5).
[20] *ibid*, 26(5).

object or been given it or had it bequeathed to them. The Treasure Valuation Committee is empowered to provide a reward to the acquirer in these circumstances.

Any breach of this duty is a criminal offence and could result in 51 weeks' imprisonment, a level 5 fine, or both.

16.16 The case of *Attorney General of the Duchy of Lancaster v G E Overton (Farms) Ltd* [1982] 1 All ER 524 remains the authority defining the limits of the Crown's right to treat objects as treasure trove. It limited the Crown's right to treasure trove to objects of gold and silver and for an article to be so described it must contain a substantial amount of precious metal, which would be decided as a question of fact by a jury. Lord Denning observed that an object should have gold or silver content of 50% or more before it can be described as a gold or silver object; see p 530 paras e and f.

17

Secondary Legislation

17.1 Further consultation upon the 2009 Act ended on 1 July 2010 and views were invited upon the content of secondary legislation.

The legislature hopes to finalise secondary legislation during the second half of 2011 with a planned implementation date of April 2012. This timetable may be amended as the new Coalition Government consider the legislation.

A final version of the Charter for Bereaved People will also be completed around 2012 following final consultation in 2011. The Charter lists a number of services which should be delivered to bereaved people to enable them to better participate in Coroner investigations.

The consultation paper published on 11 March 2010[1] is an expansive document, running to some 170 pages, and covers all aspects of the new legislation in nine distinct chapters. The document, whilst inviting responses, provides a useful insight into how the legislature sees the coronial system developing as a result of the 2009 legislation. This is of significance, particularly given that secondary legislation is yet to come into force and will indicate the tone of the final Act as it will appear in April 2012.

Deaths to be Reported to a Senior Coroner

17.2 The consultation paper emphasises that the policy is designed to ensure that Coroners have appropriate deaths reported to them and that there is clarity between the role of the Coroner and the new Medical Examiner, which the Act creates. It is anticipated that the introduction of Medical Examiners will have the benefit of tackling the over-reporting of deaths to Coroners, which takes place within the current system, while at the same time ensuring that all deaths are scrutinised independently. The paper goes on to state that presently 45 per cent of deaths are reported to Coroners each year and that this is a 15–20 per cent higher rate than in any other country that has Coroners with responsibilities broadly similar to those in this country.

---

[1] *Reform of the Coroner System Next Stage: Preparing for Implementation*, 11 March 2010 (CP06/10).

17.3 Presently there are no statutory duties on doctors to refer deaths to a Coroner and the only specific duties fall on Registrars;[2] on Prison Governors, to report the death of an inmate; and on the Commanding Officer or Commandant, to report the death of a person in the United Kingdom in Naval quarters or in an Army or Air Force establishment.

The 2009 Act introduces a new death certification system in England and Wales to run parallel with the coronial system.

17.4 By virtue of the Registration of Births and Deaths Regulations 1987, a death, even an apparently natural death, can only be certified without reference to the Coroner if the attending doctor has seen the deceased after death or within 14 days before the death. Otherwise, as the consultation document points out, the Registrar must refer the death to the Coroner.

Interestingly the consultation document observes that in the legislature's view the 14-day time limit is too short. It is observed that, with the developments of palliative care in particular, the legislature believe that either the limit should be higher, 21 or 28 days, or there should be no limit at all and that it should be left to the discretion of the attending practitioner, in discussion with a medical examiner where necessary, to determine whether the death should be reported to a Coroner under one of the other categories for referral.

Transferring Cases From One Coroner Area to Another

17.5 These measures are intended to bring flexibility into the coronial system and take account of the needs of a bereaved family to have a prompt investigation and inquest, conducted in accordance with national standards, and wherever possible, in relation to the inquest, held at a geographically convenient location.

17.6 The drafters of the legislation expect that Local Authorities will continue to be responsible for the funding of a reformed Coroners system, and for meeting expenses incurred in an investigation.[3] Regulations made under section 43 of the 2009 Act will set out the process for notification of transferred investigations, which are anticipated to come into play in a number of circumstances:[4]

a) When the death requiring investigation occurred overseas.
b) When the death occurred in England and Wales – when someone was on holiday or on business – but the immediate family lives in a different part of the country.
c) When the death occurred near the boundaries of two coroner areas but the bereaved family live on the side of the boundary where the death would not normally be investigated.

---

[2] See the Birth and Deaths Regulations 1987 (SI 1987/2088).
[3] chapter 3, para 19 of the Consultation Paper (p 26).
[4] *ibid*, chapter 3, para 2 (p 22).

d) If there is a major incident, or there is a major outbreak of disease, where there are many casualties.

e) Where there are unexpected surges in reported deaths to particular coroners.

f) Where the coroner believes he or she has a conflict of interest in conducting the investigation, perhaps through knowing the deceased well.

g) Where the coroner is subject to a formal complaint, which has been accepted for investigation, by a party to the case.

Post-mortem Examinations and Retention of Bodies

17.7 The consultation document on secondary legislation emphasises that the purposes of these reforms are in part to achieve greater consistency between Coroners in circumstances when they commission a post-mortem examination, and that the bereaved family are provided with better opportunities to be informed about the purpose and outcome of examination.

The consultation document[5] makes it clear that at a fundamental level the purpose of a Coroner's post-mortem examination is to provide the Coroner with sufficient information to carry out his or her legal duty of establishing the cause of death, when it is unknown or uncertain, so a decision may be made as to whether an inquest is required or the death can be registered without an inquest. The document goes on[6] that there are other important reasons for a Coroner's post-mortem examination and in particular that they can play a key role in preventing future deaths, particularly in identifying whether there is a specific underlying cause such as an inherited genetic defect that was responsible for the death and may be present in other family members, or may be passed on to future generations. The consultation paper also observes that such post-mortem examinations may help to inform the development of public health policy more generally.

From the perspective of the bereaved family these observations as to the increased latitude of future Coroners' post-mortem examinations are to be welcomed.

The consultation document emphasises that a key factor in the new legislation remains that the view of the bereaved family should, as far as possible, be taken into account throughout the coronial investigation and that this applies to post-mortem examinations.[7]

Again, the legislature emphasises that the costs will usually be met by the Local Authority responsible for the particular coronial area.[8]

It was the government's stated intention that bodies should be released to the family for burial or cremation after no more then thirty days unless otherwise

---

[5] *ibid*, chapter 3, para 12 (p 30).
[6] *ibid*, chapter 3, para 13 (p 30.
[7] *ibid*, chapter 3, para 14 (p 30).
[8] *ibid*, chapter 3, para 19 (p 31).

ordered by the Chief Coroner (now possibly a judge). It is anticipated in the consultation paper[9] that in reality the vast majority of bodies will be released more quickly than this and particularly where the body does not provide assistance in any future criminal prosecution.

Coroner Investigations – Entry, Search and Seizure

17.8 The consultation paper states that these powers are primarily intended for two purposes, first in the case of deaths which are reported to Coroners where they themselves conduct an investigation – for example hospital deaths where the cause of death is unnatural or unknown – and secondly where deaths have been, or are being, investigated by another organisation such as the police, the Health and Safety Executive, the Prisons and Probation Ombudsman or the Independent Police Complaints Commission, and where, either on receipt of interim information from the organisation or of the organisation's final report, the Coroner decides he or she wishes to secure further information to assist in fulfilling his or her own responsibilities.

The consultation documentation recognises that under the Coroners Act 1988, Coroners do not have any power to enter and search premises or to seize evidence. Similarly, the Coroners Rules 1984 do not provide the Coroner with these powers. In practice, once the police are present at the scene of a death, irrespective of whether they have had to make forcible entry to the premises, they have a responsibility to make their own assessment, which may involve the collection of evidence to enable them to determine whether a death is suspicious or unnatural. The 2009 Act gives Coroners new statutory powers to enter and search land or property and seize items which are relevant to their investigations.

17.9 Crucially, the consultation paper states[10] that the new provisions are not intended to extend the number of cases which Coroners are responsible for directly investigating, or to cut across the roles of other investigators. The paper goes on to observe that other than in the most exceptional circumstances, the powers are unlikely to be discharged by the Coroner personally in the immediate aftermath of the death being discovered. They are primarily intended, as the consultation paper stresses, for situations either where the police have immediately eliminated the possibility of the death being suspicious but where the information they have provided to the Coroner leads him or her to request the police to seize specific items if the owner of the material is unable or unwilling to consent to the material being removed; or where a Coroner has already received an investigator's report, and the Coroner decides that further evidence is required in relation to the case. By way of

---

[9] *ibid*, chapter 3, para 34 (p 34).
[10] *ibid*, chapter 4, para 4 (p 37).

factual example, the consultation paper states that this could be in premises either where the death occurred, or where the body was discovered, or premises where the Coroner believes there is material relevant to the death.

The legislature makes it clear[11] that it has never been its intention to set up alternative and parallel Coroners' investigations when other organisations already have a duty to investigate a death and nor is it intended that Coroners should manage such investigations or be able to intervene directly in how such investigations are conducted.

It is important to note that the drafters of the legislation propose that the new procedure for search and entry will mirror, where possible and appropriate, sections 15 and 16 of the Police and Criminal Evidence Act 1984 regarding safeguards and execution, and section 21 of the 1984 Act in relation to processes for carrying out entry, search and seizure.[12]

Disclosure of Information by Coroners

17.10 Again, it is the stated aim within the consultation document[13] that one of the previous government's key aims was to improve the standing and involvement of bereaved families in investigations. The consultation document stresses that a significant way of achieving this is to ensure that they have the opportunity to access the material which the Coroner will be taking into account in coming to his or her decisions.

It is acknowledged within the consultation paper that the main principles of the disclosure regime are set out in the Charter for Bereaved People at paragraph 19, which states that family members will 'have a right, on request, to see reports of any post-mortems carried out'. Paragraph 25 of the Charter states:

> disclosure of all relevant documents to be used in an inquest will take place, on request, free of charge and in advance of an inquest, to those family members whom the coroner has determined have an interest in the investigation.[14]

Paragraph 26 of the Charter qualifies the position by stating that 'it is possible, for legal reasons, that not all documents that the coroner intends to use at an inquest will be able to be disclosed, or disclosed in full'.[15]

Secondary legislation will be intended to build on clear protocols of disclosure.

---

[11] *ibid*, chapter 4, para 5 (p 38).

[12] *ibid*, chapter 4, para 10 (p 39).

[13] *ibid*, chapter 5, para 1 (p 45).

[14] Ministry of Justice, *Charter for bereaved people who come into contact with a reformed coroner system* (January 2009).

[15] The Charter's approach has been endorsed by Parliament.

17.11 An analysis of how the consultation paper sees the future of disclosure is revealing. As a preamble to the observations relating to disclosure, the consultation paper emphasises that the key references to disclosure in the Charter for Bereaved People, although only mentioning family members, must also express in spirit a system which does not overlook the rights of other interested persons.[16]

It is an expressed aim of the legislature[17] that all disclosure must be consistent with three main principles:

(i) The Draft Charter for Bereaved People (provided for by section 42 of the 2009 Act.) This document states that usually all relevant documentation for an inquest should be disclosed on request in advance of an inquest to those family members whom the coroner has determined have an interest in the investigation.

(ii) The new appeals system (section 40 of the 2009 Act), under which interested persons may appeal against certain coroner decisions. If coroners disclose information this will help to ensure that any interested person has the material they need in order to consider whether to appeal a coroner decision at the relevant point of the investigation.

(iii) Article 2 inquests. A general principle of disclosure will be consistent with the obligation enshrined under Article 2 of the Convention.

17.12 The consultation paper also emphasises that the general principle of disclosure should meet recommendation 42 of the MacPherson Report on the Stephen Lawrence enquiry, which observed '42. That there should be advanced disclosure of evidence and documents as of right to parties who have leave from a coroner to appear at an inquest'.

17.13 Revealingly, the consultation paper indicates that it is not proposed that interested persons should have all disclosable material provided to them automatically, or that if one interested person requests disclosure it should be automatically sent to all others. The document emphasises that the key point is that they should be made aware that they are entitled to request the information. It is considered that it will be a matter for them as to whether they make the request.[18]

17.14 Those who have drafted the legislation anticipate that a substantial amount of material may be subject to disclosure from the following organisations:

• The Police
• The Independent Police Complaints Commission
• The Health and Safety Executive
• The Prison and Probation Ombudsman

---

[16] Consultation Paper (n 1 above) chapter 5, para 4 (p 45).
[17] *ibid*, chapter 5, para 19 (p 48).
[18] *ibid*, chapter 5, para 22 (p 49).

- The Ministry of Defence Service Inquiries
- Marine, Air and Rail Accident Investigation Branches.[19]

The Conduct of the Inquest

17.15 The trend of future secondary legislation is that rule 16 of the Coroners Rules 1984, which currently provides for a formal opening, adjournment and closing of an inquest should be reformed.[20] In the reformed system Coroners will open investigations rather than inquests and they will not be required to open investigations in court. The legislature anticipates that matters relating to the identification of the person who has died and to certification of the death can be dealt with at that stage and in an appropriate environment.

In relation to evidence the consultation paper proposes that there should be provisions similar to rules 37 and 37A on the admissibility of documentary evidence and public inquiry findings.[21] The consultation paper observes that under the current rule 37, the coroner may admit as evidence at the inquest documentary evidence which he or she considers relevant and which, in their opinion, is unlikely to be disputed, unless a person from a defined group, in other words, an interested party, objects to it being admitted. The coroner may also accept evidence, even if it is objected to, if in his or her opinion the maker of the document would be unable to give oral evidence within a reasonable time-scale. Presently documents made by persons who are now deceased may be admitted if the coroner thinks that they are relevant. In the present system, documentary evidence can be read aloud as part of the inquest proceedings unless the coroner directs otherwise.

Rule 37A provides for public inquiry findings to be admitted as documentary evidence in instances where an inquest has been resumed following an adjournment following the establishment of an inquiry under the Inquiries Act 2005 into matters relating to the death in question.

The consultation process leading to ultimate secondary legislation has recognised[22] that rule 37 may, in practice, be unduly complicated and reforms are being considered which will alleviate this difficulty.

17.16 The rationale behind the abolition within the 2009 Act of references to 'inquisitions' and 'verdicts' is explained in the consultation document as removing terms which are more appropriate to adversarial proceedings and 'can lead to misconceptions about what an inquest may achieve'.[23]

---

[19] *ibid*, chapter 5, para 23 (p 49).
[20] *ibid*, chapter 6, para 14 (p 55).
[21] *ibid*, chapter 6, para 16 (p 56).
[22] *ibid*, chapter 6, para 17 (p 56).
[23] *bid*, chapter 6, para 21 (p 57).

After the implementation of the 2009 Act a coroner will make a 'determination' in respect of questions about the identity of the deceased and how, when and where they came by their death; and findings in respect of matters that need to be ascertained to enable a death to be registered.[24]

There are also indications within the consultation paper that in the future open verdicts will be abolished. Instead coroners may be required to return a narrative determination in any case where they are unable to attribute one of a number of specified determinations.[25]

17.17 Schedule 5, paragraphs 1 and 2 of the 2009 Act deal with the coroner's power to summon witnesses. Presently the procedure for summoning witnesses is informal and the new Schedule 5 does not set out any practical mechanisms which might be used to summon witnesses. Secondary legislation is anticipated in this area and the creation of rules to govern the criteria.

Secondary legislation is also anticipated in relation to unsworn evidence, where there is currently no provision for a coroner to accept such oral evidence. Section 45(2)(a) of the 2009 Act allows for rules to make provision about evidence, including the provision requiring evidence to be given on oath other than in prescribed circumstances. The consultation paper notes that this opens the way for oral evidence to be accepted in certain limited circumstances, unsworn. The preferred view of the Ministry of Justice is that all witnesses at an inquest must give evidence under oath, unless they are under the age of 14 or if the coroner is otherwise unable to be satisfied that the witness has sufficient understanding of the responsibility involved in taking an oath in which case the coroner may permit the witness concerned to give unsworn evidence to the inquest.

17.18 The 2009 Act further introduces the concept of suspending investigations as outlined in Schedule 1 of the Act. Presently proceedings can be adjourned.[26] Such adjournments occur, for instance, where an Inspector or representative of the relevant enforcing authority is not present; where a person whose conduct has been called into question is not present; when requested by the Chief Officer of Police; when requested by the Director of Public Prosecutions; in circumstances where it appears to the Coroner that the death is likely to be due to an offence under the Road Traffic Act 1972 or the Suicide Act 1961, and a person might be charged with such an offence; or where the deceased had a relevant association with visiting Armed Forces.

The Ministry of Justice proposes that new rules will be drafted to make provision for adjourning inquests.

---

[24] Section 10 of the Coroners and Justice Act 2009.
[25] Consultation Paper (n 1 above) chapter 6, para 28 (p 59).
[26] Coroners Rules 1984 (SI 522/1984) as amended, rr 23, 25–29, 32 and 35.

Appeals and Complaints

17.19 The Ministry of Justice intends to pilot new procedures. Such pilots were expected to happen between April 2012 and March 2013 with the aim of establishing a system nationally from April 2013.[27]

The legislature does not anticipate that the appeals system should be used by an interested person as their first choice. It is hoped and anticipated that dissatisfaction can be resolved through an explanation of the reason for a decision, and those responsible for secondary legislation expect to see this built into the appeals process.

The Ministry of Justice has stated in consultation documentation that the appeals process should be available free of charge to those who wish to use it.[28]

The Ministry of Justice, within the consultation paper leading to secondary legislation, has also come to a preliminary view as to the procedure in relation to appeals to the Chief Coroner, which may be relevant if any judge assumes the now defunct role.

It emphasised that references to the Chief Coroner should also include references to the Deputy Chief Coroner, as the former Chief Coroner's powers could be delegated. The Chief Coroner was expected to determine the method of considering the appeal, whether it be on paper or orally. It was the expressed intention of the legislature that the majority of appeals would be considered on paper and would ensure quick resolution to matters in dispute. Only a very small number of cases were anticipated to be held orally due to complexity of fact, circumstances and evidence.[29]

The consultation documentation indicates that it is considered that there should be a maximum of 15 working days to appeal for most cases and a limit of 60 working days to make an appeal against a decision to discontinue an investigation before an inquest and against the decision given at the end of an inquest.[30]

Training of Coroners, Their Officers and Staff

17.20 This is covered by section 37 of the 2009 Act. It was anticipated that there will be separate training on new procedures, probably beginning in late 2011 and early 2012 for those who will be working in the reformed system.[31] The broad headings for training include

- Overview of the reformed system
- Interaction with the medical examiner system
- New forms

[27] Consultation Paper (n 1 above) chapter 7, para 2 (p 67).
[28] *ibid*, para 7 (p 68).
[29] *ibid*, chapter 7, para 28 (p 72).
[30] *ibid*, chapter7, para 29 (p 73).
[31] *ibid*, chapter 8, para 3 (p 76).

- Charter for Bereaved People, including investigations into specific types of deaths
- Practical skills and procedures on those Act provisions which will have a direct effect on working practices.

Death Registration Procedures

17.21 The expressed purpose of the Ministry of Justice in providing death registration arrangements for bereaved families is to give them an option of a short certificate of death to use for administrative or other purposes where the cause of death does not need to be disclosed. This may be because, it is observed in the consultation document, an organisation, such as a bank or utility company, only requires confirmation of the fact of death.

Presently only full death certificates are available.

The new provisions include the power to prescribe a fee for the short certificate.

APPENDIX 1

APPEALS

COURT OF APPEAL
(ON A QUESTION OF LAW)

ADMINISTRATIVE
COURT
(ON JUDICIAL REVIEW)

CHIEF CORONER

CORONER

APPENDIX 2

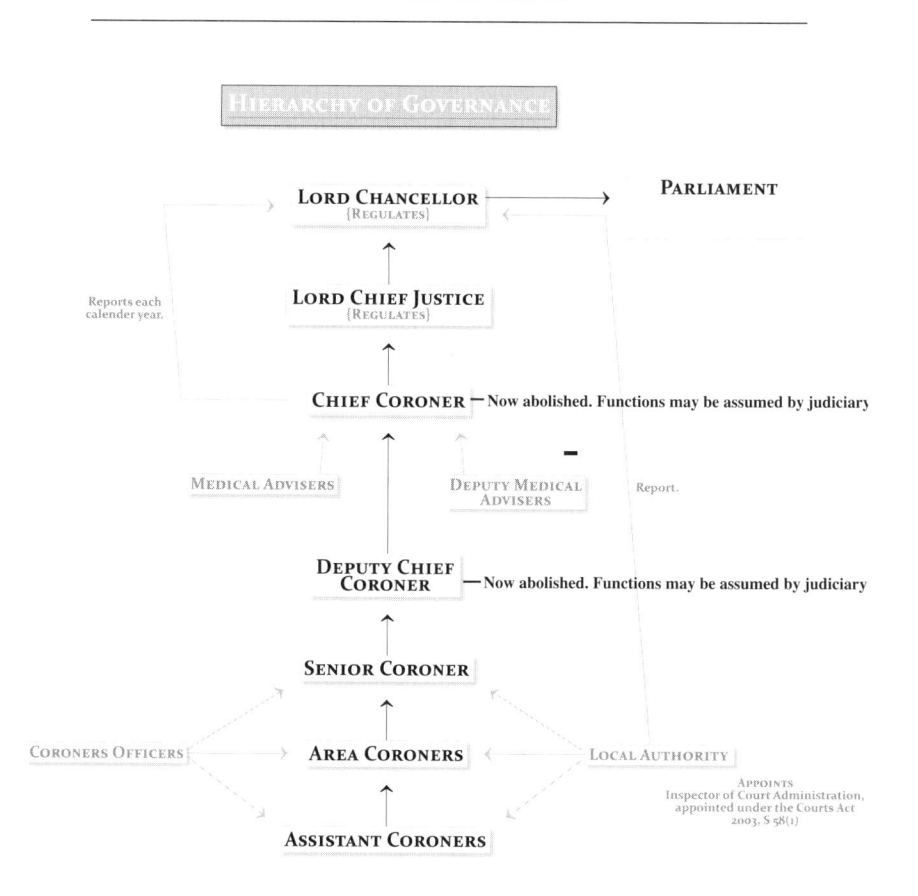

LORD CHANCELLOR
{REGULATES}

PARLIAMENT

Reports each
calender year.

LORD CHIEF JUSTICE
{REGULATES}

CHIEF CORONER — Now abolished. Functions may be assumed by judiciary

MEDICAL ADVISERS

DEPUTY MEDICAL
ADVISERS

Report.

**DEPUTY CHIEF
CORONER** — Now abolished. Functions may be assumed by judiciary

SENIOR CORONER

CORONERS OFFICERS

AREA CORONERS

LOCAL AUTHORITY

APPOINTS
Inspector of Court Administration,
appointed under the Courts Act
2003, S 58(1)

ASSISTANT CORONERS

INDEX

Index